A DEVOTIONAL

NIGHT LIGHT

FOR PARENTS

DR. JAMES & SHIRLEY
DOBSON

Multnomah®Publishers *Sisters, Oregon*

NIGHT LIGHT FOR PARENTS
published by Multnomah Publishers, Inc.

© 2002 by James Dobson, Inc.
International Standard Book Number: 1-59052-454-3

Cover image by State/Alamy

Unless otherwise indicated, Scripture quotations are from:
The Holy Bible, New International Version
© 1973, 1984 by International Bible Society,
used by permission of Zondervan Publishing House
Other Scripture quotations:
The Holy Bible, New King James Version (NKJV)
© 1984 by Thomas Nelson, Inc.
The Holy Bible, King James Version (KJV)
The Living Bible (TLB) © 1971.
Used by permission of Tyndale House Publishers, Inc.
All rights reserved.
Revised Standard Version Bible (RSV)
© 1946, 1952 by the Division of Christian Education
of the National Council of the Churches of Christ
in the United States of America
The New Testament in Modern English, Revised Edition (Phillips)
© 1958, 1960, 1972 by J. B. Phillips

Multnomah is a trademark of Multnomah Publishers, Inc.,
and is registered in the U.S. Patent and Trademark Office.
The colophon is a trademark of Multnomah Publishers, Inc.

Printed in the United States of America

For information:
MULTNOMAH PUBLISHERS, INC. • P.O. BOX 1720 • SISTERS, OR 97759

Library of Congress Cataloging-in-Publication Data
Dobson, James C., 1936–
Night light for parents/ James and Shirley Dobson.
       p. cm.
ISBN 1-57673-928-7
       1-59052-454-3
1. Parenting. 2. Parenting--Religious aspects--Christianity. 3. Family. 4. Child rearing. I. Title.
HQ755.8 .D623 2002
242/.645 21   2002512548

05 06 07 08—10 9 8 7 6 5 4 3

We dedicate this book to the millions of moms and dads today who are lovingly and sacrificially pouring their lives into the next generation. There is no greater responsibility in living than training and guiding these precious kids and, ultimately, introducing them personally to Jesus Christ. It is toward this end that these suggestions and prayers have been prepared. May God bless each of you as you read along with us, day by day.

Jim and Shirley Dobson

CONTENTS

Introduction

Many years have come and gone since our first child was born. An instant and irrational love affair blossomed that day between this new father and his baby daughter, Danae Ann, who took center stage in the Dobson household. How deeply I loved that little girl! She would stand in the doorway each morning and cry as I left for work, and then run giggling toward me with her arms stretched upward when I arrived at home each evening. You would have thought we had been separated for months. I wondered: Would I ever love another child as much as this one?

My question was answered five years later when a little lad named James Ryan made his grand entrance into the world. I fell in love all over again. He was my boy—the only son I would ever be privileged to raise. What a joy it was to watch him grow and develop and learn. How proud I was to be his dad—to be trusted with the well-being of his soul. I put Ryan to bed every night when he was small, and we laughed and we played and we talked about Jesus. I would hide his sister's stuffed animals around the house, and then we would turn out the lights and go "big game hunting" with flashlights and a toy rifle. Ryan never tired of that simple game.

But those early developmental years came and went so quickly, and right before our eyes, the kids suddenly grew up. Danae finished high school and went away to college. After graduating, she set about making an exciting life of her own. It was very difficult for Shirley and me to let her go, but we took comfort in the fact that Ryan had five more years at home. But again, the years passed in a blur of activity, and Ryan began thinking about going off to college some two thousand miles away. This time, however, there was no one at home to fill the void he would leave. The empty nest had arrived in a single day, leaving Shirley and me unprepared for what that cataclysmic change would mean in our lives.

We had known for years, of course, that the moment of release was coming. I had written, spoken, and counseled others about the experience of "turning loose," but it is a different matter when it happens to you. I admit without embarrassment that Ryan's departure hit me like the blow from a hammer. Packing and storing his stuff was an especially nostalgic process, as we worked our way through a massive accumulation of junk in his room. Ryan had been a collector of things no one else would want—old street signs, broken models, and favorite fishing rods. The entire family got tetanus shots before we plunged into the debris. Finally, on our last evening together, Shirley and Ryan loaded the remaining boxes and emptied the last drawer. The job was finished. His suitcases were packed. Our son was ready to go.

Ryan came into my study about midnight, and we sat down for another of the late-night chats that I had cherished over the years. He has always liked to talk at the end of the day. I won't tell you what we said in that final conversation because it is too personal to share.

The next morning we drove as a family to the airport. There I was, driving down the freeway, when an unexpected wave of grief swept over me. I thought I couldn't stand to see him go. It wasn't that I didn't look forward to what the future held. No, I mourned the end of an era—the culmination of a precious time of my life when our children were young and their voices rang in the halls of our house. I couldn't hide the tears as I parked the car and entered Burbank International Airport. Ryan was to depart from Gate 18, but I couldn't sit and cry in the waiting area. So I took a long walk though the concourse and returned as the passengers were boarding. Then we hugged good-bye and sent our youngest off to Chicago. I knew that Ryan would be home many times after that, but being on his own would change both of us forever. The parent-child relationship would take on an entirely different character. That is the way it should be, but I've never liked irreversible change, especially when it involves people I love.

Shirley and I drove in silence to the home where our beloved son and daughter had grown from babies to young adults. There I lost it again! The house we left three hours earlier in a whirlwind of activity and ringing phones had been transformed in our absence. It had become a monastery—a morgue—a museum. The quiet was deafening to us both. Every corner held a memory that wafted through the air.

I meandered into Ryan's room and sat on the floor by his bed, where his crib had once stood. I could almost see him as a toddler—running and jumping into my open arms. What a happy time that was in my life. The ghost of a kindergartner was there, too, with his brand-new cowboy clothes and his Snoopy lunch pail. Those images remained vivid for only a moment, and then a seven-year-old boy appeared before me. He was smiling, and I noticed that his front teeth were missing. His room was filled with bugs and toads and a tarantula named Pebber. As I reached out to hug the boy, he slowly disappeared. Then a gangly teenager strolled through the door and threw his books on the desk. He looked at me as if to say, "Come on, Dad. Pull yourself together!"

My own words from years earlier then echoed in my ears. I remember saying in a speech to parents that I was already thinking about what would happen soon in our home. The day was coming, I said, when "the bicycle tires would be flat, the skateboard would be warped and standing in the garage, the swing set would be still, and the beds would not be slept in. We will go through Christmas with no stockings hanging by the fireplace, and the halls will be very quiet. I know these times will soon be here, and I realize it has to be so. I accept it. I wouldn't for anything try to hold back our son or daughter when it comes time to let them go. But that will also be a very sad day because the precious experience of parenting will have ended for me." Alas, the day I had anticipated for so many years arrived in a single morning.

If you're thinking that I am hopelessly sentimental about my kids, you're right. The greatest thrill of my life has been the privilege of raising them day by day. Still, I did not expect such intense pain at the time of Ryan's departure. I thought I was prepared to handle the moment, but I realized just how vulnerable I was—and still am—to the people I love.

In the larger sense, however, it is not merely the end of formal parenting that shook my world when Ryan left. I grieved for the human condition itself. When he boarded that plane in Los Angeles, I comprehended anew the brevity of life and the temporary nature of all things. Later, as I sat on the floor in his room, I heard not only Ryan's voice, but also the voices of my mother and father, who laughed and loved in that place. Now they were gone too. One day, Shirley and I will join them—first one, and then the other.

We are just "passing through," as the gospel songwriters used to say. All of life boils down to a series of happy hellos and sad good-byes. Nothing is really permanent, not even the relationships that take root in a healthy home. King David said it best: "As for man, his days are as grass: as a flower of the field, so he flourisheth. For the wind passeth over it, and it is gone; and the place thereof shall know it no more" (Psalm 103:15–16, KJV). Yes. I felt the chilly breeze of change blowing through my heart in the early days of the empty nest, and I understood its meaning.

What an incredibly important scriptural concept David gave us. If we really grasped the numbering of our days, we would surely be motivated to invest ourselves primarily in eternal values. Would a fifty-year-old man pursue an adulterous affair if he knew how quickly he would have to explain his dalliance before his God? Would a woman make herself sick over petty in-law conflict or other silly frustrations if she knew how little time was left to her? Would men and women devote their lives to the pursuit of wealth and status symbols if they realized how soon their possessions would be torn from their trembling hands? It is the illusion of permanence, you see, that distorts our perception and shapes our selfish behavior. When eternal values come in view, it becomes our greatest desire to please our Lord and influence as many others for Him as possible, beginning with our own sons, daughters, and loved ones.

I ask each of my readers this important question today: If we *truly* believe that the eternal souls of our children hang in the balance—that only by winning them for Christ can we spend eternity together with them in heaven—will we change the way each day is lived? Will we ignore and neglect so great an opportunity if our eyes are fully opened to this awesome responsibility? I think not. I pray not.

As for you mothers and fathers who still have kids at home, may I urge you to keep this biblical truth in view as you race through the days of your lives? Don't permit yourselves to become discouraged with the responsibilities of parenting. Yes, it is an exhausting and difficult assignment, and there are times when you will feel like throwing in the towel. But I beg you to stay the course! Get on your knees before the Lord and ask daily for His strength and wisdom. Finish the job to which He has called you! There is no more important task in living, and you will understand that assignment more clearly when you stand where Shirley and I are today. In the blink of an eye, you will be hugging your children good-bye and returning to an empty house. You will pause for a moment to utter a prayer that the values and lessons you've imparted over the years have taken root in your sons and daughters and that they will bear fruit for the kingdom for the rest of their lives.

That is why we are bringing you this devotional book—to help with what we might call "first priorities." We want to encourage you as a mother or father to give yourselves enthusiastically to the spiritual welfare of your kids. Everything we have experienced in our work on behalf of families supports this profound understanding—that the greatest chance for successful parenting lies in dependence on the everlasting precepts of the Christian faith. Teach your kids about Jesus Christ, about heaven and hell, and about the foundational truths of the Word of God. Pray daily for them, and help them grow in faith. If your children enter adulthood with a clear concept of who God is and what He wants them to do, you will have achieved the greatest accomplishment in life.

We believe this book will help you reach that objective while lifting your spirits along the way. *Night Light for Parents* is designed for Mom and Dad to enjoy together at the end of the day—or, if you are a single parent, in a few minutes of quiet reflection alone. Like *Night Light*, our original devotional for couples, it features twenty-six weeks (six months) of devotionals on important topics for your family: spiritual training, prayer, character, discipline, rest, tough times, and many more. A new theme is introduced each Sunday, along with an inspirational story and my brief commentary. Sessions on Monday through Friday address the theme through Scripture verses, prayers, our insights and suggestions, and a few provocative questions. Then on Saturday, Shirley concludes the week with her own thoughts.

If you are tired, frustrated, or discouraged—if you feel that your efforts as Mom or Dad aren't making a difference—then this book is for you. There is hope in these pages, as well as practical and spiritual wisdom. We pray that you will sense the Lord's encouragement and blessing as you read each devotional. Our heavenly Father is ready to light the way for *all* His beloved children to a wondrous eternity with Him.

By the way, I should end this introduction with a brief update about our empty nest. My period of "mourning" lasted about thirty days, during which I didn't think I could take it. But guess what? Something interesting happened about that time: The new family constellation began to sound like a pretty good idea. The house stayed cleaner, adolescent noise and chaos gave way to serenity, and Shirley and I had much more time for each other. It turns out that God's plan is best after all. Now we enjoy a wonderful relationship with our grown children, not as parents who bear the responsibility for our kids' behavior, education, and training, but as friends who share an entirely new kind of bond that is just as rewarding as were the first eighteen years. Shirley and I talk with or hear from Danae and Ryan nearly every day, and we are so proud of them both. Most important, they are serving the Lord and carrying on the values and principles taught during their impressionable years. That is the most gratifying experience of all.

We hope you enjoy *Night Light for Parents* and find within it many practical ideas and inspirational stories for application in your own home. We would love to hear from you in the days ahead.

Jim (and Shirley) Dobson

Passing On the Faith

FOOTSTEPS

by Dennis Rainey

*S*amuel was always the natural athlete in our family. Since I had played junior-college basketball and baseball, I hoped that our son might follow in my footsteps.

As a child, Samuel played Little League ball for a couple of years with older boys and did well. But when he turned thirteen, he really began to excel in tennis. We loved attending his matches and tournaments. We drove hundreds of miles, taking him all over the state to play singles and doubles in tournaments. He brought home trophies and ribbons, and he once battled the number-one player in the state in his age group to match point before losing in a tiebreaker.

Samuel was ranked seventh in the state when his game began to slide. His coach didn't understand why he wasn't getting to balls that earlier he had reached with ease. Thinking it might be his shoes, we took him to an orthopedic specialist for a proper fitting. The problem only got worse.

After Samuel's fourteenth birthday, we took the entire family to a FamilyLife marriage conference in Dallas. That weekend we noticed that Samuel wasn't keeping up with the rest of us as we walked to dinner and later when we hurried to catch a plane at the airport.

The following Monday morning we went to a doctor's office with Samuel and were soon numb with disbelief as the neurologist announced, "Your son has a form of muscular dystrophy. He will most likely never be confined to a wheelchair, but he will never run again. His days of tennis and sports are over." Months later a trip to the Mayo Clinic confirmed the earlier diagnosis.

Although Samuel's disease was not life threatening, we felt as though a dream had died for a young man and his parents.

The next four months were tough because Samuel refused to quit tennis. Most matches he tripped and fell facedown on the asphalt, losing in straight sets. Many of his opponents, who had no way of knowing what was going on, mocked and laughed at him. (He and a partner did win a doubles tournament once, with a miraculous come-from-behind victory.)

Finally, Samuel hung up his tennis racket, admitting that his playing days were over.

Late one afternoon as I was driving Samuel home from a doctor visit, we were talking about what his disease meant to him as a young man. I was struggling to keep my emotions composed while trying to comfort him. I was battling my own feelings about a fourteen-year-old boy who would never field grounders again. Never play basketball with his brother. Never jog with his dad.

But Samuel ended up comforting me.

In the twilight of late afternoon, he turned to me and with a boyish grin said, "Well, Dad, I guess you don't need legs to serve God."

I couldn't talk. As I brushed away a stream of tears, all I could do was reach across the seat and give him a hug.

Samuel is not perfect. He's still spreading his wings and, like all of us, learning constantly what it means to be a disciple of Christ.

But riding in the car with me that afternoon, he showed me that he was a young man whose identity went far beyond tennis, whose character was weathering a stiff challenge, whose relationship with God and family was sustaining him, and whose mission for God transcended any physical limitations he would face in his lifetime.

I had hoped that Samuel would follow in my athletic footsteps. I was delighted to realize that he was choosing a far more meaningful path.

LOOKING AHEAD...

Is anything more difficult for a parent than watching a son or daughter go through pain, whether it's physical, emotional, or spiritual, or a combination of the three? You want desperately to take away the hurt, yet there is nothing you can do. Or is there?

It's true that many of life's difficult moments can't be avoided. Times of crisis are inevitable. But you *can* equip your children to face the hardships to come. It's the most important task you'll ever undertake.

We'll be talking this week about your primary job as mom or dad: helping your kids establish a relationship with the Lord. Their faith in almighty God will guide and protect them, give them strength, and place them on the path that leads to an eternity with Him. No matter how severe the challenges, our heavenly Father will provide your children with the comfort they need, when they need it. And when *you're* hurting, He'll do the same for you—perhaps even through your own son or daughter.

JCD

RELAY RACE

*I have no greater joy than to hear that
my children are walking in the truth.*
3 John 1:4

The vital mission of introducing your children to the Christian faith can be likened to a relay race. First, your parents run their lap around the track, carrying the baton, which represents the gospel of Jesus Christ. At the appropriate moment, they hand the baton to you, and you begin your journey around the track. Finally, the time comes when you must get the baton safely into the hands of your child. But as any track coach will testify, *relay races are won or lost in the transfer of the baton.* This is the critical moment when all can be ruined by a fumble or miscalculation. Any failure is most likely to occur in this exchange. Once firmly gripped, however, the baton is rarely dropped on the backstretch of the track.

As parents, our most important reason for living is to get the baton—the gospel—safely into the hands of our children (John 3:3). Unless our sons and daughters grasp the faith and take it with them on their journey through life, it matters little how fast they run. When they cross that finish line with their commitment to Jesus Christ intact, they—and you—will bask in the applause of heaven!

Before you say good night...

- How, if at all, did your parents hand off the baton of faith to you?
- Are you preparing your own children for a smooth handoff?
- What more can you do to show your kids this most profound need?

Heavenly Father, our most fervent desire is to one day be together with our children in eternity. Grant us strength and wisdom as we seek to lead our children to You, especially in those critical handoff moments. Amen.

EARLY TRAINING

> *Train a child in the way he should go,*
> *and when he is old he will not turn from it.*
> Proverbs 22:6

When you construct a plan for introducing your children to Jesus, you may want to make your motto "the earlier the better." In a recent nationwide poll, researcher George Barna learned that children ages five through thirteen have a 32 percent probability of accepting Christ as their Savior. That rate drops dramatically, to just 4 percent, for kids ages fourteen through eighteen. And those who have not become Christians before age nineteen have only a 6 percent probability of doing so during the rest of their lives!

Spiritual training of children should begin at their earliest moments of awareness and continue through the teen years. The most important year, however, may be age five. That is when they are open and tender to the call of Christ. Some kids come to a fork in the road at this point. Either they begin to internalize what they are taught and make it their own, or Bible stories and lessons become like fables that don't apply to the real world. Your careful instruction during this period can lay the faith foundation that will guide your children throughout their earthly lives—and lead them into a joyous eternity.

Before you say good night...

- Where do your kids stand right now regarding faith in Jesus Christ?
- Does the level of spiritual training you're providing match the ages of your kids?
- How does the spiritual training you received as a child influence your faith today?

Dear Jesus, You are the master teacher. Help us to follow Your example as we train our children—to say the right words at a time when their ears will hear so that they will become devoted followers of You. Amen.

Imprinting

*Teach them to your children...so that your days and
the days of your children may be many.*
Deuteronomy 11:19–21

e recommended last night that you give extra attention to the spiritual training of your children at age five, when they are most open to your teaching. This idea may concern you. You might prefer that your child be allowed to decide for himself on matters of faith and God. We can respond to this concern with an illustration from nature. After a gosling hatches from his shell, he will become attached, or "imprinted," to the first thing he sees moving near him—which is ordinarily mother goose. If mama goose is absent, however, any mobile substitute will do. In fact, a gosling will become imprinted easily to a blue football bladder dragged by on a string. A week later, he will fall in line behind the bladder as it scoots past. Time is the critical factor; the gosling is vulnerable to imprinting for only a few seconds after he hatches. If that opportunity is lost, it cannot be regained.

In a similar way, there is a brief period when children are most receptive to instruction about God and about right and wrong. When parents choose to withhold religious training from their small child, allowing him to "decide for himself," they almost guarantee that he will "decide" in the negative. If you want your kids to enjoy a meaningful faith, you must give up any attempts at objectivity and instead "teach [these words of Mine] to your children" (Deuteronomy 11:19).

Before you say good night...
- Are we holding back in the spiritual training of our kids? If so, why?
- Can we harm our kids by withholding our instruction?

Dear God, thank You for the privilege of teaching our children about You. Let us make the most of the opportunities You give us, not allowing anything to come between our kids and an intimate relationship with You. Amen.

DILIGENT TEACHING

Do not forget the things your eyes have seen....
Teach them to your children and to their children after them.
Deuteronomy 4:9

As you teach your children about God, you would be wise to heed the words of Moses. His message to parents is that we should talk about spiritual matters continually:

Impress [My commandments] on your children. Talk about them when you sit at home and when you walk along the road, when you lie down and when you get up. Tie them as symbols on your hands and bind them on your foreheads. Write them on the doorframes of your houses and on your gates.
Deuteronomy 6:7–9

If we take away anything from this passage, it is that we must make the spiritual development of our children our highest priority. Nothing comes close to it in significance. By God's grace, our efforts to establish a vibrant faith in our two now-grown children, Danae and Ryan, have been successful, which is our highest achievement in life! If you follow Moses' advice and are diligent in revealing the Lord, His Word, and His ways to your kids, the probability is great that you will achieve the supreme prize of parenthood.

Before you say good night...

- How persistent are you in instructing your children about God?
- Is teaching your kids about God your top parenting priority?
- What practical ideas can you implement that follow Moses' advice?

Father, forgive us for too often losing sight of our responsibility as parents. We want to obey Your commands and impress them on our children. By Your Spirit, help us to consistently draw our family closer together and closer to You. Amen.

THE GOOD NEWS!

"Whoever believes in him
shall not perish but have eternal life."
John 3:16

You may be reading this book tonight without ever having made a commitment to Jesus Christ. The best gift you can give your children—and yourself—is the decision to put your trust in Him. All of us have been afflicted with a disease called sin, which means that we are in a state of rebellion against God. This curse is embedded in our very natures. Scripture tells us it is impossible to be good or righteous enough to cleanse us of this wickedness, regardless of how hard we try (see Romans 3:23; 5:8; 6:23).

Fortunately for us, however, God's infinite love demanded that He provide a remedy for the human family. His wonderful answer was to send His only Son, Jesus Christ, to endure on the cross at Calvary the punishment we deserve. Jesus' death and resurrection three days later are your passage from a meaningless existence to an eternity of joy and freedom. He offers you a gift of new life. All you have to do is repent of your sin and put your faith in Him. This is the meaning of our human existence—the *only* satisfactory explanation for why we are here and where we are going. No wonder it's called the Good News!

How can you introduce your children to Christ if you don't know Him intimately? If you haven't given your heart to Jesus, will you do so right now with the prayer below?

Before you say good night...

- Have you claimed the gift of eternal life offered by Jesus Christ?
- If not, what is preventing you from making that commitment?

Lord Jesus, I am thankful beyond words for Your sacrifice. I am a sinner who needs You and believes in You. Help me to serve You, obey You, and follow You. Please forgive all my sins and grant me a new life for eternity with You! Amen.

DIVINE HELP

Pray without ceasing.
1 Thessalonians 5:17, NKJV

When confronted with the awesome responsibilities of parenthood—not to mention the incredible evil in today's world—it's no surprise that many parents feel an urgent need to pray continually for their children. When Danae was about three years old, Jim and I realized that as parents we needed divine help. We began fasting and praying for Danae, and later for Ryan, almost every week (a practice that I continue to this day). Our prayer went something like this: "Lord, give us the wisdom to raise the precious children You have loaned to us, and above all else, help us bring them to the feet of Jesus. This is more important to us than our health or our work or our finances. What we ask most fervently is that the circle be unbroken when we meet in heaven."

God has not only heard this prayer, but also blessed it in ways we never anticipated. Our prayer time has become a project that Jim and I enjoy *together*, drawing us closer to each other as we draw closer to God. In addition, the act of fasting each week serves as an important reminder of our priorities: It's difficult to forget your highest values when one day out of seven is spent focusing entirely on them. Finally, our children were influenced by these acts of discipline. When they observed us fasting or praying, it gave us the opportunity to explain why we did these things, how much we loved them, and how much we loved and trusted the Lord.

God hears and honors—in His perfect timing—our petitions on behalf of our children. If you want the very best for your sons and daughters, I urge you to call on the greatest power in the universe in frequent prayer.

SMD

Spiritual Training

LIVING AND LEARNING

by Robin Jones Gunn

We were caught in downtown traffic when the thin woman approached our car at a red light.

"Please," she said, tapping on the closed window. "Please, can you help me?"

My husband rolled down the window and we all heard the wail of the baby in her arms.

"I need milk for my baby. Can you give me some money?"

My husband pulled a twenty-dollar bill from his pocket and handed it to her as the light turned green. We drove away and I frowned. *What kind of beggar wears that much makeup? How many drivers has she hit up today?*

It was our seven-year-old daughter who spoke first. "Do you think she'll go buy milk now?"

I gave a muffled "humph." My husband said, "I don't know."

"Then why did you give her the money?" our eleven-year-old son asked.

My husband didn't hesitate before answering. "Because God asked me to be a cheerful giver. I'm not responsible for what she does with the money. She'll have to answer to God for that. I'm only responsible for my part, which in this case was to give cheerfully."

Humph. I still wasn't convinced. It wasn't like we had an abundance of twenty-dollar bills to hand out. We were on a very tight budget.

Budgets were something our kids knew all about. We sat them down as soon as they started receiving an allowance and taught them how to budget their money. We also talked a lot about responsibility. And as for honesty, we called them into the living room and gave a grand lecture on always telling the truth.

According to all the Christian parenting books, we were doing it right, teaching our children character based on biblical principles. But it was easy to call a family meeting. What I found more difficult was taking advantage of the daily opportunities to teach that seemed to pop up at the most inopportune times.

Like the time I bought two pairs of jeans for our son and made it all the way home before discovering the department store had only charged me for one pair. It was the clerk's mistake, and I really didn't have time for another trip downtown. Still, I remembered that honesty lecture we'd given the kids, so after I picked up our daughter from school, I took the jeans and the receipt and tried to pay for the second pair. The clerk didn't quite know what to do, so she called for her supervisor to intervene. I explained again as my daughter listened. The supervisor sent me to customer service and again I tried to pay.

"Why are you doing this?" the clerk asked. I was beginning to wonder myself. Then my daughter reminded me.

"God would have known," Rachel said quietly. She tugged on the strap of my purse. "Tell her you're just trying to be honest, Mom."

My frustration didn't immediately evaporate, but I began to understand that I was teaching my daughter something that would stay with her much longer than any talk I gave. Our kids were watching our lives and learning from the choices we made.

Our son is now a tall teenager. He doesn't have a regular job, but money comes to him in various ways. His last birthday produced some serious income, and he was excited about buying a new paintball gun. The next week at church I noticed him slip a folded twenty-dollar bill into the offering plate.

Quickly doing the math, I realized he'd given twice what a tithe would have been on his birthday money. He wouldn't be able to buy that paintball gun now.

Stunned and tearfully proud of the way he'd given in such a humble way, I turned to catch a glimpse of his face.

There was a grin across that firm jaw of his, and at that moment he looked so much like his father. What really warmed this mother's heart, though, was knowing that we had passed on more than a family resemblance.

LOOKING AHEAD...

This true story by Robin Jones Gunn sounded very familiar when I read it. It should have, because the same thing happened to me in the parking lot of a restaurant a few years ago. A woman with a baby blocked my path with her car and began crying hysterically. She said she absolutely had to have twenty dollars immediately and didn't have time to explain. When I asked again why she needed the money so desperately, she blurted out, "Oh, please help me. I can't go into the reason. I just have to have it." I handed her twenty dollars and she drove off crying.

Was I taken in by a scam? Probably. Then why did I cooperate? I didn't have a child with me to impress or influence, so that wasn't my motivation. I gave the money for the same reason Robin's husband handed twenty dollars to the woman with a baby. I was taught by my parents to give to those in need. Generosity is a central feature of the Christian ethic. When Scripture tells us to "give to the one who asks you" (Matthew 5:42), it does not say "give only if the money will be used wisely" or "give only if you know you'll get it back." Oh, I know what you're thinking right now—that it is stupid to allow yourself to be duped, and I agree. But until all the facts are known, I choose to do what appears to be right and let God deal with the other person.

This principle of giving to others is only one component of the strong spiritual foundation we must pass on to our children. Scripture admonishes us to "Train a child in the way he should go, and when he is old he will not turn from it" (Proverbs 22:6). There is an assumption in that proverb, however. We as parents can't train a child in the way he should go unless we *know* which way he should go.

To help with that task, we are providing material in the next week related to what I call a "checklist for spiritual training." This little self-test will walk you through a carefully conceived, systematic approach to the faith instruction of your children. Many of these items require maturity that they lack, and we should not try to make adult Christians out of our immature youngsters. But we can gently teach them these concepts during the impressionable years of childhood. This may be the most important challenge you will face as parents.

The six scriptural concepts that follow can serve as a guide as you nurture your children—especially during their first seven years. The concepts and supporting questions are "targets" toward which you can nudge your boys and girls. When consciously taught, they will give your children the foundation on which all future doctrine and faith will rest. Bathe the entire effort in prayer and He will guide your paths.

JCD

CHECKLIST FOR SPIRITUAL TRAINING

Concept 1. "Love the Lord your God with all your heart" (Mark 12:30).

__ Is your child learning of the love of God through the love, tenderness, and mercy of his parents? (Most important.)

__ Is he learning to talk about the Lord and to include Him in his thoughts and plans?

__ Is he learning to ask Jesus for help whenever he is frightened or anxious or lonely?

__ Is he learning to read the Bible?

__ Is he learning to pray?

__ Is he learning the meaning of faith and trust?

__ Is he learning the joy of the Christian way of life?

__ Is he learning the beauty of Jesus' birth and death?

Concept 2. "Love your neighbor as yourself" (Mark 12:31).

__ Is he learning to understand and empathize with the feelings of others?

__ Is he learning not to be selfish and demanding?

__ Is he learning to share?

__ Is he learning how to be kind to others?

__ Is he learning to accept himself?

Concept 3. "Teach me to do your will, for you are my God" (Psalm 143:10).

___ Is he learning to obey his parents as preparation for later obedience to God? (Most important.)

___ Is he learning to behave properly in church—God's house?

___ Is he learning a healthy appreciation for both aspects of God's nature: love and justice?

___ Is he learning to cooperate with and submit to authorities outside of self: parents, teachers, police, et cetera?

___ Is he learning the meaning of sin and its inevitable consequences?

Concept 4. "Fear God and keep his commandments, for this is the whole duty of man" (Ecclesiastes 12:13).

___ Is he learning to be truthful and honest?

___ Is he learning to keep the Sabbath day holy?

___ Is he learning the relative insignificance of materialism?

___ Is he learning the meaning of the Christian family and the faithfulness to it that God intends?

Concept 5. "But the fruit of the Spirit is…self-control" (Galatians 5:22–23).

___ Is he learning to give a portion of his allowance (and other money) to God?

___ Is he learning to control his impulses?

___ Is he learning to work and carry responsibility?

___ Is he learning to tolerate minor frustration?

___ Is he learning to memorize and quote Scripture?

Concept 6. "He who humbles himself will be exalted" (Luke 14:11).

___ Is he learning to be appreciative?

___ Is he learning to thank God for the good things in his life?

___ Is he learning to forgive and forget?

___ Is he learning the vast difference between self-worth and egotistical pride?

___ Is he learning to bow reverently before the God of the universe?

LOVE THE LORD

"Love the Lord your God with all your heart."
Mark 12:30

I (JCD) will never forget the day I took my daughter, Danae, then four, for a bicycle ride. Neither of us realized at the time that I had positioned her new passenger seat too close to the front wheel. We were flying down the road when Danae thrust her foot into the spokes. In a terrifying instant, both of us were thrown to the pavement; Danae's tooth was knocked loose and her foot bloodied.

Kneeling over my wounded child after that accident was one of the most painful experiences of my life. Danae remembers it vividly as well. She later wrote, "My father gathered me in his arms and ran to the house. He cried as he ran, saying over and over, 'Babe, I'm so sorry I hurt you!' The tenderness of my father on that distressing afternoon has come to symbolize his love for me through the years." Apparently, in the agony of those moments, Danae realized—perhaps for the first time—just how precious she is to me and how deeply I care about her. It was one of her first pictures of how much God loves her, too.

Are your children learning about the love of God through your love for them? Are they learning to talk about the Lord, to include Him in their thoughts and plans, to turn to Jesus when they are anxious or lonely? The best way to encourage intimacy between your kids and the Lord is to demonstrate His love in their lives each day.

Before you say good night...

- Are you modeling God's love and tenderness to your kids each day?
- How can you help them understand the love of God?

Father, we understand that the best way to teach our children to love You and serve You is to love and serve You ourselves. Forgive us for the times we've hurt our kids, and show us the path that will bring us closer to You. Amen.

LOVE YOUR NEIGHBOR

"Love your neighbor as yourself."
Mark 12:31

A traveler was walking along a road when robbers suddenly attacked him. They tore his clothes, beat him, and left him to die. Eventually a priest walked down the same road, but when he saw the man, he passed on the other side. Later, a local man came upon the scene, but he, too, passed on the other side. Finally, a stranger from another land walked down the road, noticed the beaten man, and rushed to his aid. He bandaged the man's wounds, helped him onto his own donkey, and transported him to an inn to take care of him. The next day he paid the innkeeper to look after the man.

You are no doubt familiar with this story of the Good Samaritan (Luke 10:30–37). Have your children heard it, too? Jesus told the parable to show us who our neighbors are—everyone around us—and how we should lovingly respond to their needs. Does the elderly woman on the corner need help with her yard? Does your teen know a classmate who needs a friend? Opportunities to serve are all around us.

As you teach your children to love their neighbors as themselves, you might ask: Are they learning to understand and empathize with others' feelings? Do they resist the urge to be selfish and demanding? Are they learning to share? We're never closer to God than when we seek to love one another.

Before you say good night...

- Have your children ever seen you act as Good Samaritans?
- Do your kids show concern for others?
- What can you do specifically to encourage love for others?

Lord, when You walked this earth, You always taught from real-life situations. Help us by Your own Spirit to teach our children about Your great love in the midst of the hassles and challenges and opportunities of our busy lives. Amen.

WALKING IN HIS WILL

Teach me to do your will, for you are my God.
Psalm 143:10

We should always be grateful for God's clear instructions for successful living and for revealing how we can gain a glorious eternity with Him. Yet simply reading and understanding God's will for us isn't enough. We must also choose in obedience to follow it—and that's the difficult part. So often, we are too headstrong to submit.

The mother of a strong-willed four-year-old once said to her daughter, "Now, Cathy, you're just going to have to obey me. I'm your boss, and I have the responsibility to lead you. That's just what I intend to do." Little Cathy thought for a minute, and then replied, "How long does it have to be that way?" Even at age four, this child was already yearning to forge her own path. Most of us were just as determined when we were kids.

It's vital that your sons and daughters learn to obey you as preparation for later obedience to God. It's not always easy to instill a spirit of obedience in your kids, but it's worth the effort. Walking in the will of God always is.

Before you say good night...

- Are your kids learning a healthy appreciation for the importance of obedience?
- Do they understand that they must yield to many forms of benevolent authority?
- Are they learning the meaning of sin and its consequences?
- Are you setting a proper example by walking in the will of God yourself?

Dear Lord, please give us the patience and the will to be consistent in our rules, to insist on complete obedience, and—when we must—to follow through with discipline. Be our strength and help, we pray. Amen.

HEALTHY FEAR

Fear God and keep his commandments,
for this is the whole duty of man.
Ecclesiastes 12:13

You can hardly watch a movie, pick up a magazine or novel, or listen to the radio today without hearing or seeing the Lord's name taken in vain. Even Christians use the phrase "Oh God!" in everyday language. As a society, we seem to have lost our reverence for and fear of the Father.

Maybe that's why the Lord plainly instructs us to be careful about speaking His name. In fact, He made it the third of the Ten Commandments: "You shall not misuse the name of the LORD your God" (Exodus 20:7). Our Father knows that to show disrespect for His name—to allow it to be used as a common curse—is to treat the King of the universe with disdain and vulgarity. Even the angelic beings in His presence say, "Holy, holy, holy is the Lord God Almighty" (Revelation 4:8).

King David understood and respected Jehovah and His mighty power: "You have heard my vows, O God; you have given me the heritage of those who fear your name" (Psalm 61:5). If we want our families to understand that reverence, we must honor His name in word, thought, and deed. Reflect daily on His glory; let your voice fill with respect when you speak of Him; turn off movies, TV programs, and videos that degrade or trivialize His name. Above all, teach your kids why "The fear of the LORD is the beginning of wisdom" (Proverbs 9:10).

Before you say good night...
• Does your family have a healthy fear of the Lord?
• How can you model reverence for God's name and Word?

Father, remind us to treat Your name with great reverence and honor. Forgive us if we've spoken of You in a light or frivolous way. We know that our children are watching and listening...and so are You. Amen.

THE SELF-CONTROLLED CHILD

But the fruit of the Spirit is…self-control.
Galatians 5:22–23

Many parents take a passive approach to guiding and disciplining their children because they want their kids to learn self-control. But since young people lack the maturity to generate self-discipline, the good intentions of these parents usually fail. Their kids enter adulthood without ever having learned how to manage their own lives or control their own impulses.

Consider the example of Doug, a young man who has never learned to curb his temper or his tongue. His parents consistently ignored their son's angry outbursts during childhood, assuming he would eventually learn to control this problem on his own. Years later, Doug lands his first full-time job, but quickly gets into a heated dispute with his boss and is fired. It is only the first of many disappointments ahead.

Your children need help in developing self-discipline and self-control. Allow them, within reason, to suffer the unpleasant consequences of their mistakes, such as walking to school when they miss the bus or paying for the repairs when they put a dent in the family car. Most important, encourage them to spend time in the Word of God and to invite Jesus into their hearts. When they give their lives to Him, they will begin to enjoy the fruits of the indwelling Holy Spirit (Galatians 5:22)—including self-control.

Before you say good night…

- Are you allowing your kids to experience the consequences of their actions?
- In what new ways could you help your children develop self-control?

Father, help us to stand firm when we feel weak, to remain steady when we'd rather shrug our shoulders, and to lead our children with patience and wisdom. Let us be good examples ourselves as we seek to develop self-control in our kids. Amen.

A HUMBLE HEART

"He who humbles himself will be exalted."
Luke 14:11

Robertson McQuilkin, as reported in his book *A Promise Kept*, served as president of a thriving seminary and Bible college in South Carolina for more than twenty years. His wife, Muriel, supported him in many ways, including as an excellent cook and hostess when they entertained guests of the college in their home. They were an effective ministry team.

Then Muriel's health declined. Tests confirmed her doctor's fears; she had Alzheimer's disease. In time, Muriel's abilities failed and Robertson became increasingly responsible for her basic needs, which included feeding, bathing, and dressing.

With Muriel's needs escalating and his responsibilities at the college unchanged, Robertson faced a difficult decision: Should he place Muriel in an institution? He felt that God had called him to service as a college president. Yet he also knew that the Lord had another calling for His children—to "clothe yourselves with humility toward one another" (1 Peter 5:5). Robertson resigned from his position so that he could better care for Muriel. It was his turn to humbly serve his wife.

Robertson was startled by the response to his choice. Husbands and wives began renewing marriage vows. Pastors told the story to their congregations. Friends eventually urged him to write about the experience. What had been, in hindsight, the obvious response to a troubling circumstance seemed to touch a chord in many hearts.

When you put your partner's needs ahead of your own, as Robertson McQuilkin did, your children will notice. Your example of sacrificial love will leave a lasting impression and encourage them to apply a giving spirit to others. Your kids will find favor with God when they follow your lead and approach life with thankful and humble hearts.

SMD

The Privilege of Prayer

INNOCENT PETITIONS

by Robin Jones Gunn

When we lived in Nevada, my daughter Rachel had a best friend named Kristin. We moved to Portland, Oregon, only a few days before Rachel's first day of second grade. Each night we talked about her new school and prayed together before she went to bed.

The night before school started, Rachel prayed that Jesus would give her a new best friend at this school and that her name would be Kristin. I felt compelled to alter her prayer but decided to let it go. How do I tell my child she shouldn't be so specific with God?

The next morning, Rachel stood in front of the mirror while I combed her hair. She seemed lost in thought, and then suddenly she announced to me that Jesus was going to give her a new best friend. Her name would be Kristin, and she would have brown hair, just like the Kristin in Nevada.

I quickly ran through all my mental notes on prayer. What would be the best way to explain to this child that prayer is not telling God what we have in mind for Him to do, but rather seeking His mind? I tried a few flimsy sentences. All fell flat. She seemed undaunted. I drove her to school, still unable to find a way to protect her from her own prayer. I was afraid she would experience a spiritual crisis when she arrived at school and found no brunet Kristin in her class. What would that do to her innocent faith?

We entered the classroom, and Rachel found her name on her new desk. She lifted the top and began to examine the contents. I sat down at the desk next to hers and decided this would be a good time to explain how praying isn't like wishing. It's not magic. You can't ask God for something and expect it to materialize at your command. She needed to be willing to accept whatever new friends God brought to her.

I was about to plunge in, when out of the corner of my eye I noticed the name of the student who would occupy the desk next to Rachel.

There, in bold black letters, was printed *Kristin.*

I could barely speak. "Rachel," I finally managed in a whisper, "look! There *is* a Kristin in your class. And she's going to sit right next to you!"

"I know, Mom. She's the one I prayed for."

The bell rang, and I practically staggered to the back of the classroom as the students began to come in. Rachel sat up straight, folded her hands on her desk, and grinned confidently.

I glued my eyes to that door. Four boys entered. Then a girl with blond hair who took a seat in the front row. Two more boys and then, there she was! She sauntered shyly to the "Kristin" desk, caught Rachel's welcoming grin, and returned the same.

I probably don't need to mention that she had brown hair—down to her waist.

Or that everything I really needed to know about prayer I learned in second grade.

LOOKING AHEAD...

Prayer is one of God's most mysterious and remarkable gifts to us. It is our lifeline to heaven, our means to the most holy of relationships, our opportunity to directly express our praises and desires to the Creator of the universe. There is a power in this simple act that cannot fully be explained, yet can never be denied: "The prayer of a righteous man [or child] is powerful and effective" (James 5:16).

Of course, not every request made on your knees will be answered as quickly or easily as Rachel's prayer for a friend. But encouraging your family to pray is always the right choice—in good times, in hard times, in moments of anxiety, and during periods of joy. If any gift from our heavenly Father is worth passing on to our children, it is the privilege of prayer. Let's talk about it this week.

JCD

A HEAVENLY RELATIONSHIP

Devote yourselves to prayer.
Colossians 4:2

The Bible places great emphasis on prayer. We read many examples of how important prayer was to Jesus (Luke 5:16). We are taught that prayer should be for God's benefit and not to gain favor in the eyes of men (Matthew 6:5–6), and that we need not use "many words" in an attempt to impress Him (v. 7). We are even given examples of the words we should use (vv. 9–13).

But why, exactly, is prayer so important to our Lord? Incredibly, it is an expression of His desire to have a *relationship* with us. Though it is impossible to explain why, our Lord wishes to know us intimately—to have a personal, two-way conversation with each of His children. Though He can read our minds, He wants us to seek Him, to love Him, and to talk with Him daily. The reason is that there is no relationship in eavesdropping!

As a father or mother, you naturally desire a close relationship with your kids. You appreciate hearing about their new discoveries and joys. When they tell you they are afraid, you quickly offer reassurance. Our heavenly Father, who loves us even more than we love our own children, responds to our prayers in the same way. Scripture tells us that "the prayer of the upright pleases him" (Proverbs 15:8). That's true for you, your spouse, and your kids. Let's please our loving Lord by seeking Him often in prayer.

Before you say good night...

- How is your prayer relationship with the Lord?
- How can you encourage each other, and your kids, to pray more often?

Heavenly Father, we are humbled that You would desire a personal relationship with us. We so want to enjoy holy intimacy with You. Help our family draw closer to You through the privilege of prayer. Amen.

POWER FOR GENERATIONS

*"I prayed for this child,
and the LORD has granted me what I asked."*
1 Samuel 1:27

My (JCD's) great-grandfather George McCluskey prayed every morning from eleven to noon for his children and for future generations of his family. Toward the end of his life, he announced that God had made him a promise: Every member of four generations of his family would become Christians. That promise has been working itself out in remarkable ways. By the time I came along, every family member from my great-grandfather to me not only had accepted Christ, but also had been or were ministers. H. B. London, my cousin and a member of the fourth generation, is also a minister. I am the only one who did not feel specifically called to this service. Yet considering the hundreds of times I have talked to audiences about the gospel of Christ, I feel like an honorary member of the team!

My great-grandfather is long dead, but he still provides the richest source of inspiration for me. If you want to have that kind of impact on your family, we suggest you get on your knees daily and seek God's power and blessing through prayer—not only for your children, but for future generations as well.

Before you say good night...

- How often do you pray for your grandchildren and your great-grandchildren yet to come?
- What time of day works best for you to pray for your family?
- How can you increase your commitment to praying for your kids?

Dear God, we are humbled that You make Your mighty power available to us through prayer. May all our requests honor You and release Your best for us, our children, and generations of our family to come. Amen.

ANYTIME, ANYWHERE

When I called, you answered me.
Psalm 138:3

One rainy night, I (SMD) was alone and working in the kitchen. I suddenly had a strong urge to pray for my daughter, Danae, who was out with a friend. At first I ignored the impression, but it was so intense that I put down what I was doing and prayed right then for Danae's safety, calling for a legion of angels to protect her.

A while later, a policeman came to our home and told me that Danae and her friend had been in an accident on a mountain road. The car she was driving had hit a slick mixture of oil and gravel and flipped over, sliding on its top within a few feet of a five-hundred-foot precipice—a sheer drop-off with no guardrail. Both Danae and her friend suffered minor injuries, but neither was seriously hurt. I am so thankful that I heeded that urge to pray—I can still picture those angels, standing wing tip to wing tip, providing a safe guardrail.

The Lord wants us to "pray continually" (1 Thessalonians 5:17). If you or anyone in your family feels even the slightest nudge to pray, I encourage you to set aside what you are doing and start talking to God—anytime, anywhere! The power of prayer is only effective when we use it.

Before you say good night...

- Are you ready to pray anytime you feel a heavenly nudge?
- Have you ever felt specifically prompted by God to pray? What happened?
- Do you understand that "arrow prayers" can be sent without uttering even a word and that they are heard and received in heaven?

Dear Lord, thank You for Your love for us, Your interest in even the small details that make up our days, and Your desire to protect us from harm. Enable us to be ready to heed Your call to prayer, anytime, anywhere. Amen.

PEACE IN OUR TIME

Present your requests to God. And the peace of God...
will guard your hearts and your minds.
Philippians 4:6–7

A husband arrived home from work and found the washing machine spewing out suds, the refrigerator on the fritz, and crushed cereal nuggets scattered in every room. His three-year-old had the chicken pox, his eight- and ten-year-old boys complained of upset stomachs, and the baby was covered head to toe with melted chocolate chips. In the middle of this disaster scene was his wife, who managed a weary smile and muttered, "Welcome home."

There's no question that life can be chaotic. Sometimes we're so busy, tired, and stressed that we feel we don't have time to pray. Yet these are the days we need to be talking with the Lord most of all. When you pray—for yourselves and others in need—you can't help feeling a sense of God's love for you and your family. You're reminded of His awesome power and how capable He is of handling your situation. You begin to feel the joy, hope, and peace that are always available in the Lord.

The apostle Paul urged that "requests, prayers, intercession and thanksgiving be made for everyone...that we may live peaceful and quiet lives in all godliness and holiness" (1 Timothy 2:1–2). When a tornado of unexpected circumstances strikes your home, why not gather for a brief time of family prayer? The chaos may not instantly vanish, but we promise that you'll be able to deal with it better.

Before you say good night...

- Do you feel too busy to pray? If so, how can you change this?
- Are you showing your kids how to turn to God in times of stress?

Almighty God, only You can bring peace and order to our chaotic existence. When the problems of this world seem too overwhelming, gently draw us near so that we may discover anew Your calming touch. Amen.

KEEP PRAYING

Wait for the LORD; be strong and take heart.
Psalm 27:14

I (JCD) know of a mother and father who prayed for their three children before they were born and who continue to speak daily to the Lord on their behalf. Yet their middle daughter has chosen to reject their faith. She lives with a twice-divorced man and has no intention of marrying him. She has had at least two abortions, and her language is offensive. Angry and frustrated, these parents wrote to me, asking about their "ineffective" prayers.

Our prayers *do* unleash the power of God in the lives of others. We have the privilege, and the responsibility, of entering into intercessory prayer for our loved ones and holding their names and faces before the Father. In return, God makes the all-important choices crystal clear to those individuals and brings positive influences into their lives. But He will not force Himself on anyone. A person must *choose* to repent and believe in the name of Christ to claim the gifts of forgiveness and salvation.

To put it another way, the Lord will not save a man or woman against their will—but He has a thousand ways to make them more willing. That's why we mustn't blame God when our prayers seem to go unanswered—and why we "should always pray and not give up" (Luke 18:1), anticipating the moment our loved ones finally and joyfully turn to Him.

Before you say good night...

- Are you ever discouraged by what seems to be ineffective prayer?
- Do you pray consistently even when you don't see immediate results?
- Are you teaching your children to do the same?

Dear Father, in our impatience, we sometimes become discouraged that our prayers seem to go unanswered. Yet we know that You are always listening and always at work! Help us to remain faithful, to pray without ceasing, and to never give up on our loved ones who so desperately need to come to You. Amen.

THE MAIN COURSE

I will praise you, O Lord my God, with all my heart.
Psalm 86:12

*M*ost of us have little trouble remembering to pray during times of crisis. I certainly called on the Lord the night a burglar startled me out of my sleep and again on the evening that Jim suffered a stroke. We do pretty well at bringing other requests before Him, too. We know that Jesus said, "Ask and you will receive, and your joy will be complete" (John 16:24). These are easy prayer concepts to teach our children.

But our prayerful communication with the Lord has another purpose: worship. After all, God is not a "genie in a bottle" waiting in heaven for us to send a laundry list of needs and wants. He is worthy of our praise and is pleased when we come before Him with humble reverence. He wants to be appreciated, just as we do.

Praise and adoration are not merely "appetizers" in the lives of believers—they are part of the main course. David, who gave us so many wonderful words of praise in the Psalms, put it this way: "Ascribe to the LORD the glory due his name.... Worship the LORD in the splendor of his holiness" (1 Chronicles 16:29).

In the same way, praise and worship are essential to an effective and satisfying life of prayer. When Jesus taught His disciples how to pray, He *began* with praise: "Our Father in heaven, hallowed be your name" (Matthew 6:9).

Our loving Lord is the sovereign Creator of the universe. He loves us as His own children and has given us every good thing that we have; He is worthy of our praise every moment. Let's remember to focus on *Him* when we pray and to teach our children to do the same. It will move us away from being self-centered, filled with worry and distress, to being God-centered, with joy and peace in our hearts.

SMD

Model Parents

LAVENDER MEMORIES

by Sandra Picklesimer Aldrich and Bobbie Valentine

As Cotha Prior strolled past the new shop that sold body lotions and soaps, the lavender-wrapped bars displayed in the window caught her attention. Her daughter would like those. Once inside, Cotha picked up the closest bar and held it to her nose. The fragrance carried her back to her childhood.

She remembered Margie, the little girl in her fifth grade class who always was poorly dressed and whose bathing habits were, well, not one of her regular habits. Even at that young age, Cotha knew how important the opinions of her friends were, so although she felt sorry for Margie, she couldn't risk being friends with her.

Then one afternoon, as young Cotha colored the states on her homework worksheet, she casually mentioned Margie to her mother, who stopped in the middle of stirring the stew to ask, "What's her family like?"

Cotha didn't look up. "Oh, really poor, I guess," she answered.

"Well, it sounds as though she needs a friend," Mrs. Burnett said. "Why don't you invite her to spend Friday night with you?"

Cotha looked up quickly then. "You mean here? Spend the night with me? But, Mom, she smells."

"Cotha Helen." Her mother's use of both names meant the situation was settled. There was nothing to do but invite Margie home. The next morning, Cotha hesitantly whispered the invitation at the end of recess while her friends were hanging up their jackets and combing their hair. Margie looked suspicious, so Cotha added, "My mother said it's okay. Here's a note from my mother to give to yours."

So two days later they rode the school bus home while Cotha tried to ignore the surprised looks on her friends' faces as they saw the two of them together. Had two fifth grade girls ever been quieter? Cotha thought of other times when she'd been invited to spend the night with a friend. They would talk and giggle all the way to their stop.

Finally Cotha gave a determined little huff and said to Margie, "I've got a cat. She's going to have kittens."

Margie's eyes lit up. "Oh, I like cats." Then she frowned as though recalling a painful memory and added, "But my dad doesn't."

Cotha didn't know what to say then, so she feigned interest in something outside the school bus window.

Both girls were silent until the bus rolled to a stop in front of the white house with green shutters.

Mrs. Burnett was in the kitchen. She greeted Cotha and Margie warmly and then gestured toward the table, which was set with two glasses of milk and banana bread. "Why don't you girls have a little snack while I tend to dinner," she said.

When the banana bread was finished, Mrs. Burnett handed each child identical paper-doll books and blunted scissors. Dressing the paper women in shiny dresses gave them something in common to talk about. By the time they washed their hands for dinner, they were chatting enthusiastically about school.

After the dishes were done, Mrs. Burnett said, "Time to take a bath before bed, girls." Then she held out scented soaps wrapped in lavender paper. "Since this is a special night, I thought you might like to use fancy soaps," she said. "Cotha, you first, and I'll wash your back for you."

Then it was Margie's turn. If she was nervous about having an adult bathe her, she didn't show it. As the tub filled, Mrs. Burnett poured in a double capful of her own guarded bubble bath. "Don't you just love bubble baths, Margie?" she asked as though the child bathed in such luxury every day.

She turned to pull Margie's grimy dress over her head, then said, "I'll look away as you take the other things off, but be careful climbing into the tub. The bubble bath makes it slippery."

Once Margie was settled into the warm water, Mrs. Burnett knelt down and soaped the wet washcloth heavily before rubbing it over the child's back.

"Oh, that feels good," was all Margie said.

Mrs. Burnett chatted about how quickly Cotha and Margie were growing and what lovely young women they were already. Repeatedly she soaped the washcloth and scrubbed Margie's gray skin until it shone pink.

Through the whole thing, Cotha was thinking, *Oh, how can she do that? Margie is so dirty.* But Mrs. Burnett continued to scrub cheerfully, then washed Margie's hair several times. Once Margie was out of the tub, Mrs. Burnett dried her back and dusted her thin shoulders with scented talcum. Then, since Margie had brought no nightclothes, Mrs. Burnett pulled one of Cotha's clean nightgowns over Margie's now shining head.

After tucking both girls under quilts, Mrs. Burnett leaned over to gently kiss them good night. Margie beamed. As Mrs. Burnett whispered, "Good night, girls," and turned out the light, Margie pulled the clean sheets to her nose and breathed deeply. Then she fell asleep almost immediately.

Cotha was amazed that her new friend fell asleep so quickly; she was used to talking and giggling for a long time with her other friends. To the sound of Margie's gentle breathing, Cotha stared at the shadows on the wall, thinking about all her mother had done. During Margie's bath, Mrs. Burnett had never once said anything to embarrass the girl, and she'd never even commented about how grimy the tub was afterward. She just scrubbed it out, quietly humming the whole time. Somehow Cotha knew her mother had washed more than Margie's dirty skin.

All these years later, the adult Cotha stood in the fragrant store, the lavender soap still in her hand, wondering where Margie was now. Margie had never mentioned Cotha's mother's ministrations, but Cotha had noticed a difference in the girl. Not only did Margie start coming to school clean and pleasant on the outside, but she had an inside sparkle that came, perhaps, from knowing someone cared. For the rest of the school year, Cotha and Margie played at recess and ate lunch together. When Margie's family moved at the end of the school year, Cotha never heard from her again, but she knew they had both been influenced by her mother's behavior.

Cotha smiled, then picked up a second bar of the lavender soap. She'd send that one to her mother, with a letter saying that she remembered what her mom had done all those years ago—not only for Margie, but for Cotha as well.

Wouldn't it be interesting to talk to Margie, now undoubtedly an adult, about her recollections of the "sleepover"? I would guess that the love and care given by Cotha's mom to a dirty, bewildered little girl made a lifelong impact on her. It certainly had that effect on Cotha, who was watching carefully.

As parents, we often intentionally set out to teach our children the lessons they'll need for life. Many of us forget, however, that in our unguarded moments we're *still* teaching our kids. The simple things we do each day—helping a neighbor change a flat tire, letting an elderly woman ahead of us in the line at the supermarket, or giving a bath to a lonely young girl—say more than the most stirring lecture.

Children pick up their parents' values in the routine experiences of everyday living, and most of this teaching is done with very few words. That's true for small matters and for the most important instruction of all—the values and principles found in Scripture. I hope you will keep this in mind as we talk about "model" parenting over the next week: Your kids are watching you every minute, and much of what they see will be remembered for a lifetime.

JCD

"I Love You, Daddy"

In everything set them an example by doing what is good.
Titus 2:7

*I*t's a well-known fact that kids identify their parents—and especially their fathers—with God. One day when I (JCD) was out of town on business, Shirley asked our son, Ryan, then two years old, to pray before their meal. Though Ryan had watched his mother and me pray at mealtimes, he had never been asked to say grace before. The invitation startled him, but he folded his little hands, bowed his head, and said reverently, "I love you, Daddy. Amen."

When Shirley later told me what had happened, the story unsettled me. I hadn't realized the degree to which Ryan linked me with his heavenly Father. I wasn't even sure I wanted to stand in those shoes! But I had no choice, and neither do you. We parents have been given the awesome responsibility of representing God to our vulnerable little children. That's why it is critically important for us to acquaint our kids with the nature of God—in particular His unfathomable love and His justice. Your example can lay a firm foundation of faith for your children.

Jesus said, "The Son can do nothing by himself; he can do only what he sees his Father doing" (John 5:19). Let's reveal the heart of God at home with our every deed.

Before you say good night...

- Do your kids identify you with God?
- Do your actions at home reveal the nature of God?
- What can you change to set a better example for your children?

O Lord, help us to remember that no matter what we do, others are watching—little eyes, grown-up eyes, and Your eyes, too. Help us to live carefully, handling life as a precious treasure, leaning on You for strength. Amen.

LEGACY OF A GOOD MAN

A good man leaves an inheritance for his children's children.
Proverbs 13:22

D r. Willis B. Dobson was a good man. He was also my (JCD's) uncle. He earned his Ph.D. in Shakespearean English at the University of Texas and taught for more than forty years at a small Christian college. He worked for peanuts compared to what he could have earned at a state university, but he had other priorities than acquiring wealth. When his beloved wife succumbed to cancer, Uncle Willis rededicated his life to the service of others. At age seventy he began a taxi service for what he called "old people." He set up a refreshment stand in front of his house for the trash collectors. One frigid night in December, Uncle Willis and his son, Bill, walked past a drunken man sitting on a curb. My uncle suddenly stopped, went back, and placed his overcoat around the man's shoulders. "Why did you do that?" asked Bill. "That coat is brand-new."

"Because," Uncle Willis replied, "I have two coats and that man has none."

Willis B. Dobson was simply following the command of his God (see Luke 3:11). He never received great acclaim for his selfless commitment to others, but he was remembered with deep affection by his family and was a role model for me. I hope I can leave that kind of legacy to my family.

Before you say good night...

- Are you modeling an attitude of service to your kids?
- What were your most selfless acts in the last week? In the last year?
- How can you do more for others?

Dear Father, the months and years speed by so quickly. Help us to live purposefully, remembering that our legacy to our children has little to do with money—and everything to do with how we heed and obey Your Spirit. Amen.

KNOW WHERE YOU'RE GOING

Those who plan what is good find love and faithfulness.
Proverbs 14:22

Early in their marriage, FamilyLife ministry cofounders Dennis and Barbara Rainey decided to go away for a weekend. Their goal was more than a couple days of relaxation. Separately, they each created a list of values that they wanted to one day teach their children. After making their lists, Dennis and Barbara came together and settled on their top five family values. That project was a wonderful time of sharing for the Raineys that also established "true north" for their journey as parents. In later years, Dennis and Barbara had a written record to refer to when child-rearing issues arose. In fact, Dennis still carries that dog-eared piece of paper with him wherever he goes.

Whether you write your values list on paper or in your heart, it's important to recognize where you are leading your family. As Yogi Berra once said, "You got to be very careful if you don't know where you're going, because you might not get there." Your children will discover and embrace the values that matter—love for each other, kindness, integrity, devotion to God—only if you have the right map to lead them there. Choose your values wisely (see examples in Matthew 7:12; Romans 12:9–13; 1 Corinthians 16:13–14; 2 Peter 1:5–7)—then stay on the trail!

Before you say good night...

- Do you have a plan for leading your family?
- What are your family's top five values?
- Are you passing on your values to your kids?
- How can you do a better job of this?

Lord Jesus, apart from You, we wouldn't even know where to start. Help us to lead our children; help us to set the pace toward a godly life. Show us what You value most so that we might live those values within our home...and before a watching world. In Your strong name, amen.

COURSE CORRECTION

[The Lord] guides the humble in what is
right and teaches them his way.
Psalm 25:9

A blizzard had confined our family and our guests to a ski lodge for three days, giving us a major case of cabin fever. Finally, on Sunday, we awoke to clear slopes and a brilliant blue sky. But what were we to do? Our family had made it a lifelong policy to attend church on the Sabbath and refrain from skiing or going to professional athletic events (we respect the fact that many Christians take a different view of this issue). On this particular Sunday, I (JCD) rationalized, deciding that an exception was in order. I announced, "It's such a beautiful day. We can have our devotions tonight. I think it's okay to ski." Everyone was jubilant—or so I thought.

A few minutes later I found my eleven-year-old son crying. "Dad," Ryan said, "I have never seen you compromise before. If this was wrong in the past, then it's still wrong today." My son's words hit me like a blow from a hammer. I eventually regained my composure and said the words he needed to hear: "Ryan, you're right." Instead of skiing that day, we went to church in a nearby town. We extended our trip and had a marvelous time on the slopes the next day.

It's vital to set a consistent, biblical example for your children—but your willingness to humbly admit to and correct any deviations from that course may be the most important lesson of all.

Before you say good night...

- Are you willing to admit your mistakes to your children?
- Are you compromising your standards for the sake of convenience?

Lord, as You know, we are prone to wander. Please give us strength to continue on the path You've given us to walk, grace to admit when we've drifted off course, and perseverance to hold fast to Your ways. Amen.

FAITHFUL ROLE MODELS

Follow my example, as I follow the example of Christ.
1 Corinthians 11:1

Unlikely as it sounds, I (JCD) made the decision to become a Christian at three years of age. I remember the occasion clearly. I was attending a Sunday evening church service and was sitting near the back with my mother. My father was the pastor; he invited those who wished to do so to come forward, and I joined them. I recall crying and asking Jesus to forgive my sins. It is overwhelming for me now to imagine the King of the universe caring about an insignificant kid barely out of toddlerhood!

Not all children will heed a call to faith that early or dramatically, of course—nor should they be expected to. Yet it is important to note that my own conversion at that young age was possible because of my parents' example. From my first days, I saw them on their knees, praying and talking to the Lord. They later told me that I attempted to pray before I learned to talk, imitating the sounds I had heard.

If you set a faithful example beginning with the day your sons and daughters are born, they will never forget what they have seen and heard. Even if they reject God later, the remnant of those early memories will be with them for the rest of their lives—and may well bring them back to the fold. As parents, this is our privilege and duty as outlined in Scripture: "Bring them up in the nurture and admonition of the Lord" (Ephesians 6:4, KJV).

Before you say good night...

- How is your faith example influencing your kids' walk with God?
- Do you need to pray for a stronger, more visible faith?

Our Father, how will our children know You unless they see us seeking You above all else? By Your own strength, grant that our ways would match our words. As our children look to us as an example, may they see Jesus. Amen.

HELPING HANDS

You became imitators of us and of the Lord.
1 Thessalonians 1:6

I already knew that children are prone to imitate their parents, but it was the "Siggie shave" incident that brought this fact home to me.

Danae was two years old the first time she noticed Jim shaving in the morning. She was fascinated and watched every detail as he soaped his face and applied a razor to his skin. We should have known that Danae would try what she had seen. The next morning, I came into the bathroom and hardly recognized our dachshund, Siggie, who was sitting in his favorite spot on the furry lid of the toilet seat. Danae had covered his head with lather and was systematically shaving the hair from his shiny skull! I screamed, "Danae!" which sent Siggie and his barber scurrying for safety. It was strange to see our frightened dog with nothing but ears sticking up on the top of his bald head.

Our kids' tendency to imitate provides an opportunity for their parents to teach them. Invite your children into the kitchen when you are preparing breakfast, explain what you are doing, and allow them to stir the pancake batter. Teach them how to fold the clothes from the dryer. Show them how to mow the lawn. Demonstrate how to scrub away the dirt on the doors and windows of your car when it's time for a wash. Then bow your head to thank God for giving your family food to eat, clothes to wear, and a place to live. In this way you teach your children, "Whatever you do, do it all for the glory of God" (1 Corinthians 10:31).

It's true that you may not finish your daily duties as quickly with the "help" of little hands, but showing your children how to properly complete tasks at home—especially when handled in a positive, fun manner—can give them a wonderful sense of accomplishment, help them develop good attitudes about work, and create an enriching time for the whole family. You'll be setting an example that will benefit your children *and* yourself in the years ahead.

SMD

Being "Dad"

REMODEL JOB

by Bob Welch

$\mathcal{I}$ was sitting in a bathtub full of moldy Sheetrock when my thirteen-year-old son asked the question: "Can you take me golfing sometime?"

I had a bathroom to remodel. It was fall, and the forecast for the next week was for 100 percent chance of Oregon's liquid sunshine. I wanted to say no. "Sure," I said. "What did you have in mind?"

"Well, maybe you could, like, pick up Jared and me after school on Friday and take us out to Oakway."

"Sounds good."

Friday came. The showers continued. As I looked out the window, moldy Sheetrock seemed the saner choice. But at the appointed hour, I changed from home-improvement garb to rain-protection garb and loaded the boys' and my clubs in the back of the car. In front of the school, Ryan and Jared piled in. Ryan looked at me with a perplexed expression.

"What's with the golf hat, Dad?" he said.

It was, I thought, a silly question, like asking a scuba diver what's with the swim fins.

"Well, I thought we were going to play some golf."

A peculiar pause ensued, like a phone line temporarily gone dead.

"Uh, you're going *too?*" he asked.

Suddenly, it struck me like a three-iron to my gut: I hadn't been invited.

Thirteen years of parenting flashed before my eyes. The birth. The diapers. The late-night feedings. Helping with homework. Building forts. Fixing bikes. Going to games. Going camping. Going everywhere together—my son and me.

Now I hadn't been invited. This was it. This was the end of our relationship as I had always known it. This was "Adios, Old Man, thanks for the memories, but I'm old enough to swing my own clubs now, so go back to your rocking chair and crossword puzzles and—oh yeah—here's a half-off coupon for your next bottle of Geritol."

All these memories sped by in about two seconds, leaving me about three seconds to respond before Ryan would get suspicious and think I had actually expected to be playing golf with him and his friend.

I had to say something. I wanted to say this: *How could you do this to me? Throw me overboard like unused crab bait?* We had always been a team. But this was abandonment. Adult abuse.

This was Lewis turning to Clark in 1805 and saying: "Later, Bill. I can make it the rest of the way to Oregon without you." John Glenn radioing Mission Control to say thanks, but he could take it from here. Simon bailing out on Garfunkel during "Bridge over Troubled Water."

Why did it all have to change?

Enough of this mind-wandering. I needed to level with him. I needed to express how hurt I was. Share my gut-level feelings. Muster all the courage I could find, bite the bullet, and spill my soul.

So I said, "Me? Play? Naw. You know I'm up to my ears in the remodel project."

We drove on in silence for a few moments. "So, how are you planning to pay for this?" I asked, my wounded ego reaching for the dagger.

"Uh, could you loan me seven dollars?"

Oh, I get it. He doesn't want *me,* but he'll gladly take *my money.*

"No problem," I said.

I dropped him and Jared off, wished them luck, and headed for home. My son was on his own now. Nobody there to tell him how to fade a five-iron, how to play that tricky downhiller, how to hit the sand shot. And what if there's lightning? What about hypothermia? A runaway golf cart? A band of militant gophers? He's so small. Who would take care of him?

There I was, alone, driving away from him. Not just for now. Forever. This was it. The bond was broken. Life would never be the same.

I walked in the door. "What are you doing home?" my wife asked.

I knew it would sound like some thirteen-year-old who was the only one in the gang not invited to the slumber party, but maintaining my immature demur, I said it anyway.

"I wasn't *invited,*" I replied, with a trace of snottiness.

Another one of those peculiar pauses ensued. Then my wife laughed. Out loud. At first I was hurt. Then I, too, laughed, the situation suddenly becoming much clearer.

I returned to the bathroom remodel, and as I worked I began realizing that this is what life is all about: change. This is what father and son must ultimately do: change. This is what I've been preparing him for since he first looked at me and screamed in terror: not to play golf without me, but to take on the world without me. With his own set of clubs. His own game plan. His own faith.

God was remodeling my son. Adding some space here. Putting in a new feature there. In short, allowing him to become more than he could ever be if I continued to hover over him. Just like when I was a kid and, at Ryan's age, I would sling my plaid golf bag over my shoulder and ride my bike five miles across town to play golf at a small public course called Marysville that I imagined as Augusta National.

I remember how grown-up I felt, walking into that dark clubhouse, the smoke rising from the poker game off to the left, and proudly plunking down my two dollars for nine holes. Would I have wanted my father there with me that day? Naw. A boy's gotta do what a boy's gotta do: grow up.

A few hours later I heard Ryan walk in the front door. I heard him complain to his mother that his putts wouldn't drop, that his drives were slicing, and that the course was like a lake. He sounded like someone I knew. His tennis shoes squeaked with water as he walked back to where I was working on the bathroom.

"Dad," he said, dripping on the floor, "my game stinks. Can you take me golfing sometime? I need your help."

I wanted to hug him. Rev my radial-arm saw in celebration. Shout, "I'm still needed!" I wanted to tell God, "Thanks for letting me be part of this kid's remodel job."

Instead, I got one of those serious dad looks on my face and stoically said, "Sure, Ry, anytime."

LOOKING AHEAD...

As Bob Welch suddenly realized in the story above, a father's job is to train his children to take on the world. The moment will come when your kids will walk away from the comforts of home and begin their own exciting journey into independence and adulthood. To prepare for that transition, your children desperately need your love, leadership, and guidance throughout their growing-up years. A father's role in that assignment is different from that of the mother, but no less important. The impact and responsibility of dads in raising kids cannot be overestimated. Fathers are central to God's design for successful families.

Dad, we've designed this week especially for you. (Mom, we still want you to participate, too!) I hope it will encourage you in preparing your kids for the adult years to come.

JCD

FATHER OF ALL FATHERS

"My Presence will go with you, and I will give you rest."
Exodus 33:14

You don't need a license or a diploma to become a father, yet the job description is one of the toughest imaginable. According to Scripture, a father encourages and comforts his children, urging them to "live lives worthy of God" (1 Thessalonians 2:11–12). He is charged with the instruction (Proverbs 1:8–9) and discipline (Hebrews 12:10) of his offspring. He is expected to provide "good gifts" for his children (Matthew 7:9–11). Harder still, a father must not "exasperate" his children as he does these things. Instead—and most important of all—he is to "bring them up in the training and instruction of the Lord" (Ephesians 6:4).

In the face of these enormous responsibilities, you may feel like a high school dropout interviewing for a job as a nuclear physicist—you know that your résumé doesn't measure up! But don't be discouraged. Scripture tells us that our heavenly Father will assist us in each of life's heavy responsibilities: "The LORD will guide you always; he will satisfy your needs" (Isaiah 58:11). You can depend on almighty God, the Father of all fathers, for strength in every parenting challenge—no matter what your qualifications might be.

Before you say good night...

- What are your strengths as a father?
- What areas of fatherhood do you most need to work on?
- Are you depending on God for answers to challenges with your kids?
- How can you do better in trusting the Lord as a dad?

(father) Dear Lord, I sometimes feel overwhelmed by the mighty responsibilities of fatherhood. Help me to come before You daily, humbly asking for Your wisdom as I seek the best for my children. Amen.

A FATHER'S INFLUENCE

"He will turn the hearts of the fathers to their children,
and the hearts of the children to their fathers."

Malachi 4:6

Bill Haughton, president of a large construction firm, had hired and managed thousands of employees. He was asked, "When you are thinking of hiring an employee—especially a man— what do you look for?" His answer may surprise you. He said, "I look primarily at the relationship between the man and his father. If he felt loved by his dad and respected his authority, he's likely to be a good employee."

Haughton may have been familiar with the biblical story of Eli. A priest of Israel, Eli had two sons, Hophni and Phinehas. Eli apparently failed to discipline his children when they were young; the two sons did not respect their father. They rebelled against him and against the Word of God, appropriating the people's animal sacrifices for their own meals and threatening anyone who resisted them (1 Samuel 2:12–17). When Eli heard about what his sons were doing, he spoke to them, but they ignored his warnings (vv. 23–25). Their actions offended God, eventually bringing on judgment (3:11–13) and death (4:17).

Dad, never underestimate the incredible influence you have on your children. It can make the difference between disaster and lives that are successful and pleasing to Him.

Before you say good night...

- How did your dad influence the person you've become today?
- What kind of impact do you think you're having on your kids?
- Are you the kind of father God wants you to be?

(father) Almighty God, thank You for the privilege of fatherhood. I want so much to lead my children onto right paths for their lives. Despite my sometimes inadequate efforts, let my kids achieve the holy plan You've set out for them. Amen.

FATHERS AND SONS

"I will be his father, and he will be my son."
2 Samuel 7:14

*S*omeone has said, "If you connect a boy to the right man, he seldom goes wrong." I (JCD) fully believe that to be true.

The full force of my own father's contribution hit me years ago when he lay in the hospital after a heart attack. As I stood by his bedside, I thought back to the happiest moments of my childhood—how we would rise early on a wintry morning, pull on our hunting clothes, and head twenty miles outside of town to a favorite place we called "the big woods." He'd get me situated under a little tree, and then we'd wait for the sun to come up, watching the squirrels and birds and chipmunks. Those moments with my dad were priceless. They made me want to be like him—to choose his values as my values, his dreams as my dreams, his God as my God.

Are you cultivating common ground with your son? Sharing hobbies or other interests now will encourage open communication during the turbulent times ahead. It will plant the seeds for a mutual faith—and a friendship that can last a lifetime.

Before you say good night...

- As a child, did you share any hobbies with your dad?
- What are your favorite memories of those times?
- What activities do your children enjoy sharing with you? What new ones could you try?
- How can common activities build a mutual faith?

(father) Lord, help me to be sensitive to the interests and needs of my son(s). Give us grace to create memories that will strengthen our relationship and draw us closer together, and closer to You. Amen.

Fathers and Daughters

I ask that we love one another.
2 John 1:5

If you have a daughter, Dad, one of your primary tasks is to set the tone for her future relationships with men. If you are warm and nurturing, she'll eventually look for a husband with similar qualities. If you communicate that she's beautiful and feminine, she'll be inclined to see herself that way. If you blend love and discipline in a way that conveys strength, your daughter will be more comfortable with a give-and-take marriage characterized by mutual respect. But if you reject your daughter, she's likely to spend her life trying to find a man who can meet the needs you never fulfilled in her heart.

One wonderful way to build up your daughter is to take her on regular "dates," which can begin even in the preschool years and extend to the teens. Let her help plan these outings. Then open doors for her, help her with her chair, and listen attentively when she speaks. Treat her with the same consideration and respect that Scripture prescribes for your wife (1 Peter 3:7). You'll create a feeling of self-worth and begin to establish her standards for a husband, if she chooses to marry. We can't imagine a better wedding present for a father to give his precious daughter.

Before you say good night...

- How would you describe your relationship with your daughter?
- What is your daughter's current attitude toward men?
- What can you do better to prepare your daughter for a successful marriage?

(father) Heavenly Father, I want my daughter(s) to know how much I love and value her. Let my every word and deed encourage her today and help shape her into the woman You want her to be. Amen.

HOLD ON TIGHT

Those who have been given a trust must prove faithful.
1 Corinthians 4:2

A mother at a church where I (JCD) was a guest speaker told me tearfully that her husband had recently divorced her, devastating her two sons. "They miss their daddy every day," she said. "They don't understand why he doesn't come to see them. The older boy, especially, wants a father so badly that he reaches for every man who comes into our lives."

The next morning I spoke again at their church. The same mother and her boys greeted me after the service, and I shook the older boy's hand. Then something happened that I was not fully aware of at the time—the boy did not let go of my hand! He gripped it tightly, preventing me from welcoming others around us. To my regret, I unconsciously grasped his arm with my other hand and pulled myself free. Only later did I remember and realize how desperately this lad needed a man in his life.

Dad, your sons and daughters will often reach for your hand in the years ahead. When they do, I urge you to hold on tight! This is doubly true if you are divorced or separated. Now more than ever, your children need assurance of a love that "always protects, always trusts, always hopes, always perseveres"…and "never fails" (1 Corinthians 13:7–8).

Before you say good night...

- In what ways do your kids "reach" for you?
- What are the biggest challenges of being a single dad?
- What is toughest about being the child of a single dad?
- What specific things can you do to reassure your kids that you'll always be there for them?

Dear God, no matter what our family circumstances, let us never waver from our charge as parents! Please forgive us for so often failing our children and You. Help us to be worthy of Your trust in us to lead and love our kids. Amen.

FATHERLY LOVE

Mordecai had taken her as his own daughter.
Esther 2:7

*T*his week we've addressed the awesome privileges and responsibilities of fathers. I'd like to speak tonight to a group of dads who are especially close to my heart: stepfathers.

My own father was an alcoholic. As a child I often hid when he arrived at our run-down home in the early morning hours, drunk and shouting threats. I remember finally praying to God in desperation: *If Dad isn't going to change, then please get us out of this house and give us the kind of father that will love and provide for us.*

After much suffering related to my father's continued drunkenness and an illicit relationship, my parents divorced when I was in sixth grade. My mother, brother, and I moved to a tiny house where at last we could sleep through the night in peace. A year later, my mother married a man who had been a confirmed bachelor. My new stepfather was a faithful husband and good provider. Though he wasn't a Christian at the time, both he and my mother later committed their lives to Jesus.

I am so thankful that the Lord answered my prayer and delivered this wonderful man to our family. Joe Kubishta brought high moral standards, warmth, and much-needed stability into our lives. My mother, my brother, and I fell for his sunny disposition and big smile. Even though I wasn't his "real" daughter, he showed me the fatherly respect and kindness I had longed for.

If you are a stepfather, I encourage you to display the same caring and sensitivity toward your stepchildren. They may not accept you as openly as I did Joe; they may even want nothing to do with you. Underneath such outward appearances, however, are vulnerable girls and boys yearning for a man who will demonstrate genuine fatherly love.

No matter what your family situation, I implore you to be the kind of father that our heavenly Father calls you to be. Your commitment will be the answer to a little child's prayers.

SMD

Being "Mom"

ALONE TIME FOR MOM

by Crystal Kirgiss

*A*ll I needed this morning was a half hour alone, thirty minutes of peace and quiet to help preserve my sanity. No mom-do-this, mom-I-need-that, mom-he-hit-me, mom-I-spilled-juice-on-the-couch.

Just me, a hot Calgon bath, and solitude.

I shouldn't dream so big.

After getting the two oldest off to school, I settled the youngest in front of *Barney* and said, "Honey, listen closely. Your mommy is going to crack. She's losing her marbles. She's teetering on the edge of permanent personality damage. This is happening because she has children. Are you following me so far?"

He nodded absently while singing, "Barney is a dinosaur in our imagination…"

"Good. Now, if you want to be a good little boy, you'll sit right here and watch *Barney* while Mommy takes a nice, hot, quiet, peaceful, take-me-away bath. I don't want you to bother me. I want you to leave me alone. For thirty minutes, I don't want to see you or hear you. Got it?"

Nod.

"Good morning, boys and girls…" I heard the purple wonder say.

I headed to the bathroom with my fingers crossed.

I watched the tub fill with water. I watched the mirror and window steam up. I watched the water turn blue from my bath beads. I got in.

I heard a knock on the door.

"Mom? Mom? Are you in there, Mom?"

I learned long ago that ignoring my children does not make them go away.

"Yes, I'm in here. What do you want?"

There was a long pause while the child tried to decide what he wanted.

"Um…can I have a snack?"

"You just had breakfast. Can't you wait a few minutes?"

"No, I'm dying. I need a snack right now."

"Fine. You can have a box of raisins."

I heard him pad off to the kitchen, listened as he pushed chairs and stools around trying to reach the raisin shelf, felt the floor vibrate when he jumped off the counter, and heard him run back to the TV room.

I sank back into the water.

Knock, knock, knock.

"Mom? Mom? Are you in there, Mom?"

Sigh. "Yes, I'm still in here. What do you need now?"

Pause. "Um…I need to take a bath, too."

Right.

"Honey, can't you wait until I'm done?"

The door opened just a crack.

"No, I really need to take one now. I'm dirty."

"You're always dirty. Since when do you care?"

The door opened all the way.

"I really need to take a bath, Mom."

"No, you don't. Go away."

He stood in the middle of the bathroom and started taking off his pajamas.

"I'll just get in with you and take a bath, too."

"No! You will not get in with me and take a bath! I want to take my own bath! I want you to go away and leave me alone!" I began to sound like the three-year-old with whom I was arguing.

He climbed onto the edge of the tub, balancing carefully, and said, "I'll just get in *with* you, okay, Mom?"

I started to shriek, "No! That is not okay! I want my own bath, all by myself! I don't want to share! I want to be alone!"

He thought for a moment and said, "Okay. I'll just sit here and you can read me a book. I won't get in, Mom, until you're done." He flashed me a knockdown charming smile.

So I spent my morning alone time reading *One Fish, Two Fish* to a naked three-year-old who sat on the edge of the tub with his chin resting on his knees, arms wrapped around his bent legs, slight smile on his face.

Why fight it? It won't be long before I have all the alone time I want. And then I'll probably wish I had a lot more together time.

LOOKING AHEAD...

The job of mom isn't easy, is it? A mother must be a resident psychologist, physician, theologian, educator, nurse, chef, taxi driver, fire marshal, and occasional police officer. And if she succeeds in each of these responsibilities, she gets to do it all over again the next day. It's no wonder that mothers like the one in the story above so desperately need—and so rarely find—a few minutes to themselves.

Most mothers I know deserve a medal (mine certainly did!) for the passion they have for their children and for what they endure while raising them. These mothers would literally lay down their lives to protect the youngsters entrusted to their care.

We're dedicating this week to you, Mom. Cherish your together time with your kids, and always remember that you hold a special place in God's heart.

JCD

UNIQUELY QUALIFIED

*"Can a mother forget the baby at her breast
and have no compassion on the child she has borne?"*
Isaiah 49:15

From the beginning of life, children need their mothers like they need no one else. A baby in the womb depends on his mother for the nutrients that help him develop. After birth, the quality of bonding between mother and child can have lifelong implications. For example, a Harvard University study found that 91 percent of men who did not enjoy a close relationship with their mothers in their early years developed coronary artery disease, hypertension, ulcers, and alcoholism by midlife; only 45 percent of men who recalled maternal warmth and closeness had similar illnesses.

This is only one of the countless reasons why we encourage you to care for your baby yourself and avoid day-care facilities unless there is no reasonable alternative. Research on this subject consistently supports this recommendation. If you are a single mom, you may have no choice. Do the best you can, and don't feel guilty! Yet if your financial situation requires you to work, ask yourself: Could I cut back on my hours? Could I work from home? Are there other ways to spend more time with my child?

Every precious newborn needs five things to thrive: touch, connection, permanence, nurturance, and reassurance. By God's design, no one is better qualified to provide those conditions than mom.

Before you say good night...

- Are you giving your kids consistent, loving attention?
- Are you seeking God's will on how to raise your kids?
- What can you do to make more time for the children?

(mother) Lord, it is so hard to balance the needs of my children with the realities of life. Help me to be the best mother I can be, grant me wisdom to make wise choices, and give me peace when I am doing all that I can. Amen.

TAKING CARE OF MOM

> *"This is the resting place, let the weary rest."*
> Isaiah 28:12

ow well I (SMD) remember the day I put my son, Ryan, then four months old, on the dressing table to change his diapers. As soon as I removed the wet garments, he made like a fountain and "initiated" the wall and a picture of Little Boy Blue. I cleaned up his mess, then left to answer the telephone. While I was gone, Ryan was struck by an attack of projectile diarrhea; he machine-gunned the nursery. I bathed him, scoured the room, and dressed him in sweet-smelling clothes. Exhausted but grateful that the ordeal was over, I affectionately put Ryan on my shoulder—and was horrified to feel him dump his breakfast down my neck!

These memories of the difficult moments of child-rearing have given me a special tenderness for moms. They need care and nurturing, too. The Lord knows that even dirt produces more bountiful crops with periodic rest (Leviticus 25:4–5). So it is for mothers. It's a good idea, then, to regularly do something you enjoy—play tennis, go shopping, stop by the gym, or simply "waste" an afternoon. Go out on dates with Dad, invite a neighbor over for coffee, join a church Bible study or a Mothers of Preschoolers (MOPS) group. Most important of all, take time for quiet fellowship with the Lord. A few of these breaks in the routine will keep you fresh for the next round of diaper-changing with your little darlings.

Before you say good night...
- Are you pushing yourself too hard? Do you need more breaks?
- Husbands, can you help provide your wife with times to refresh?

(mother) Dear God, it's so easy for me to fall into a frantic routine and neglect my own needs. Show me the activities and friends that You want for me, and open my heart to Your leading as I take care of my family and myself. Amen.

"IS BREAKFAST READY?"

There will be...glory, honor and peace
for everyone who does good.
Romans 2:9–10

Though I (JCD) have always respected the talents of mothers, my appreciation for them soared when my son, Ryan, was three years old. Shirley broke her leg while skiing (she claims it was an accident), granting me the chance to do *her* thing for a few weeks. It was a shocking experience. My first day on the job, Ryan interrupted my deep, dreamy sleep with a loud cry at 6 A.M. As he howled, I staggered toward his room, then nudged open the door. The crying abruptly stopped and a cheery voice asked, "Is breakfast ready?" I trudged into the kitchen and stared at the cabinets, hoping something quick and simple would tumble out. Ryan followed, peppering me with questions such as "Are we having bacon?" and "Why isn't the milk poured?" Finally, exasperated with his unresponsive new "mother," Ryan sighed and said, "I'm getting so tired of you!"

Isn't that often the story of motherhood? You give up your own needs to care for your beloved offspring—yet they fail to appreciate or even notice it. Be assured, however, that *God* notices. Every sacrifice, large or small, brings a smile to His face and joy to heaven. That's worth remembering the next time your child is howling at 6 A.M.

Before you say good night...
- What do you find most discouraging about motherhood?
- What can the kids and your spouse do better to help you?
- In what ways does God value mothers? (See Exodus 20:12; Leviticus 20:9; Proverbs 23:22; Isaiah 66:13; John 19:26–27.)

(mother) Heavenly Father, thank You for the blessing of motherhood. Give me strength and encouragement to face its challenges as I seek to fulfill and enjoy Your ordained plan for our family. Amen.

THE GLAMOROUS LIFE

Don't be deceived, my dear brothers.

James 1:16

*M*any women feel that the job of "mom" is boring and monotonous—and they are right! But so is practically every other occupation. I (JCD) once stayed in a hotel next to the room of a famous cellist. I could hear him through the walls (believe me!) as he practiced hour after hour. He did not play beautiful symphonic renditions; he repeated scales over and over. As the cellist strolled onstage that evening, I'm sure many in the audience thought, *What a glamorous life!* Some glamour. He spent the entire day alone in his hotel room.

Few of us enjoy heart-thumping excitement each moment of our professional lives. How thrilling is the work of a medical pathologist who examines bacterial cultures from morning until night or a dentist who spends his days drilling and filling? The job of a homemaker can be about as boring as most others. Yet in terms of significance, no job can compete with a mother's task of shaping and molding a human being in the morning of life (though humanists would have us believe otherwise).

Not every woman chooses to be a mother, of course, but those who do are worthy of our admiration and respect. "Children," we are told in Scripture, "are a blessing" (Psalm 37:26, TLB). If so, then mothers are His loving gift to them.

Before you say good night...

- If you're a full-time mom, do you feel God is pleased with your service to Him as a mother?
- If not, what changes do you wish you could make?
- How can your spouse help you make those changes happen?

(mother) Dear Lord, You have called me to the incredibly important job of being a mom. Help me to experience the satisfaction of resting in Your will. Amen.

STRENGTH TO CARRY ON

Our competence comes from God.
2 Corinthians 3:5

very mother deserves our support and admiration, but the single mom (or dad) merits a double dose. She must locate available and safe child-care services, work for eight or more hours every day, pick up the kids, stop by the grocery store, then come home to cook dinner, wash the dishes, change the diapers, help with the homework, bathe the preschoolers, read a story, dry a tear, say a prayer, and tuck the kids into bed. Then, after perhaps twelve hours of such toil and mothering responsibilities, she must tackle the household chores. It's an assignment that will overwhelm even the most skillful and dedicated parent. That's why those of us in two-parent families must reach out in Christian love to single moms and their children.

No matter what your circumstances, Mom, your best avenue to success is daily dependence on the Lord. Without regular prayer and supplication on behalf of your children, your task is simply too daunting. When you're feeling that one more runny nose or whiny cry will send you over the edge, lay your burdens at His feet. The "Father of compassion and the God of all comfort" (2 Corinthians 1:3) will give you the strength to carry on.

Before you say good night...

- Do you know a single mother who needs encouragement and help?
- When you feel discouraged, do you turn to the Lord for solace?
- Do you regularly seek direction in Scripture?

Father of compassion and comfort, thank You for loving and caring for us! We know that no matter how difficult the journey, You are there to pick us up and point us in the right direction. Wrap us daily in Your arms as we do the same with our children. Amen.

A SUCCESSFUL MOM

*"Your mother was like a vine in your vineyard
planted by the water; it was fruitful and
full of branches because of abundant water."*
Ezekiel 19:10

*M*y mother was a very strong woman when she was young. It was only through her wisdom and devotion that I survived the emotional pressures of my early childhood.

To keep her family fed, Mom found a job at a fish cannery. She was required to work unpredictable hours; many times she would be called at three or four in the morning. I marveled at her ability to hold a job and do the shopping, cooking, housekeeping, and laundry under such stressful circumstances.

Despite the difficulties, Mom was tremendously successful in the two areas of parenting that matter most. First, she convinced my brother and me that she loved us. Second, even though she was not a practicing Christian, she understood that attending the local evangelical church was important for her children. Mom would not go with us (Sunday was her "catch-up" day), but she insisted that my brother and I get involved. She pulled back the blankets every Sunday morning and ordered us to get ready for church. We often complained and moaned, but to no avail. Now I am so thankful for her insistence. It was in that little neighborhood church that I was introduced to Jesus Christ and eventually invited Him into my heart. A few years later, Mom came to know Him, too.

You may be facing your own difficult circumstances as a mother right now. Perhaps your kids' childhoods aren't turning out the way you'd planned. But don't worry about achieving perfection as you raise your children. Cast your "anxiety on him because he cares for you" (1 Peter 5:7) *and* your kids. Show your children your love and teach them to love the Lord. A mother who accomplishes that is doing just fine.

SMD

Safe at Home

STAY!

by Jodi Detrick

$\mathcal{I}$t felt so good to be curled up on the couch after spending most of the day on the go. I had just put the teakettle on and was relaxing while watching the Boston Pops Orchestra on television. Jana, our eleven-year-old music-loving daughter sat in the big blue chair nearby, while across the room Don lounged in the recliner, a book in his hands as usual.

Anne Murray was the guest soloist with the orchestra, and it was easy to reminisce as she sang songs popular in my youth. When one particular love ballad came on, "Could I Have This Dance" (for the rest of my life), my eyes met Don's and we smiled at each other. The song had once been a favorite of ours.

Spontaneously, I rose from the couch and with a grand bow toward Don said, "Would you care to dance, sir?" With a gleam in his eye, he met me in the middle of the living room. The funny thing is that dancing had never been part of our courtship. Neither of us had ever really danced in our lives.

I giggled as we tried to assume a waltzing position and started swaying to the music.

"I think you're supposed to do something with your feet," Don said, and he began to shuffle his steps this way and that. I laughed even harder as we stepped in a pattern that would cause Arthur Murray to roll over (gracefully) in his grave. Jana watched quietly from her chair as we continued our clumsy dance and even stole a kiss or two between our bouts of laughter.

Just then the teakettle, with no invitation from the conductor, brashly added its off-key whistle to the music, signaling an abrupt end to our fun. Breathless, I pushed myself away from Don's arms to go rescue the teakettle.

"No...stay!" Instantly, Jana was off her chair and scurrying into the kitchen.

"It's okay, Jana. I'll get it," I started to protest. But I was too late; Jana pulled the kettle off the burner and turned off the heat.

Once again her words came, and the intensity of command in her young voice caught me off guard.

"No...stay!" This time I could see her arm go up and toward us like a miniature traffic cop hailing an oncoming truck. So we again swayed and stumbled to music that ended all too soon.

Later, as everyone prepared for bed, I wondered about the seriousness on Jana's sweet little face and her strange, earnest command. As she climbed between her sheets, I sat on her bed for "tucking in" time. We talked for a few minutes, as we always do, about special needs we could pray about together. Our prayer list ranged from school issues to the war in Bosnia and many things in between. Then she added one more item.

"Mom," she said softly, "my friend's parents still aren't sleeping in the same room anymore, and now they aren't even talking."

This close schoolmate had recently confided in Jana about her parents' marital struggles. Jana carried her friend's heavy burden seriously, bringing it only to me to take to Jesus in prayer. Together we asked God to please heal this marriage and end the deep sadness in this girl's heart.

"Jana, is she worried that her parents will split up?" I asked.

"I guess. She really doesn't like to talk about it much."

"I understand," I said.

And now I did. So many of Jana's friends were from homes that had been ripped apart by divorce. She had seen, through the young eyes of her peers, the painful aftermath. Now, once again, a friend's happiness and security—this time, a very close friend—were being threatened by the potential divorce of her parents.

I understood. "No...stay!" was a plea to us. It really said, "Please stay in love...stay committed to each other and to our home...keep laughing together...stay partners even when you step on each other's toes in the crazy dance of marriage." It said, "No, don't let the busyness of your lives, the whistling lure of other teakettles, of pleasure in other places, separate your embrace…no, don't be too tired and too preoccupied to hear the music of young love…keep lighting up when you look into the other's eyes across a room. Just…stay."

By this time, everyone was asleep in my home except for me and the One who never sleeps. We talked quietly for a while, and then before I crawled into bed beside my slumbering dance partner, I promised Him again that I would stay.

LOOKING AHEAD…

Our world is changing, and not always for the better. Today's kids must contend with dangers that were virtually unheard-of during my childhood: school shootings, gang wars, illegal drugs, sexual molesters, kidnappers, and terrorists. Yet the greatest threat to a child's sense of security and well-being has nothing to do with these outside forces. It is, instead, the fear that Mom and Dad might one day break up the family.

Kids desperately want and need a stable, secure environment in which to grow. It's what God wants for your family, too. We'll offer several suggestions this week about how you can provide an atmosphere of safety and stability for your children. It all starts with a commitment between you and your partner to nurture your relationship—that wonderful and challenging "dance of marriage."

If you are reading this tonight as a single mom or dad, I especially want to offer you a word of encouragement. Children who have suffered the loss of a parent through divorce or death are particularly vulnerable to uncertainty about the future and fears of abandonment. Your kids need extra reassurance that you will always be there for them. Kind words and gentle hugs, as well as consistent application of boundaries, express your love *and* commitment to provide a stable environment for your children.

You and your kids can also draw comfort from passages in Scripture written especially for you: "A father to the fatherless, a defender of widows, is God in his holy dwelling" (Psalm 68:5). Perhaps the best news for you and your family is simply knowing that you are never alone: "Surely I am with you always, to the very end of the age" (Matthew 28:20). Jesus is standing right beside us every moment.

JCD

MAKING THE MOST OF MARRIAGE

Marriage should be honored by all.
Hebrews 13:4

*D*aniel and Debbie fell deeply in love and married eight years ago. About five years later, however, they found themselves drifting apart. Their hectic schedules and the responsibilities of raising a family had stolen the joy from their relationship. Equally disturbing was the fact that their two young children were becoming increasingly irritable and anxious.

Both parents realized that a change was needed. They committed to each other that they would go on a "date" together every Sunday, even if it was something as simple as relaxing over a cup of coffee at the mall. Gradually, those weekly dates made a difference. Daniel and Debbie began to talk, to enjoy each other again, and to spend more moments together in the Word and in prayer. At the same time, the attitude of their children improved dramatically.

Granting love and attention to your kids goes a long way toward establishing a stable atmosphere at home. But the *best* way to foster security in young hearts and minds is to cultivate your relationship with your spouse. When children see, close-up, your ironclad commitment to each other—as well as your unshakable faith in Jesus Christ—they'll begin to develop a sense of assurance about their own future that is likely to stay with them for the rest of their lives.

Before you say good night...

- Is your marriage solid at the core? What can you do to improve it?
- Are you demonstrating love and respect for each other?
- Do your kids *know* how much your marriage means to you?

Father, You know how we are formed. You understand that we are weak and made of dust. For the sake of our children, Father, and for the sake of Your holy name, strengthen the bond between us as husband and wife. Amen.

WE'LL BE THERE

The winds blew and beat against that house; yet it did not fall,
because it had its foundation on the rock.
Matthew 7:25

When you spoke your marriage vows to your spouse and committed yourself to loving and caring for that person for the rest of your life, you made a holy promise to your husband or wife, as well as to the Lord. You may not have realized then that you were also making a commitment to a few special people who weren't even in the church that day—your children.

When fears and troubles threaten to overwhelm your sons and daughters, they will need to be able to hang on to the rock that is your marriage relationship. Security for children is rooted almost entirely in their parents. For the sake of your marriage and your children, you might want to adopt a Bill and Gloria Gaither tune, "We'll Be There," as the theme song for your family. The lyrics read, in part: "We'll be there...when you need us to hold you tight...when...you're scared of the dark...when you dream your first dreams...when you stand or you fall...when you go on a date, and you're out too late, and you quietly slip up the stairs.... You can count on it. We'll be there."

As described in Scripture, the winds *will* blow and beat (Matthew 7:25) against the house that is your marriage. Yet if you keep your holy commitment and depend on the truth and power of God's Word, your "house" will stand firm, providing a lasting haven for your family.

Before you say good night...

- Are your kids observing anything at home that makes them insecure?
- What more can you do to make each other and your family feel secure?

Lord Jesus, we do want to have a marriage that everyone in our family can depend on. Help us to take the commitment of marriage seriously, ever relying on Your Spirit and Word to provide the holy foundation for our lives. Amen.

LIVE IN PEACE

Live in peace with each other.
1 Thessalonians 5:13

Kellie, a sensitive six-year-old, enters the kitchen and discovers her parents arguing. "You don't care about me!" her red-faced mother shouts at her father, who stands in the corner with his arms crossed. "Every time I ask you to do something you make an excuse. Marrying you was a big mistake!" "Mistakes can be fixed," the father snaps back. "I never asked for a marriage like this!" Now upset herself, Kellie runs to her bedroom and covers her head with a pillow.

We all know that conflict is inevitable in marriage. But how often do we pause to consider the impact of our battles on others? Even when the combatants make up, the fallout of harsh words or acts can linger not only between Mom and Dad, but also in the minds of their kids.

Imagine how you would feel if you were suddenly aware of conflict between God, Jesus Christ, and the Holy Spirit. It would be a devastating moment, one that would shake the foundations of your faith. That's how kids feel about ever-present strife between parents. We urge you to "live in peace with each other" and make the most of your relationship as husband and wife—for your own sake, and for the sake of sons and daughters who depend on you to provide a nurturing environment at home.

Before you say good night...

- Do you argue in front of your children?
- How does it seem to affect them?
- What can you do to provide a more nurturing atmosphere for your kids?

O Lord, how we sometimes struggle to live in peace with each other! Show us the hurtful impact of our angry words and deeds, and help us to bring a holy unity to our marriage and family as we seek to know and follow You. Amen.

LEAVING WORRY BEHIND

"May there be peace within your walls."
Psalm 122:7

When the horrific images of September 11, 2001, flashed across our televisions, the emotions in households across the nation plunged into a traumatic mix of shock, anger, sorrow, and fear. One of those was the Dean home, where nine-year-old Erik watched television reports with wide eyes. Soon the questions began to spill out: "Mom, did people die in those buildings? Why would someone do that? Would they come here?"

The dangers of this age threaten to introduce worry and anxiety into every family. That's why Jesus said, "Do not worry about your life.... Who of you by worrying can add a single hour to his life? Since you cannot do this very little thing, why do you worry about the rest?" (Luke 12:22, 25–26). You bring stability to your family when you cast your burdens on the One who can bear all our burdens (Psalm 68:19).

There is another reason to cast your anxieties on Him. As parents, you set the tone for the attitude of your children in times of crisis. We advise you to shelter them to some degree. Answer their questions about world events, but reserve details for older kids. Teach your children basic safety precautions, reassure them of how committed you are to their protection and well-being, and remind them that God is in control of all our lives. When we shield our kids from the dangers of the world, we allow them to sleep with smiling faces and calm hearts.

Before you say good night...

- Do your children *know* that God is in control of your lives?
- What can you say and do to reassure your kids during times of crisis?

Father, show us how to respond wisely to a fallen and often violent world. Our children need to know that You are always their source of comfort and strength. Grant us freedom from worry as we cast our burdens on You. Amen.

FAMILY TRADITIONS

*These days should be remembered and
observed in every generation by every family.*
Esther 9:28

*I*n today's hurry-up society, it's easy for frantic husbands and wives, as well as their harried children, to feel isolated and lonely. They begin to feel more like a busy cluster of people simply living together in a house than a living, breathing family with a linked character and heritage.

One way to avoid this disconnection is to establish traditions that encourage closeness and fellowship. For instance, for many years the Dobson family has enjoyed several traditions during the holidays that center around food. Each year during Thanksgiving and Christmas, the women prepare marvelous turkey dinners with all the trimmings. Another favorite at these times is a fruit dish called ambrosia, containing sectioned oranges and grapes. The family peels the grapes the night before the big day. We look forward to these gatherings not just for the food, but for the laughter and warm family interaction that occurs when we come together.

Even more beneficial are traditions that reinforce God's love for His children, such as attending church as a family, reading Scripture together, and singing songs of praise. They bring a sense of identity and belonging to marriages and families, providing a wonderful reminder that we are all brothers and sisters in the family of God.

Before you say good night...

- What were your favorite family traditions as a child?
- What new traditions could you implement to benefit your family?

Dear God, we praise You as the refuge and strength of our marriage and family. May the traditions that we establish bring glory and honor to Your name even as they bring each of us closer together in love. Amen.

OUR SOURCE OF SECURITY

The Lord is faithful, and he will strengthen and protect you.
2 Thessalonians 3:3

*C*hristian singer Rebecca St. James faced a test of faith the year her family moved from Australia to Nashville, Tennessee. Two months after they arrived in America, Rebecca's father lost his job. Rebecca, her parents, and her five siblings were left on the other side of the world with no other family, no close friends, no car, no furniture, no income, and a new brother or sister on the way. They felt lost and couldn't help wondering if God knew what He was doing.

But the St. Jameses didn't give up on God in their time of crisis. They responded in the only way they knew how—by sitting on the floor as a family and praying. Soon after, the Lord began providing. Groceries and furniture were delivered to their doorstep. A family donated a car. An anonymous friend even paid for Rebecca's new sister, Libby, to be born in a hospital. God *did* have a plan.

When your children feel discouraged or that their lives are out of control, talk to them about Jeremiah 29:11: "'For I know the plans I have for you,' declares the LORD, 'plans to prosper you and not to harm you, plans to give you hope and a future.'" When they are afraid, show them how to pray as David did: "You are my hiding place; you will protect me from trouble and surround me with songs of deliverance" (Psalm 32:7). When they are anxious, teach them to put their burdens before God to find the holy peace that guards hearts and minds (Philippians 4:6–7).

We've offered several tips this week about how to provide security and stability for your children. The best advice we can give you, however, is to remember that the true source of security for children and their parents is always our loving and merciful God.

SMD

Time for Your Kids

FAMILY PICTURE

by Gary Rosberg

J was sitting in my favorite chair, studying for the final stages of my doctoral degree, when Sarah announced herself in my presence with a question: "Daddy, do you want to see my family picture?"

"Sarah, Daddy's busy. Come back in a little while, honey."

Good move, right? I *was* busy. A week's worth of work to squeeze into a weekend. You've been there.

Ten minutes later she swept back into the living room. "Daddy, let me show you my picture."

The heat went up around my collar. "Sarah, I said come back *later*. This is important."

Three minutes later she stormed into the living room, got three inches from my nose, and barked with all the power a five-year-old could muster: "Do you want to see it or don't you?" The assertive Christian woman in training.

"No," I told her, "I don't."

With that she zoomed out of the room and left me alone. And somehow, being alone at that moment wasn't as satisfying as I thought it would be. I felt like a jerk. (Don't agree so loudly.) I went to the front door.

"Sarah," I called, "could you come back inside a minute, please? Daddy would like to see your picture."

She obliged with no recriminations and popped up on my lap.

It was a great picture. She'd even given it a title. Across the top, in her best printing, she had inscribed: "OUR FAMILY BEST."

"Tell me about it," I said.

"Here is Mommy [a stick figure with long yellow curly hair], here is me standing by Mommy [with a smiley face], here is our dog Katie, and here is Missy [her little sister was a stick figure lying in the street in front of the house, about three times bigger than anyone else]." It was a pretty good insight into how she saw our family.

"I love your picture, honey," I told her. "I'll hang it on the dining-room wall, and each night when I come home from work and from class, I'm going to look at it."

She took me at my word, beamed ear to ear, and went outside to play. I went back to my books. But for some reason I kept reading the same paragraph over and over.

Something was making me uneasy.

Something about Sarah's picture.

Something was missing.

I went to the front door. "Sarah," I called, "could you come back inside a minute, please? I want to look at your picture again, honey."

Sarah crawled back into my lap. I can close my eyes right now and see the way she looked. Cheeks rosy from playing outside. Pigtails. Strawberry Shortcake tennis shoes. A Cabbage Patch doll named Nellie tucked limply under her arm.

I asked my little girl a question, but I wasn't sure I wanted to hear the answer.

"Honey...there's Mommy, and Sarah, and Missy. Katie the dog is in the picture, and the sun, and the house, and squirrels, and birdies. But Sarah...*where is your Daddy?*"

"You're at the library," she said.

With that simple statement my little princess stopped time for me. Lifting her gently off my lap, I sent her back to play in the spring sunshine. I slumped back in my chair with a swirling head and blood pumping furiously through my heart. Even as I type these words into the computer, I can feel those sensations all over again. It was a frightening moment. The fog lifted from my preoccupied brain for a moment—and suddenly I could see. But what I saw scared me to death. It was like being in a ship and coming out of the fog in time to see a huge, sharp rock knifing through the surf just off the port bow.

Sarah's simple pronouncement—"You're at the library"—got my attention big-time. I resolved right then to change—to be a daddy who was *there* for his kids, who didn't spend every moment studying or at the office, who was an active participant in his children's lives. Sure, it might slow down my career ambitions a bit. But I desperately wanted my daughter to know that she was the pride and joy of my life—and that she could show me her latest drawing anytime.

It was time for this daddy to get back in the picture.

LOOKING AHEAD...

How well I understand the struggle Dr. Rosberg describes in tonight's story. Shortly after the birth of my daughter, Danae, I finished my Ph.D. and the whole world seemed to open up to me. Radio and television opportunities were there for the taking, and a book contract sat on my desk. I was running at incredible speed, just like every other man I knew. Although my pursuits were bringing me professional rewards, my dad wasn't impressed. He wrote me a long and loving letter, gently expressing how great a mistake it would be if I continued to pour every resource into my career and failed to meet my obligations to my wife and infant daughter. He said that my occupational success would be pale and unsatisfying if I lost the love of those I cared about most. Those words shook me to the core and made me reexamine my priorities.

Satan once attempted to entice Jesus with the "authority and splendor" of this world (Luke 4:6). He will try the same with you, making every effort to lure you away from your family with temporary treasures and pleasures. When your day is so filled with "important" activities that you don't have a moment for your spouse or children, it's a victory for the devil. Don't listen to him!

Time is a precious resource that, once lost, can never be recovered. Let's spend it in a way that creates joyful, eternal memories for the loved ones under our roofs.

JCD

UNDER THE BIG TOP

I want you to be wise about what is good.
Romans 16:19

*J*osh was so excited. The day had finally arrived. After lunch, his father was taking him to the circus! Then the phone rang. As Josh listened to his father speak, his heart sank. Something about urgent business that required his father's attention downtown. With tears in his eyes, Josh got up from the kitchen table and began walking slowly toward his room. Then he heard his father say, "No, I won't be down. It will have to wait." Almost in disbelief, Josh hurried back to the table and saw his mother smiling at his father. "The circus will come back, you know," she said. "I know," his father answered. "But childhood won't."

We *do* have choices in how we spend our days. Yes, there are consequences if we put off an assignment at work or postpone cleaning the house. But when the alternative is taking time for your son or daughter, what is the better choice? After all, when Jesus asked two fishermen named Peter and Andrew to "Come, follow me" (Mark 1:17), did they respond with, "Not now, Jesus, we have important work to do"?

We encourage you to weigh your options carefully as you plan your schedule. Sometimes an afternoon under the big top is the best appointment of all.

Before you say good night...

- Do you ever appear to value your work over the kids?
- What is God saying to you about the amount of time you spend with your children?
- How can you increase your time together as a family?

O Lord of time and eternity, You know very well how fleeting is the opportunity to encourage our children. Open our eyes so that we might cherish such moments and not let them slip away. In Jesus' name, amen.

JUST SAY NO

Train the younger women to love their husbands and children, to be self-controlled and pure, to be busy at home.

Titus 2:4–5

*F*rench naturalist Jean-Henri Fabre once conducted an experiment with processionary caterpillars, so called because of their genetic inclination to follow one another. He lined them up around the inner edge of a flowerpot and watched them march in a circle. Then he put pine needles, their favorite food, in the center of the pot. The caterpillars continued to walk without breaking rank. Finally they rolled over and died of starvation, just inches from their ideal food source.

Many of today's moms are a bit like these furry little creatures. They trudge around in circles from morning until night, wondering how they can get everything done. Many are employed full-time while also taking care of families, chauffeuring kids, fixing meals, cleaning the house, and trying to maintain marriages, friendships, and spiritual obligations. It's a breathless way of life we call "routine panic."

If we've just described *your* life, realize that it doesn't have to be this way. The tendency for families to take on too many commitments is rampant these days, but it can be avoided by employing one little word: No. As the apostle Paul wrote, we are "to say 'No' to ungodliness and worldly passions, and to live self-controlled, upright and godly lives in this present age" (Titus 2:12). Self-control starts with saying no to frantic living—and yes to a more orderly existence.

Before you say good night…

• Are you overcommitted? What could you cut from your schedule?

• Do you end current obligations before adding new ones?

Save us, Father, from our addiction to constant motion and endless commitments. Grant us courage to rethink our priorities, to say no instead of yes. Lord, give us the self-control that will bring peace and rest to our family. Amen.

QUANTITY AND QUALITY

Every prudent man acts out of knowledge,
but a fool exposes his folly.
Proverbs 13:16

The old debate about which is best for your children, "quantity time" or "quality time," shouldn't be a debate at all. Your children need both. After all, when you look forward all week to an evening at your town's finest and most expensive restaurant, you won't be satisfied with a huge serving of steak that tastes awful. Nor will you settle for a tiny bite of the best steak ever. No, at those prices, you deserve quantity *and* quality! And that's just what your kids deserve from you.

Of course, some of us deceive ourselves. We think we're giving our children the undivided attention they need. But you're missing the target if you have a football game on television while you play Monopoly with the kids, or read the paper while "helping" them with homework, or drive them to the office to color while you work, or take them to one movie at the multiplex while you watch another. Sure, your kids may enjoy some of these activities, but they also know the difference between an involved parent and one who's merely pretending. They deserve "sincere" love (Romans 12:9).

Like the fool in the book of Proverbs, we'll eventually expose our folly if we try to fake significant interest in the lives of our kids. Let's be "prudent" parents and give them our best effort.

Before you say good night...

- Do you ever try to substitute a few "quality" minutes for significant time with your kids?
- Do you give the kids your full attention when you're with them?

Lord, thank You that even as You direct the stars and planets, You still hear our feeble cries and give us Your attention. Help us, Lord, to be like You. Help us to listen to our children, to make time for them, and to let them know in a thousand ways how much they are loved. Amen.

THE TIME CHALLENGE

> *"Is not this the kind of fasting I have chosen...?*
> *Not to turn away from your own flesh and blood?"*
> Isaiah 58:6–7

*S*etting aside time for the kids is a challenge for any family, but it's doubly so when Mom and Dad are divorced. Yet if you are willing to make a few sacrifices, your kids will benefit significantly.

We know of a divorced mother and father who have rearranged their professional lives so that each can spend substantial parts of their week with Zach, their four-year-old son. John, a former golf instructor, gave up his job at the clubhouse because it filled up his weekends. Now he takes care of Zach on Saturdays and Sundays, then leaves him with Zach's mother, Stephanie, each weekday morning. John works during the day at his new job as a sales associate while Stephanie spends that time with Zach. Then Stephanie, who arranged to work the night shift in her job as a nurse, leaves Zach with John for the evening and overnight. The result is that Zach feels loved and cared for by both of his parents.

Establishing complementary schedules with your ex-spouse will not always be easy, or even possible. Yet after the pain and uncertainty that inevitably follow a family breakup, your child needs you more than ever. Phone calls and gifts won't substitute for what your child wants most from you—a mom or dad who is *there* every moment possible.

Before you say good night...

- How do your kids respond when you give them one-on-one time?
- If you are divorced, how do you think your kids feel about the breakup of your family? What can you do to help them?

Lord, we read these words and wonder how we will accomplish these things. Without You, we can never be the parents we want and need to be. Have mercy on us, and fill us with Your grace and wisdom—and staying power! Amen.

LET'S GET TOGETHER

If we walk in the light, as [God] is in the light,
we have fellowship with one another.
1 John 1:7

When was the last time you had friends drop by unexpectedly for a visit? For many of us, it's been entirely too long. There was a time when families made a regular habit of driving over to a friend's home for an afternoon of good conversation and a piece of banana cream pie. It was one of life's special little pleasures.

That kind of spontaneous camaraderie is difficult to achieve in today's fast-paced world. We seldom, if ever, drop in on friends unannounced. Even if we did, they would probably have to cancel a string of appointments in order to be with us. So we career through our days, glancing at our watches and wondering why we don't have many close friendships.

It takes time to build a relationship, whether it's with a friend, your spouse, or your son or daughter. And the moments you'll truly cherish often occur not during a scheduled activity, but in the freedom of unstructured and unpressured time together. The apostle Paul wrote, "Let us not give up meeting together, as some are in the habit of doing" (Hebrews 10:25). He was speaking specifically about fellowship with believers, but it applies just as much to fellowship with friends and family. Make time to simply "be" with the people you care about. You'll never regret it.

Before you say good night...

- Do you wish you had more unstructured time as a family?
- How long has it been since your friends dropped by for a visit?
- Do you have a meaningful social life, or do you think only about work or obligations?

Father, we need the blessing of time together as a couple, as a family, and with the friends You have brought into our lives. Forgive us if we've isolated ourselves or become self-centered. Help us make time for each other for Jesus' sake. Amen.

SPELLING TEST

Let us not love with words or tongue
but with actions and in truth.
1 John 3:18

Writer Jeannie Williams tells a story about a five-year-old named Joey, who was asked by his kindergarten teacher to draw a picture of something he loved. He drew his family, then took a crayon and colored a red circle around the stick figures. He wanted to write a word at the top of the picture, so he approached his teacher's desk. "Teacher," he asked, "how do you spell—" Before he could finish the question, the teacher told him to sit down and not interrupt the class. Joey folded the paper and stuck it in his pocket.

When Joey got home, he saw his mother preparing supper. "Mom," he asked, "how do you spell—" She cut him off with, "Joey, can't you see I'm busy right now? Why don't you go outside and play?"

That evening, Joey approached his father. "Daddy, how do you spell—" His father interrupted without looking up from his newspaper. "Joey, I'm reading right now. Why don't you go outside and play?"

It was more than twenty years later when Joey—now Joe—sat with his five-year-old daughter, Annie, in his lap. They were looking and laughing at a picture she had drawn of their family. Suddenly, Annie jumped up and ran into the kitchen. She returned a moment later with a pencil and positioned it over the top of the picture.

"Daddy," she asked. "How do you spell *love?*"

Joe looked thoughtful for a moment. Then he gently gathered Annie in his arms and guided her hand as she formed each letter. *"Love,"* he said, "is spelled T-I-M-E."

Don't you agree with Joe? When we tell our children that we love them, the words carry a hollow ring unless we back them up "with actions and in truth." God loves us so much that He sent His Son to die for us. He cares for us so deeply that He makes Himself available to us every moment through prayer. Our loving Lord is always ready to spend time with His children. When our own kids seek us out, we must be ready and willing to do the same.

SMD

"I Will Give You Rest"

THREE DAYS OF JOYE

by Sandra Byrd

My shaking hand dialed the phone to cancel a hair appointment. One ring, two. I held back the tears.

Unexpectedly, my friend Joye, instead of the salon, answered the phone. Wrong number. I burst out crying before apologizing and hanging up.

I'd never understood winter blues. The start of a new year had always meant fresh beginnings, back to school or work. But this year, instead of my happy, let's-keep-those-New-Year's-resolutions-going attitude, I was run-down, depressed, and apprehensive about another round of responsibilities. Years of busyness and gutting it out had come home to call. The emotional toll was high.

Please, God, I prayed through a fog of fatigue and discouragement, *help me.*

Five minutes after that fervent prayer, the doorbell rang. I wiped my eyes and pulled a brush through my hair. *Go away,* I thought. It rang again, and again. I finally opened the door—to Joye.

"I'm here to help," she announced. She threw her arms around my weak shoulders, ignoring my faltering refusal. Bundling my children up against the early January chill, she helped me with my coat as if I were a child, too. We buckled into her car for the five-block ride to her house. I tried to argue, but like frosty breath hanging in the air just a minute before disappearing, my protests evaporated against her warm resolve.

When we arrived at her home, she settled me on a cozy couch, tucking me under a soft, well-loved blanket, then shooed away her kids and mine to play downstairs. I felt silly. But after five minutes of thumbing through a magazine, I closed my eyes. While I napped on the couch, the children romped through an unexpected play day.

At noon, Joye brought me a tray with lunch. Tears sprang up again and I smiled. Once I'd told Joye that my mother had made tomato soup with a chunk of cheddar cheese at the bottom whenever I was sick as a girl. She'd remembered.

The next day I felt better, but Joye insisted that we come over again. My children laughed as she painted clown faces on them with costume makeup. I giggled, too—my first giggle in months. This day, Joye baked and served warm Monster Cookies. Her mother had prepared them for her when she was a girl.

On the third day I maintained that I was fine, but Joye said, "We're having so much fun, why not come over for one more day?" So I sat on her couch while she went about her housework. I'd forgotten how much a mother and wife needs a few hours now and then to renew herself—and how wonderful it felt!

Later that afternoon, we sat in Joye's kitchen sipping hot cocoa. She pulled three tiny plastic cups out of her junk drawer and began stuffing them with potting soil. "What are you doing?" I said, savoring a mini-marshmallow as it dissolved against my tongue.

"You need a hobby," Joye said. She snipped the best, strongest leaf off of each of her three prized African violets. "It will help you relax." She tucked one leaf into the rich soil in each planter. "Soak these when you get home, then let them dry out. Don't water them again until they're completely dry. In a few weeks they'll sprout roots, and then in a couple months they'll blossom. It'll be the first sign of spring."

Now, me and my brown thumb were highly skeptical that anything would grow in my house, much less something without roots to begin with. But sure enough, one month later each of those plants budded several tiny leaves, proof of unseen roots thriving below the soil. Months later I settled the growing plants into larger pots, preparing them to withstand my move to a new home across town.

After I got unpacked in the new house, I invited Joye and her kids over for lunch. "Look at my violets!" I proclaimed as she walked into the kitchen. I smiled like a mother boasting of her children's latest achievement.

"They're thriving," Joye agreed, counting almost a hundred heady purple and pink blossoms among the three plants.

I hugged her. "And so am I."

Like the once-weary mother in tonight's story, we all need rest to thrive. It's not just a convenience that we try to squeeze into our schedules or an indulgence for those who aren't willing to work hard. Regular times of quiet and stillness are a spiritual and biological necessity. Many members of the animal kingdom, as well as certain plant species, will hibernate or lie dormant through the winter months in order to survive. We humans have a much harder time acknowledging the natural rhythms of life.

But God knows about our overzealous tendencies. He created us. That's why He commands us to set aside a day each week to rest, pray, and rejuvenate. He understands how much we need regular periods of renewal and how easy it is for us to put them off. In today's hurry-up culture, families will often try to do it all—work, school, church, social events, and an endless array of swim meets, acting classes, and piano lessons. Life begins to feel like a runaway freight train.

Want to get off the train before it crashes? Let's talk this week about ways to make that happen.

JCD

KEEPING IT HOLY

"Be still, and know that I am God."
Psalm 46:10

The Lord doesn't mince words when discussing the Sabbath. He included it among His most important instruction to His people, the Ten Commandments: "Remember the Sabbath day by keeping it holy. Six days you shall labor and do all your work, but the seventh day is a Sabbath to the LORD your God. On it you shall not do any work" (Exodus 20:8–10).

The Sabbath is to be a holy time, devoid of work and dedicated to worship, prayer, and praise. When we honor God as a family, we begin to sense the depth of the love, peace, and power that are available to us.

God *commands* us to keep the Sabbath holy. (They are the Ten Commandments, after all, not the ten suggestions!) But how, you ask, can you make Sunday—or whatever day you choose as your Sabbath rest—a holy day in the midst of life's many distractions? You can start by unplugging the phone and computer, and turning off the television, washer, and dryer. Begin the day and each new activity with a prayer. Join fellow believers at church. Light a candle as a reminder of the One who is the light of the world. By respecting the Sabbath, you'll discover a holy, healing calm that will revive you and your entire family.

Before you say good night...

- How often do you truly honor God as a family on the Sabbath?
- Besides what's listed above, what else can you do to keep the Sabbath holy?
- How might your family benefit from a weekly day of rest?

Father, we need the sweet calmness of a day focused completely on You. Our marriage needs it, and the kids need it, too. Show us Your desire and Your will in making this happen. The first step can be the most difficult! Guide us by Your strong hand. Amen.

OUR GREAT EXAMPLE

*Jesus got up, left the house and went
off to a solitary place, where he prayed.*

Mark 1:35

A crowd, more than two hundred strong, waited patiently in the sun on the dusty outskirts of Capernaum. One shouted, "I hear He gives sight to the blind!" Another called back, "He healed my leprosy!" A few, however, grew restless. One large man approached the small camp where His followers were staying. "Where is this Jesus?" the man demanded. "We are tired of waiting."

One of the followers stood and addressed the man in a soft voice. "He will come when it is time. He is in prayer."

We don't really know all that transpired and what was said when crowds gathered during Jesus' ministry. But we do know that Jesus frequently sought spiritual renewal and rest. We are told, for instance, that "after [Jesus] had dismissed [the crowd], he went up on a mountainside by himself to pray" (Matthew 14:23). Scripture also says that "crowds of people came to hear him and to be healed of their sicknesses. But Jesus often withdrew to lonely places and prayed" (Luke 5:15–16).

If Jesus, for whom anything was possible, chose repeatedly in the midst of His great teaching to withdraw to quiet places for prayer and rest, how much more do we need to do the same? You'll be a more effective parent—and a better example to your kids—when you imitate the perfect ways of Christ.

Before you say good night...

- How often do you spend even a few minutes of quiet time with God?
- Could you make a commitment to do this daily for the next week?

Lord, how foolish to think we could be wise and caring parents in our own strength! How we need more and more of You—Your perspective, Your power, and Your peace. Show us how and where to find time alone with You. Amen.

RAISED IN A MINIVAN

This too is meaningless, a chasing after the wind.
Ecclesiastes 4:4

Are you burning out your kids with too many scheduled activities? Are you, like Martha (Luke 10:40), allowing busyness to distract you and your family from what is truly important? These are questions worth asking. Many of today's parents want their children to experience everything that's available—motivated in part so that their kids will be able to "compete" with their peers when college scholarships are handed out. Those are laudable intentions. But are all the sports practices, singing lessons, and dance recitals worth the price?

According to recent studies, free time for kids is down to only six hours a week. Moms average more than five car trips a day running errands and chauffeuring their children. Typical of this scene, perhaps, is one Chicago-area mother of four busy children. She admitted recently that her one-year-old was practically being raised in the family minivan. "When he's not in the van, he's somewhat disoriented," she said.

When kids aren't sure which is home, the house or the family car, something is definitely wrong. Give your children downtime to play, to wonder, to "waste some time," and to just be kids. Solomon describes the relentless pursuit of knowledge and achievement, when not inspired by God, as "meaningless, a chasing after the wind" (Ecclesiastes 1:16–18; 4:4). We agree.

Before you say good night...

- Do your kids have free time every day?
- Do they *enjoy* their outside activities? Do you?
- What activities might you consider cutting from their schedule?

Slow us down, dear Lord. We've been like Martha, worried and distracted, instead of Mary, who spent time at Your feet, enjoying and adoring You. Please change our hearts by Your indwelling Holy Spirit. Amen.

AFTERNOON HIKE

He makes me lie down in green pastures,
he leads me beside quiet waters, he restores my soul.
Psalm 23:2–3

I (SMD) know of a grandmother who set out on a hike with her almost-two-year-old granddaughter, Carter. She figured that by keeping a steady pace, they could walk the mile to a meadow and back to Carter's house by the end of the afternoon.

Carter, however, had other ideas. Not long after the hike began, she stopped to examine two sticks on the trail. A few minutes later, she stopped to pick some flowers. Farther down the trail, she halted again to rest on a rock. And the grandmother began to remember that the rhythm of life for a little child is very different than the determined pace set by sophisticated adults.

Because of Carter's frequent stops, grandmother and granddaughter walked no more than a half mile that afternoon. But by the end of the hike, that was just fine with this grandmother. With Carter's help, she'd collected sticks, flowers, pebbles, and a dead butterfly. She'd also been reminded that life for a child—and perhaps for grown-ups, too—isn't so much about completion as it is about the process of getting there. When we slow our pace enough to take in the "green pastures" and "quiet waters" along the way, we'll find God right beside us, restoring our souls—just as He promised.

Before you say good night...

- When was the last time you took a family walk?
- When did you last point out any of God's handiwork to your kids?
- Is it time to slow down the pace of your lives?

Please, Lord, set the pace for our family. Help us to see again through the eyes of a child. Take upon Your shoulders the worries and strains that squeeze delight and joy from our lives. And please remind us to let our kids be kids. Amen.

THE JOURNEY IS TOO MUCH

"Come to me, all you who are weary and burdened,
and I will give you rest."
Matthew 11:28

*E*lijah had just achieved a great triumph on Mount Carmel. Now he was thoroughly drained in body and soul. The devil, who delights in attacking us when we are vulnerable, took full advantage of the situation through Jezebel's threat to kill Elijah. Exhausted and discouraged, Elijah sat down and prayed for it all to end. "I have had enough, LORD," he said. "Take my life" (1 Kings 19:4).

God heard Elijah's prayer and sent His tender answer through an angel: "The journey is too much for you" (v. 7). After sleeping, Elijah found that a meal had been prepared for him. He ate and drank and received new hope and strength to continue.

When your energy is totally depleted because of extra commitments, when you've been sick and have nothing left to give, when obstacles seem to thwart your every move—these are the moments when Satan will gather his forces for a fresh assault on your spirit. But if you respond by turning to the Lord in prayer, He *will* show you a way out of hopelessness and discouragement (see Ephesians 6:10–11). When we send our burdens to heaven and rest in His Spirit, we can always count on Him to lighten the load.

Before you say good night...

- Are you discouraged with life because you're simply too tired?
- Do you, and your kids, turn to the Lord in all moments of distress?
- When has God responded to you as He did to Elijah?

We praise Your powerful name, Lord! You are the One who makes a way where there is no way. Forgive us for limiting Your power and Your love—which have no limits at all. We offer you our lives afresh this night. Amen.

THE GIFT OF BOREDOM

This is the day the LORD has made;
let us rejoice and be glad in it.
Psalm 118:24

"Mom, I'm bored!"

Many a frustrated mother has heard those three whiny words. You may be one of them. But before you rush to fill those empty moments with a long list of suggested activities, you might stop to consider if boredom is such a bad thing.

When today's children aren't in school or occupied by after-school activities, homework, chores, and jobs, they too often turn to passive entertainment—television and video games—to fill the rest of their days. The fact is that many kids in the twenty-first century just don't know what to do with time to themselves.

Yet children need "unproductive" time to rest and recharge their batteries. It is the impetus for them to develop their inner lives, imagination, creativity, and sense of individuality. It is a time for play—not structured sports and games, but role-playing fun with stuffed animals or games where the kids make up the rules as they go. This allows children to practice negotiation and creative problem-solving. Unstructured time also provides an opportunity to encourage a love for reading in your kids—a habit that will benefit them for the rest of their lives.

Of course, too much free time can also lead to trouble. The unambitious or irresponsible teenager who avoids all structure is at greater risk for involvement with drinking, drugs, and other perils of adolescence. You'll want to channel him or her into constructive activities through church or school, or perhaps a part-time job.

Other than these exceptions, though, I believe you're wiser to allow your children a few idle moments now and then. God makes so many things for us to enjoy each day—rainbows, sunsets, birds, music, hot chocolate by a toasty fire. As you and your children begin to appreciate them, you may start to see boredom not as a curse, but as a precious gift.

SMD

Loving Discipline

Standing Tall

by Steve Farrar

When I was a sophomore in high school, we moved to a new town and a new high school. It was the typical scenario of being the new kid who doesn't know anyone. One of the fastest ways to make friends in a situation like that is to go out for a sport. In about two days you know more guys from playing ball than you could meet in three months of going to school.

Normally, I would have gone out for basketball. But I had done something very foolish. I had brought home a D on my last report card. The only reason I had gotten a D was that I had horsed around in the class and basically exhibited some very irresponsible behavior in turning in papers. My dad had a rule for the three boys in our family: If any of us got anything lower than a C in a class, we couldn't play ball. He didn't demand that we get straight A's or make the honor roll. But my dad knew that the only reason any of us would get a D was that we were fooling around instead of being responsible.

As a result, I didn't go out for basketball. Now, my dad was all for me playing ball. He had been all-state in both basketball and football in high school, went to college on a basketball scholarship, and after World War II was offered a contract to play football for the Pittsburgh Steelers. He wanted me to play. But he was more interested in developing my character than he was in developing my jump shot.

One day in my physical education class we were playing basketball. I didn't know it, but the varsity coach was in the bleachers watching the pickup game. After we went into the locker room, he came up to me and asked me who I was and why I wasn't out for varsity basketball. I told him that we had just recently moved into town and that I'd come out for basketball next year. He said that he wanted me to come out this year.

I told him that my dad had a rule about getting any grade lower than a C.

The coach said, "But according to the school rules, you're still eligible to play if you have just one D."

"Yes, sir, I realize that," I replied. "But you have to understand that my dad has his own eligibility rules."

"What's your phone number?" the coach asked. "I'm going to call your dad."

"I'll be happy to give you the phone number, but it will be a waste of your time," I said.

This coach was a big, aggressive guy. He was about six feet two inches and 220 pounds, which put him one inch shorter and twenty pounds lighter than my dad. Coach was used to getting his way. But he hadn't met my dad. I knew before the coach ever called what my dad's answer would be.

Was my dad capable of change? Sure he was. Was he going to change because he got a call from the varsity coach? Of course not. That night after dinner, Dad told me the coach had called. He told me he had told the coach no. He then reminded me of the importance of being responsible in class and that he really wanted me to play basketball. But the ball was in my court (no pun intended). If I wanted to play it was up to me. At that point, I was very motivated to work hard in class so that I could play basketball the next season.

The next morning the coach came up to me in the locker room. "I talked to your dad yesterday afternoon and he wouldn't budge. I explained the school eligibility rules, but he wouldn't change his mind. I don't have very much respect for your father."

I couldn't believe my ears. This coach didn't respect my father. Even I had enough sense to know that my dad was doing the right thing. Sure, I wanted to play ball, but I knew that my dad was a man of his word and he was right in not letting me play. I couldn't believe this coach would say such a thing.

"Coach," I said. "I can tell you that I highly respect my dad. And I also want you to know that I will never play basketball for you."

I never did. I got my grades up, but I never went out for varsity basketball. I refused to play for a man who didn't respect my dad for doing what was right. That was the end of my high school basketball career because that man coached basketball for my remaining years in high school.

Come to think of it, the real reason I wouldn't join his team was that I didn't respect *him*. He was a compromiser, and I suspected that he would do anything to win. My dad was a man of conviction and a man of character. And any coach who couldn't see that was not the kind of man I wanted to associate with. My dad was strict and unwilling to change his conviction even though it hurt him for me not to play ball. My dad was capable of change, but he was unwilling to change because he had a long-term objective for my life that the coach didn't have.

The coach wanted to win games. My dad wanted to build a son.

LOOKING AHEAD...

I would like to have met Steve Farrar's father, who clearly understood the importance of respect and discipline in raising a family. That message also got through to his son, even if it was lost on a certain high school basketball coach.

Raising children under such a system produces characteristics such as self-discipline, self-control, and responsible behavior. Some argue that these vital concepts cannot be taught—that the best parents can do is send their children down the path of least resistance, sweeping aside hurdles during their formative years. I completely reject this notion and offer an alternative I call *loving discipline*. When properly applied to our children, this alternative stimulates tender affection, builds up love and trust, encourages respect for others, and introduces the true nature of God.

Loving discipline isn't easy, and your kids won't always appreciate your efforts the way Steve Farrar did in the story above. But your children *will* thrive in an atmosphere that balances genuine love with reasonable, consistent discipline. And so will you.

JCD

GRAB THE REINS EARLY

Command and teach these things.
1 Timothy 4:11

A pediatrician received a telephone call from the anxious mother of a six-month-old baby. "I think he has a fever," she said nervously. "Well," the doctor replied, "did you take his temperature?" "No," she said. "He won't let me insert the thermometer."

Isn't it amazing that a child, who only a few months ago was helpless and dependent, is capable of defying the big adults who would try to control him? The truth is, we human beings are born with a rebellious nature. Babies are not innately "good," as some believe. Those who support this theory say that bad experiences alone are responsible for bad behavior. Scripture indicates otherwise. King David said, "In sin did my mother conceive me" (Psalm 51:5, KJV). Paul tells us that sin has infected every person who ever lived: "For all have sinned and fall short of the glory of God" (Romans 3:23). Even from birth we are naturally inclined toward rebellion, selfishness, dishonesty, and the like, with or without bad associations.

For this reason, we urge you to grab the reins of authority early in your child's life. You must train, mold, correct, guide, punish, reward, instruct, warn, teach, and love your kids during the formative years. Your purpose is to help shape and develop their inner nature, and especially in the case of strong-willed kids, to keep it from tyrannizing the entire family. Do your best; then trust that your children will turn over their souls to Jesus to cleanse them and make them "wholly acceptable" to the Master.

Before you say good night...

- Do you expect your kids to learn responsible behavior on their own?
- How can you help each other to properly use parental authority?

Father, help us to mold those aspects of ourselves and our children that make us more like You. Show us how to choose the right response to each family situation, ultimately preparing our children to turn their lives over to You. Amen.

THE DIGNIFIED MR. WALKER

[A father] must manage his own family well and see
that his children obey him with proper respect.
1 Timothy 3:4

*A*s a child, I (JCD) once spent the night with a mischievous friend who had an amazing ability to outmaneuver his parents. As we were settling down into our twin beds, Earl asked if I wanted to hear his father swear. Being a curious tyke, I naturally said yes. So at Earl's direction we continued to laugh and talk for over an hour, with Mr. Walker repeatedly telling us to be quiet in increasingly hostile tones. "It won't be long now," Earl told me. Finally, Mr. Walker's patience expired. He thundered down the hall, threw open the bedroom door, and leaped upon Earl's bed, flailing at the boy who was safely buried beneath layers of blankets. Then Mr. Walker uttered a stream of words that had seldom reached my tender ears. I was shocked, but Earl was delighted. He yelled to me over the verbal and physical onslaught, "Didja hear 'em? Huh? Didn't I tell ya? I toldja he would say 'em!"

Children can frustrate us to the core of our being. Some of them are motivated by nothing more than the sheer love of conflict and are overjoyed when they drive us to exasperation. When that happens, we have failed to manage our families well (1 Timothy 3:4). But don't lose hope—parenthood doesn't have to be this way! We'll offer an alternative tomorrow night.

Before you say good night...

- Do your kids manipulate you? How?
- What can you do to change this?
- How can you better support each other in managing your children?

Heavenly Father, so often we fail to manage our family well. We recommit ourselves tonight to searching deeper into Your holy Word for wisdom in disciplining our children, and we thank You for eternal truths we can count on. Amen.

LOVE AND CORRECTION

He who loves [his son] is careful to discipline him.
Proverbs 13:24

*L*ast night we talked about a family in which the son controlled the father. Now let's look at another family:

A six-year-old named David was asked by his mother to pick up orange peelings he'd left on the carpet. He wouldn't do it and as a result received a slap on his behind. This led to a temper tantrum. David's father then appropriately applied a paddle, saw to it that David picked up and disposed of the orange peelings, and sent him to bed (it was already past his bedtime). After a few minutes the father went to David's room and explained that God had instructed all parents who truly love their children to properly discipline them and that since they loved David, they would not permit such defiant behavior.

The next morning, David presented his mother with a stack of ten pennies and a letter that said in part, "Dear Mom and Dad, here is 10 Cints for Pattelling me when I really needed. Love yur son David."

David intuitively understood the truth available to all of us in Scripture: "The corrections of discipline are the way to life" (Proverbs 6:23). He knew that his father had applied just the right measure of loving discipline. When we parents properly balance love and correction, we'll stimulate the same respect and tender affection in our own families.

Before you say good night...

- How do you usually respond to a situation like the one with David?
- Are you doing a good job of balancing love and correction?
- If you handled this better, how might it change your family?

Dear God, we want a home filled with joy, tenderness, and mutual respect. Give us grace to find the holy combination of love and discipline that You desire for our family. Amen.

Rewarding Moments

"I will give to everyone according to what he has done."
Revelation 22:12

When trying to encourage proper behavior, a little positive reinforcement goes much further than nagging or screaming. For instance, genuine compliments for responsible acts ("Jack, thank you so much for putting your bicycle away without being told") will put a smile on your son's face and inspire him to try it again. Likewise, a chore chart that lists tasks and rewards for completing them can be extremely effective. Preschool children enjoy winning stickers for their achievements; older kids respond best to money or privileges such as use of the family car.

But is it biblical to use rewards to motive your children? We think so. Consider the words of Christ, who instructed us to give to "the poor, the crippled, the lame, the blind…. Although they cannot repay you, you will be repaid at the resurrection of the righteous" (Luke 14:12–14). Jesus, in fact, is keeping track of even our smallest acts of kindness: "If anyone gives even a cup of cold water to one of these little ones…he will certainly not lose his reward" (Matthew 10:42).

Christ knows exactly how we were made and what motivates us. If He is willing to use the promise of rewards in heaven to encourage the righteous behavior of His followers on earth, we believe parents are wise to do the same with the young "followers" in their families.

Before you say good night…
- How do you encourage good behavior at home?
- How do you feel about a system of rewards for your children?
- What types of rewards would motivate them best?

Dear Jesus, You have promised heavenly rewards for living according to Your ways and deeds. Forgive us for so often falling short! Guide us as we seek to please You in motivating our children. Amen.

A Measure of Mercy

God has bound all men over to disobedience
so that he may have mercy on them all.
Romans 11:32

I (JCD) was invited to speak at a church service many years ago, and I made two big mistakes. First, I decided to speak on the discipline of children. Second, I brought my kids to the church with me. I should have known better.

After delivering my witty, charming, and informative message, I stood at the front of the sanctuary answering questions from a group of about twenty-five parents. As I dispensed further wisdom, we all heard a crash in the balcony. I looked up in horror to see nine-year-old Danae chasing five-year-old Ryan over the seats, giggling and stumbling and running through the upper deck. It was one of the most embarrassing moments of my life. How could I go on telling the mother in front of me how to manage her children when mine were tearing down the church?

At frustrating times like these, I urge you to show a measure of mercy to your rambunctious little ones. No matter how hard you strive to implement a flawless system of discipline in your family, there will be times when it breaks down. Children *will* be children. If the Father of creation can grant mercy to His disobedient children (Romans 11:30–32), we can do the same to ours.

Before you say good night...

- Do you ever expect more from your children than you should?
- Are you merciful toward your kids even as you discipline them?
- Are you most concerned about your image or your kids' character?

Father, as we raise our daughters and sons, remind us that You are the author of their childish ways. As we teach them, lead us to attitudes of patience, understanding, and mercy. Thank You for our kids! Amen.

ACTION OVER ANGER

Man's anger does not bring about the
righteous life that God desires.
James 1:20

As a former schoolteacher, I know how important it is to practice effective discipline in the classroom and at home. One of Jim's former teaching colleagues had no clue about effective classroom management. When her fifth-grade students got out of hand, she jumped on top of her desk and blew a whistle. The only problem was, her students loved it! They spent their days plotting how to get her back on that desk.

Angry threats, screams, and whistles are highly inefficient forms of discipline. They actually create disrespect in the minds of kids. Would you respect a superior court judge who presided over his courtroom by waving his arms wildly, shouting out empty threats and warnings? I doubt it. And so it is in our homes. When we try to rule our families by our emotions, we find our kids manipulating us just like the class with the whistling teacher.

Anger is ineffective in another way; it leads us to say and do things we'll regret. Scripture repeatedly instructs us to avoid inappropriate anger: "Refrain from anger and turn from wrath" (Psalm 37:8); "Get rid of all bitterness, rage and anger (Ephesians 4:31); "Everyone should be...slow to become angry" (James 1:19). I'm not suggesting that you hide your feelings from your children. Sometimes your kids *should* know that you are upset by their actions. But when we try to control the behavior of our children through our anger, it usually ends up controlling us instead.

How, then, should a parent respond to a son or daughter's deliberate disobedience? With consistent disciplinary *action,* administered with a cool head and restrained hand. As we are reminded in Proverbs 29:11, it is the wise man—and the wise parent—who keeps himself or herself under control.

SMD

Those Young Rebels

LOVE WINS

by Patsy G. Lovell

t age thirteen, our daughter Kathleen was a lively teenager. One day she excitedly asked permission to buy a short leather skirt, one like all the other girls in her class were wearing.

I could tell she was expecting a negative response. Nonetheless, she acted surprised when I said no, and then launched into great detail how she would be the only one in class without a leather skirt. I again said no and explained my reasons.

"Well, I think you're wrong!" she retorted.

"Wrong or right, I've made the decision. The answer is no."

Kathleen stomped off, but quickly turned on her heel. "I just want to explain why this is so important to me. If I don't have this skirt, I'll be left out. And all my friends won't like me."

"The answer is no," I quietly repeated.

She puffed up like a balloon and played her final card. "I thought you loved me," she wailed.

"I do. But the answer is still no." With that, she *whumped*—a noise made only by an angry junior high kid trying to get her way. She ran upstairs and slammed her bedroom door.

Even though I had won the battle, I felt I was losing the war. Then an unexplainable thing happened: An inner voice said *Hold fast!*

The whumping noise started once more, and Kathleen appeared on the stairs. This time she was breathing fire.

"I thought you taught us that we have rights!" she screamed.

"You do have rights. The answer is still no."

She wound up again, but I cut her off. "Kathleen, I have made my decision. I will not change my mind, and if you say another word about this you will be severely punished. Now go to bed!"

She still had a few words left, but she held them in check. Visibly seething, she disappeared.

I sat on the couch, shaking and upset. Since my husband was working late, I was the only parent "on duty." None of the children had ever pushed me so far. Just when I thought our skirmish was over, I heard it again—whumping. Kathleen came down the stairs.

"Well," she announced, "I'm just going to tell you one more time…"

I met her at the bottom step, planted my hands on my hips, and looked her in the eyes. "Do not answer," I said. "Do not say anything. Turn around and go to bed. Without a single sound!"

For several minutes after Kathleen left, I stared into space and wondered what my blood pressure was. Then I heard her door open. Kathleen, her nose and eyes red from crying, walked down the stairs in pajamas and curlers. She held out her arms to me.

"Oh, Mom, I'm sorry." We hugged as she said through her tears, "I was so scared!"

"Scared of what?" I asked.

"I was scared that you were going to let me win!" she sniffed.

You were scared that I was going to let you win? I was confused for a moment. Then I realized my daughter had wanted *me* to win!

I had done the right thing—Kathleen's simple words assured me. I had held fast, and now she was holding on to me.

LOOKING AHEAD…

Do you have any idea how the mother in the preceding story felt? If you're a parent, I'm betting the answer is a resounding yes! Children rebel in every home—some more often than others, especially when strong-willed personalities are involved. These encounters can cause even the most dignified fathers and mothers to grind their teeth in frustration.

Yet you are not powerless here. There are ways to minimize such conflict, promote respectful interactions, and instill godly "habits of harmony" in your children. We're going to spend a second week discussing the concept of loving discipline, particularly as it relates to the "whumpers" in your family. You might discover how to put down some rebellions before they ever start.

JCD

MIDDLE GROUND

Wisdom is found on the lips of the discerning.
Proverbs 10:13

*S*ome mothers and fathers favor an authoritarian style of parenting for their families, while others tend toward a permissive approach. We encourage you to be wary of both extremes. In an oppressive home, a child suffers the humiliation of total domination. The atmosphere is icy and rigid, and he lives in constant fear. He is unable to make his own decisions, and his personality is squelched beneath the hobnailed boot of parental authority. Parents who employ this method at home might want to reread Ephesians 6:4: "Fathers, do not exasperate your children."

On the other hand, the child who is given no adult leadership believes the world revolves around him. He often has utter contempt and disrespect for those closest to him; he rebels regularly against his parents. Anarchy and chaos reign in his home. His mother is often the most frazzled and frustrated woman on her block. These parents would do well to embrace this passage from Scripture: "Discipline your son, and he will give you peace" (Proverbs 29:17).

The healthiest approach to child-rearing is found in the middle ground between these disciplinary extremes. Your sons and daughters will thrive in an environment where love and control are present in nearly equal proportions. If a house is built by wisdom (Proverbs 24:3), then a harmonious home is built by the consistent, balanced, and godly attitudes of parents.

Before you say good night...

- Is your parenting style more authoritative or permissive?
- Do you need to change to a more balanced approach?

Heavenly Father, grant us wisdom! We confess to making mistakes in the way we raise our children. Help us to achieve the right balance of love and leadership that You desire for our family each day. Amen.

CALLING ROBERT'S BLUFF

Children, obey your parents in everything,
for this pleases the Lord.
Colossians 3:20

*U*pon arrival for his dentist appointment, a rebellious ten-year-old named Robert refused to get in the patient chair and threatened to take off his clothes if the dentist made him sit. The dentist's reply? "Son, take 'em off." Robert did—and then, completely naked, settled into the chair and cooperated for the rest of his visit. When cavities had been drilled and filled, Robert said, "Give me my clothes now."

"I'm sorry," the wily old dentist said. "Tell your mother that we're going to keep your clothes tonight." An embarrassed Robert was forced to walk in his birthday suit through a waiting room filled with snickering patients. The next day, Robert's mother came to retrieve the clothes—and to thank the dentist. "Robert has been making unreasonable demands and blackmailing me about taking off his clothes in public for years," she said. "You are the first person to call his bluff, Doctor, and the impact on Robert has been incredible!"

Children such as Robert need boundaries. If you don't provide them, they'll threaten and push until someone else does. If you are easily "blown over" in times of confrontation, your child will not learn to yield to authority. Not only will he later defy you, but he is likely to misunderstand the ultimate authority of God. The two sources of leadership, parental and divine, are directly linked in the minds of your kids.

Before you say good night...
- Do you have a "Robert" in your home?
- Are you enforcing clear behavioral boundaries for your kids?

Dear God, just as You gave us clear boundaries for living in the Scriptures, guide us to do the same for our children. And when they cross those boundaries, grant us courage and wisdom in our response. Amen.

THE "ROD OF DISCIPLINE"

Folly is bound up in the heart of a child,
but the rod of discipline will drive it far from him.
Proverbs 22:15

You may be unsure about the notion of spanking your kids. You've heard the argument—spanking will turn your child into a violent, aggressive adult. We believe otherwise. An occasional dose of minor pain is one of nature's teachers. A child who touches a hot stove will only make this mistake once. Likewise a judicious, controlled spanking, when motivated by love and applied properly, is in keeping with the principles of Scripture (see Proverbs 23:14).

There are many conditions to proper use of spanking, though. Reserve it for moments of willful defiance only. Never spank when you are out of control. Never spank a child who is less than fifteen to eighteen months or over twelve years; spanking should taper off after age five. Spank only on the bottom (never slap a child's face or jerk his arm, which can cause serious injury). Make spanking an infrequent practice, not a regular event. Remember that corporal punishment is a tool for teaching—not for venting anger or frustration.

We most certainly do *not* advocate indiscriminate paddling of your children. Child abuse is a national tragedy! Yet there are times when a short session over a bent knee—applied with care, wisdom, and a sensible explanation—will benefit your child. After all, it *is* scriptural.

Before you say good night...
- How do you feel about spanking your kids?
- Do you or could you employ spanking properly in your family?
- In your home, what situations would warrant a spanking?

Lord, we want to be loving and effective with our discipline at home. When our children are defiant, calm our anger, heal our hurt spirits, give us wisdom, and let our actions bring us closer to each other and to You. Amen.

"THANK YOU, GRANDPA"

"Show respect for the elderly and revere your God."
Leviticus 19:32

*I*f you have been around for a while (as we have!), you've probably noticed that coarse and rude behavior is more common in today's society than in years past. We think that's a change for the worse.

Maybe it's old-fashioned, but we feel that kids should be required to say "please" and "thank you" around the house. This is just one method of reminding them that ours is not a "gimme, gimme" world. We also recommend that children maintain a level of deference when speaking to their elders—"Grandpa George" and "Aunt Alice," rather than just "George" and "Alice." Scripture teaches that children ought to respect their parents (1 Timothy 3:4) and that everyone should "Rise in the presence of the aged, show respect for the elderly" (Leviticus 19:32). This attitude of respect for our earthly elders also leads us more easily into proper respect for our heavenly Father.

Such attitudes don't happen automatically. They take root when you teach your children fundamental politeness—and when you practice it yourself! The bottom line is to create an atmosphere of mutual respect. If you can establish that in your kids' earliest years, they'll be less likely to rebel when they're older—and you'll be much better prepared to handle the uprisings that inevitably come along.

Before you say good night...

* As a family, do you show courtesy and respect to each other?
* How does demonstrating respect for others also show respect for the Lord (see Matthew 25:40)?

Loving Father, You are awesome beyond our comprehension! Help us to esteem each of Your creations and to set a respectful and reverent example for our children. Amen.

SIX STEPS

Discipline your son, for in that there is hope.
Proverbs 19:18

We've talked about the concept of *loving discipline* during the past two weeks. To give you a practical summary of our ideas, here are the six basic steps to implementing good discipline at home.

First: Define the boundaries clearly and in advance. If you haven't spelled them out, don't try to enforce them! Second: Once a child understands what is expected, hold him accountable. This may lead to a contest of wills—be sure to win those confrontations when they occur. Third: Distinguish between willful defiance and childish irresponsibility. Forgetting, losing, and spilling things are not challenges to adult leadership. Fourth: Reassure and teach as soon as a time of confrontation is over. By all means, hold your child close and explain lovingly what has just occurred. Fifth: Avoid impossible demands. Be sure that your child is capable of delivering what you require. And sixth: Let love be your guide! You *will* make mistakes with your child, but a relationship characterized by affection and grounded in God's love is certain to be healthy and successful.

These basic principles are taught throughout Scripture. They bear the wisdom of the Father Himself.

Before you say good night...

* Do you use these six steps with your kids?
* Which step is hardest for you? How can your spouse help you with that?
* Would you add anything to the steps above?

Father, we love our children so much. Strengthen our weaknesses, forgive us for our mistakes, and lead us as parents into healthy lifelong relationships with our kids. Amen.

THE ONGOING CHALLENGE

No discipline seems pleasant at the time, but painful.
Later on, however, it produces a harvest of
righteousness and peace.
Hebrews 12:11

The role of discipline in the relationship between parents and their kids is drawn directly from God's holy Word. Ephesians 6 commands children to "obey your parents in the Lord, for this is right" (v. 1) and directs fathers to "bring [children] up with Christian teaching in Christian discipline (v. 4, Phillips).

As a believer who trusts the Lord completely, I understand the significance of discipline. Yet as a mother, I also know that it's the continuing battle to *apply* proper discipline at home that so often leaves parents feeling like a failure. If you are one of these discouraged moms and dads, I urge you to take heart—you're probably doing a much better job than you think! Loving discipline *will* begin to promote an atmosphere of affection and respect if you are consistent and persistent.

I remember the first time my daughter challenged me. I was waxing the kitchen floor when Danae, then nine months old, crawled to the edge of the linoleum. I said "no" and gestured for her to stay put. She ignored me and crawled right into the sticky wax. I picked her up, set her down in the hallway, and said "no" again, this time more strongly. We repeated this scene seven times before Danae finally realized that Mom wasn't backing down; she crawled away in tears. Believe me, it wasn't the last time Danae would test her mother! Yet it did send her an early and important message: No matter how determined Danae was to get her way, I would be the one to make the rules and guide her with firmness and persistence.

It's not easy, but it *is* worth it. Do your best, seek always to discipline "in the Lord," and one day you'll see what I mean.

SMD

Encouragement for Every Day

RUN, TAMI, RUN

by John William Smith

$\mathcal{I}$ have a dear friend who lives in Dallas, and he has a daughter who is a very talented runner. The regional cross-country championships were held in my town, and he called to ask if I could pick up his wife from the airport and give her a place to stay while she was there to watch their daughter run. I was delighted to do it and so I found myself on Saturday morning witnessing the Texas Regional Cross-Country Races at Mae Simmons Park. I saw something there—a wonderful, moving thing—a thing of beauty worth telling and retelling.

It was a marvelously bright, clear, cool morning, and hundreds of spectators had gathered on the hillsides to watch. They were mostly family members who had traveled many miles—in some cases, hundreds of miles—to watch just one race. I had no child running, and so I found myself watching those who did. Their faces were intent, their eyes always picking out the only runner they were interested in; and often, when the runners were far away and could not hear their shouts of encouragement, still their lips would move, mouthing the precious, familiar names—and one other word. Sometimes they said the names audibly, but softly, as if for no ears but their own, and yet it seemed that they hoped to be heard.

"Run, Jimmy," they whispered urgently.

"Run, Tracy."

"Run."

The cross-country race is two miles for girls, three for boys. It is a grueling run—physically and mentally exhausting—over hills and rough terrain. There were ten races that morning, beginning with class 1A boys and girls and ending with class 5A boys and girls. Each race had from eighty to one hundred twenty competitors. The course ended where it began, but at times the runners were nearly a half-mile away.

As the class 5A girls' race came to a close, I watched a forty-plus-year-old mother—who was wearing patent leather shoes and a skirt and carrying a purse—run the last hundred yards beside her daughter. She saw no other runners. As she ran awkwardly—her long dark hair coming undone and streaming out behind her, giving no thought to the spectacle she made—she cried, *"Run,* Tami, *run!—Run,* Tami, *run!"* There were hundreds of people crowding in, shouting and screaming, but this mother was determined to be heard. *"Run,* Tami, *run—Run,* Tami, *run,"* she pleaded. The girl had no chance to win, and the voice of her mother, whose heart was bursting with exertion and emotion, was not urging her to win.

She was urging her to finish.

The girl was in trouble. Her muscles were cramping; her breath came in ragged gasps; her stride was broken, faltering; she was in the last stages of weariness—just before collapse. But when she heard her mother's voice, a marvelous transformation took place. She straightened; she found her balance, her bearing, her rhythm; and she finished. She crossed the finish line, turned, and collapsed into the arms of her mother.

They fell down together on the grass and cried, and then they laughed. They were having the best time together, like there was no one else in the world but them. *God,* I thought, *that is so beautiful. Thank You for letting me see that.*

As I drove away from Mae Simmons Park, I couldn't get it off my mind. A whole morning of outstanding performances had merged into a single happening. I thought of my own children and of a race they are running—a different and far more important race. A race that requires even greater stamina, courage, and character. I am a spectator in that race also.

I determined in that moment that my voice, too, would be heard above the rest. Like Tami's mother, I would not be concerned about what others thought. I would see no other runners. Whether they were in first place or last, I would urge my children to keep going. And if they faltered and seemed ready to collapse, I would run right alongside them, my words a gentle and encouraging whisper that would lift them to the finish:

"Run, children. Run."

L O O K I N G   A H E A D ...

We all weary at times of the race of life. The idea of even finishing whatever project or challenge stands before us, let alone of "winning" or doing
it exceptionally well, can seem like an impossible hurdle. That is true of
athletes, of businessmen and women, of pastors, of teachers—and most
certainly of parents and their children.

Yet the Lord sees each of us in our weakness and discouragement,
and has compassion on us: "You hear, O LORD, the desire of the afflicted;
you encourage them, and you listen to their cry" (Psalm 10:17). Though
we may feel alone, He is running alongside us, giving us the strength and
encouragement we need if only we listen for His voice.

We'll talk more this week about how the Lord encourages us, and
how much He wants us to uplift each other. Why don't you get our discussion started off right with a kind word for your spouse tonight?

JCD

Our Source of Hope

I have put my hope in your word.
Psalm 119:74

Encouragement can come from many sources, but the foundation of our strength and hope is always the unchangeable Word of God. For centuries, families have depended on the truth of Scripture to guide them in matters of faith, in the nuances of daily life, and during times of trouble. The Bible provides encouragement for the trials of today as we anticipate the joy of the hereafter.

The apostle Paul, no stranger to adversity, said to the Roman church, "Everything that was written in the past was written to teach us, so that through endurance and the encouragement of the Scriptures we might have hope" (Romans 15:4). David, one of the great heroes of the Bible, also faced many hardships (some of his own making). In these times of distress, he repeatedly turned to the Lord and His laws for deliverance: "May your love and your truth always protect me. For troubles without number surround me" (Psalm 40:11–12). The Psalms, in fact, are wonderful examples of praise and inspiration for moments of fear, insecurity, or doubt.

In our struggles as parents and as Christians, we would be wise to choose God's Word as our first option for lifting our spirits. It contains the blessed hope that brings meaning to every thought and every moment.

Before you say good night...

- What Bible verses are most encouraging to you? (See Psalm 46:1; 55:17; Luke 12:32; John 3:16.)
- Would it encourage your children if you helped them memorize Scripture?

Lord, we confess our deep and constant need for Your Word. Forgive us for depending on our own strength and wisdom—for seeking encouragement in so many shallow and unsatisfying ways. Draw us back into Scripture that sustains us in every challenge we face. Amen.

THE POWER OF WORDS

The tongue has the power of life and death.
Proverbs 18:21

*J*osh, a typical teenager in most respects, differed from his friends in at least one quite noticeable way—he had a large birthmark that covered much of his face. His unusual appearance, however, didn't seem to affect him. Josh related well with his peers and didn't act at all self-conscious.

A family friend eventually put his curiosity about this into words. "Josh, you must be aware of the large birthmark on your face," he said. "Can you tell me why it doesn't seem to bother you in the slightest?"

Josh smiled and said, "When I was very young, my father started telling me that my birthmark was there for two reasons: one, it was where the angel kissed me; two, the angel had done that so my father could always find me easily in a crowd. My dad told me this so many times that as I grew up, I began to feel sorry for the other kids who weren't kissed by the angel."

Words are an extremely potent tool, and those spoken by the people we love carry the most weight of all. Let's heed the instruction of Scripture—"encourage one another daily, as long as it is called Today" (Hebrews 3:13)—and use the power of words to bless our children at every opportunity.

Before you say good night...

- Do you consistently encourage your children through your words and actions?
- How could you be even more effective?
- How can you model encouragement to each other so your kids will see it in action?

Father, show us how to use the power of words to bring encouragement, comfort, and confidence into our children's lives. Restrain us from words that hurt and guide our tongues to bring words of light and lasting hope into our home. Amen.

TRYOUT DAY

Encourage one another and build each other up.
1 Thessalonians 5:11

An encouraging word is welcome at any time, but is needed most of all after a disappointment or failure. That's why Scripture instructs us to "encourage the timid, help the weak, be patient with everyone" (1 Thessalonians 5:14). I (JCD) am reminded of a story about Joy, a twelve-year-old who had her heart set on making the school cheerleading squad. She practiced cheers, cartwheels, and toe-touches for weeks. Yet on tryout day, Joy's best effort still fell short. She was crushed.

Joy's mother had been traveling at the time. When she returned she asked, "Joy, how did tryouts go?" "I lost," Joy answered quietly. "Really?" said her mother. She put her arms around her daughter. "Well, Joy, I am so proud of you for working so very hard, and then for having the courage to go out there and try!" The change in Joy's expression was immediate.

If Joy's mother had showed the slightest disappointment or embarrassment, Joy would have felt even worse. Emotions are contagious. We tend to "catch" the reactions of those around us and incorporate their highs and lows in our own spirits.

Your children are at their most vulnerable when they endure a terrible hurt or setback. Your attention and thoughtfulness during these moments can lessen the pain and bring you closer to your kids. Like Joy's mother, you may even find the silver lining that turns disappointment into triumph.

Before you say good night...

- Do you try to turn around disappointments in your family?
- What "encouragement strategies" can you deploy?

Lord Jesus, we need eyes like Yours—eyes that see opportunities to bring comfort out of pain, light out of darkness, hope out of despair. Open our eyes and hearts, Lord, so that we might walk our children through these years. Amen.

Up Against the Wall

"Keep up your courage, men, for I have faith in God."
Acts 27:25

few years ago, one of our Focus on the Family staff members visited Lake Powell in Utah and Arizona, a magnificent canyon lake about 185 miles long. She was especially impressed by its massive rock "sideboards" that extend hundreds of feet in the air. That night she approached one of these gigantic structures, a wall that rose at least five hundred feet above the campsite, and placed her hand on the warm rock. A thousand tiny pieces of this seemingly solid fortress crumbled in her hand. *Incredible!* she thought. *These immovable canyon walls can be stripped away by a person's fingers!*

Sometimes the barriers and obstacles that present themselves to us are like those porous walls. From a distance, they seem impenetrable and massive, but when we dare to confront them, they crumble in our hands. People like Helen Keller and Franklin Roosevelt have overcome seemingly insurmountable physical barriers. Astrophysicist Stephen Hawking, paralyzed by Lou Gehrig's disease, dictates complex mathematical computations on a computer by moving just the tips of his fingers.

When the apostle Paul's life was in danger, the Lord Himself exhorted him to "Take courage!" (Acts 23:11). If we encourage our children to do the same when they're "against the wall," they may see those walls come tumbling down.

Before you say good night...

- What are the "insurmountable" obstacles facing your family today?
- Have you confronted them directly?
- Do you lean on the Lord's strength when you tackle challenges?

Father, be with our children as they confront the daily obstacles and walls in their lives. Surround them with Your unfailing love, and show them Your power to move those things that in their eyes seem to be mountains. Amen.

A New Attitude

The lips of the righteous nourish many.
Proverbs 10:21

*I*t's difficult to maintain an encouraging spirit when you're over-whelmed by problems with your child. We know of a family that faced this predicament. Jenny was a three-year-old who was still acting like a child in the "terrible twos"; nearly every interaction between parent and child was marked by conflict. Yet the father decided that this was as good a time as any for a first "date" with his daughter: breakfast at a local restaurant. As the hot pancakes melted his butter, he felt his own disappointment with his daughter melting away. He began to tell Jenny how much she was loved and appreciated, that he and her mother had prayed for Jenny for years, that they were so proud of her.

The father stopped to eat, but never got the fork to his mouth. In a soft, pleading voice, Jenny said, "Longer, Daddy. Longer." For a second time he told Jenny why she was special…and a third time…and a fourth. Whenever he stopped, he heard the words, "Longer, Daddy. Longer."

To follow Christ is "to be made new in the attitude of your minds" (Ephesians 4:23) so that every action and word is "helpful for building others up" (v. 29). It is true with children of all ages, too. Sometimes a problem with misbehavior or rebellion can be lessened by simply taking the time to have fun together and to speak of love in very warm terms. Kids need to hear that they are respected and appreciated. And guess what—so do moms and dads.

Before you say good night…

- Are you displaying a loving, appreciative attitude toward your kids?
- What can you do this week to express this attitude to your children?

Lord, You always see the hunger for affirmation and attention and love in the hearts of our kids. Awaken us, we pray, so that we see it, too. Help us to pour out encouragement to our children as You continue to pour it into us. Amen.

TRUST HIM

Trust in the LORD with all your heart...
and he will make your paths straight.
Proverbs 3:5–6

When the decision was made years ago to move Focus on the Family from Arcadia, California, to Colorado Springs, I knew it was a positive change for the ministry—yet I did not welcome it with enthusiasm. I felt I needed the support system we had developed in California. Our friends there saw us not as ministry leaders, but as just "Jim and Shirley." We'd been in one another's weddings and had babies together. For years we'd had them over to celebrate the Fourth of July with barbecued hamburgers and games in our backyard. I grieved to leave this safe and loving circle of friends, and to say good-bye to my parents and both of our children.

In Colorado, I continued to wrestle with feeling sorry for myself and missing home, family, and friends. Yet I still prayed for the Lord's direction. One day I was standing in the bathroom preparing for work when I felt His presence. "Shirley," He seemed to say, "I'm not concerned about your happiness; I'm concerned that you are in My will, and My will is that you be in Colorado."

From that point on a new peace filled my heart. The lingering feelings of discontent left me. Though I still miss my roots and friends, I now can see God's hand in it all. I have stretched and grown in ways I couldn't have imagined. Over the years my old friends have moved, too. Only a few of those couples still live in that area of California, and we see our family almost as often now as before.

When you are discouraged about your kids, your career, your lack of friends, or anything else, don't let it stop you from speaking to God. He *will* encourage you as you seek Him: "I trust in your unfailing love; my heart rejoices in your salvation" (Psalm 13:5).

The Lord may not answer you as specifically as He did after my move to Colorado. He may not give you the answer you want at all. Yet He loves you and always responds with your best interests in mind. That's encouragement you can count on.

SMD

WEEK THIRTEEN

Money Matters

FINDERS, KEEPERS

by Faith Andrews Bedford

orty years ago on a hot August day I first experienced what it must be like to be wealthy. Mother needed milk, so I volunteered to ride my bike to town and fetch some.

I passed the school, its swings still and silent. In a little more than a month, I would be entering the sixth grade. As I came to the edge of town, I pedaled faster. I'd been saving up to buy the little horses in Mrs. Bridges's toy shop window and was eager to see if they were still there. I had only $4.25 left to save until they would be mine.

Ahead was the toy store and there, in the window, was the little horse family: a black stallion; a palomino mare, bent down as if to graze; and their little foal. I had long imagined how the trio would look on my bureau top; I would cut fresh grass every day and arrange it beneath the mare's muzzle.

Still dreaming of the horses, I nearly stepped on a lump of paper. I bent down and realized it was a roll of money. I picked it up. *It must be hundreds,* I thought, *millions!* I raced around the corner toward the grocery store, almost knocking over our neighbor Mr. Peabody.

"Look what I just found!" I said, waving the roll wildly in the air.

"Well, well, well," Mr. Peabody said. "That's quite a find. But you need to be more careful with that bike, young lady," he scowled with mock ferocity.

"Yes, sir," I said breathlessly and pushed on, a little more slowly. I leaned my bike against a tree and dashed into the store. The coldness of the milk bottle felt good against my skin as I fidgeted in the checkout line. Pushing my bike back toward the toy store, I returned to the magic spot where I'd found the money. The street was still empty.

I burst into the toy shop. The little bell on the shop's door clanged wildly. "Goodness, Faith!" Mrs. Bridges gasped, her hand flying to her throat. "Whatever is the matter?"

"Nothing." I grinned, waving the roll of bills gaily. "I've come to buy the little horses. I'm sure there's enough here."

"My, my. There certainly does seem to be. Let's count it."

Mrs. Bridges carefully counted out three tens and an endless number of ones. "You've got forty-seven dollars here, dear," she said with surprise. "Last week you told me you had eight saved up."

"Yes," I said. "But now I'm rich!"

Mrs. Bridges smiled, retrieved the little horses from the window, and put them in a bag. I took it and ran out the door shouting a thank-you over my shoulder.

The milk bottle rattled in my bike basket as I raced home. I dashed through the kitchen door just in time to find Mother hanging up the phone.

"Mother, I found a whole bunch of money!" I shouted, hugging her excitedly.

"I know," she said softly.

"You do? How?"

"That was Mr. Peabody on the phone. He told me he'd bumped into you in the village. Literally." I could feel my face redden as I recalled nearly toppling him.

"He told me about your having found the money. Then he told me he met the lady who lost it."

The heat of the day disappeared as a chill descended upon me.

"No," I whispered, tears welling up in my eyes. "It's mine."

"Faith, Faith," Mother said as she drew me close. "Mr. Peabody said that when he came out of the bank, he saw a mother with her little boy frantically searching the sidewalk in front of the electric company. When he asked her if she'd lost something, she said that she'd put the money to pay her electric bill in one pocket and her grocery money in the other. When she went in to pay her bill, the money was gone. The clerk told her they would cut off her electricity if she couldn't pay. She was desperate, Mr. Peabody said. It was a good thing he saw her."

"No, it wasn't," I cried as I buried my face in Mother's shoulder.

"There, there," she said, patting me gently. "You need to hush now.

The lady will be here soon. Mr. Peabody told her where we live."

"But I found it," I shouted, pulling away from Mother's embrace. "Finders, keepers."

Mother just looked at me.

"And besides," I sobbed, clutching the paper sack tightly, "I bought the little horses with some of that money."

"Well," Mother said quietly, stroking my hair, "I guess you'll have to take them back."

I sniffed and reluctantly realized that she was right. The money had never been mine. Not really. I knew I had done nothing to earn it. The pleasure of owning the little horses was beginning to dim. The sack grew heavy in my hands.

A few minutes later I heard a soft knock at the door. A woman's voice said, "Are you Mrs. Andrews? I think your daughter may have found the money I lost." I peeked around the corner.

"You have the right house," Mother replied. "Come in. You've had a long walk. Won't you have some lemonade?" The woman nodded. Her thin dress clung to her in the heat. One hand held a bag of groceries and the other rested on the shoulder of a skinny little boy. I had stood behind them in line at the grocery store.

Mother saw me. "This is Faith," she said, motioning me forward. "She's the one who found your money."

"In front of the electric company?" the woman asked. I nodded.

"Forty-seven dollars?"

"Yes," I said slowly, handing her the rest of her money, plus the eight dollars from my piggy bank. Relief spread across her pale face like sunshine after a rain.

"Oh, thank you," she said. "I was so frightened. I just didn't know where I was going to come up with the money to pay our bill."

"It's not all there," I mumbled in embarrassment.

"Excuse me?" she said, not quite catching my words.

"I spent some," I said, hanging my head.

"Oh," she laughed. "I'd planned to give you a five-dollar reward for finding my money and keeping it safe for me. Did you spend that much?"

I shook my head. "No, ma'am, I didn't. I only spent $4.25."

"Then here," she said, dropping three quarters into my open hand. "Here's the rest of your reward."

Mother and the lady sat in the parlor sipping lemonade and talking while I showed her son how to play Chinese checkers. Then I heard the lady say, "William will be in first grade this year."

"You will?" I asked him. He moved one of his marbles into place and nodded shyly. He looked both proud and scared.

"Here," I said, pressing one of my reward quarters into his hand. "You'll need some colored pencils." I felt at once wise and magnanimous. After all, I'd been wealthy for a moment.

The day had begun to cool by the time William and his mother left for home. I stood in our front yard and watched them turn down the lane. Then I began to pick a bit of fresh grass for my little horses.

Just before they turned the corner, I heard William call out a good-bye and thank-you. One hand was held in his mother's, but he waved the other in farewell. It was still clasped around his quarter. I could tell he didn't trust pockets.

LOOKING AHEAD...

Many of us dream, at one time or another, of suddenly acquiring great wealth—whether it's finding forty-seven dollars in the street or winning the lottery—that will transform our existence into endless bliss. Before you invest too much time in those fanciful thoughts, though, you might want to take a look at your Bible.

Jesus had more to say in Scripture about money and possessions than any other subject. He made it clear that there is a direct relationship between our spiritual lives and our attitude about money. Though many of us see our faith and our finances as important but unrelated aspects of life, the Lord views them as inseparable. He knows that when our hearts are wrapped up in accumulating wealth and material goods, we can't enjoy intimacy with Him.

Do you want your children to end up with treasure on earth or treasure in heaven? We'll take a closer look at these money matters in the days ahead.

JCD

SERVING ONE MASTER

The love of money is a root of all kinds of evil.
1 Timothy 6:10

We are very concerned about the impact of materialism on families today. During the hardships of the Great Depression, it was easy enough for parents to tell their kids that they couldn't afford to buy everything they wanted. But in these more opulent times, children see that you *can* afford to purchase their hearts' desires—if not with cash, then with your magic credit card. And then there are the advertisers that spend millions of dollars to stimulate your kids' lust for their products—toy monsters; dolls that eat, walk, and talk; designer shoes and clothes; and more. Your children begin to develop an "I need more" mentality that can be terribly destructive in their adult years. It's why so many people are hopelessly in debt today. It's what spawned a popular bumper sticker a few years ago: "He who dies with the most toys wins." The sticker should read, "He who dies with the most toys dies anyway."

Jesus delivered a very different message when a rich man questioned Him about the path to eternal life. Jesus said to "sell your possessions and give to the poor, and you will have treasure in heaven" (Matthew 19:21). The man walked away because he was unwilling to part with his wealth.

It simply isn't possible to seek, worship, and serve both God *and* money (Matthew 6:24). Now is the time to choose for your family.

Before you say good night...

- How much of your time is invested in that which is of no long-term significance?
- What can you do to reduce the influence of materialism?

Father, we know that our children's attitude toward money will be shaped to a large degree by our own. Please take us by the hand and lead us toward Your heart's desire for this important area of our lives. Amen.

TEMPORARY DEPRIVATION

He who gathers money little by little makes it grow.
Proverbs 13:11

*I*n today's "instant gratification" society, impulse shopping has become a way of life. We see a new set of golf clubs, a dress, even a minivan, and without thinking we're suddenly pulling out a credit card. But what kind of message does this behavior send to our children?

You can find the answer by watching a child open an endless stack of presents during a birthday party attended by friends. One after another, expensive gifts are tossed aside with little more than a glance and no thought to a "thank you." We shouldn't be surprised. Prizes that are won cheaply are of little value, regardless of the cost to the original purchaser.

On the other hand, the child who spends weeks doing extra chores in order to earn money for a highly sought reward learns several important lessons. He sees how honest work over a lengthy period of time causes his nest egg to grow (Proverbs 13:11). He begins to understand how goals can be accomplished through patience and persistence (Hebrews 12:1). And when the reward is in hand, he takes better care of it and appreciates it far more than if it had simply been handed to him (Psalm 128:2).

We suggest that you and your family adopt a policy of "temporary deprivation" when it comes to spending. It's ultimately more satisfying…and much less expensive.

Before you say good night...

- Do you give your kids too much?
- Are you teaching your children to earn and appreciate their rewards?
- How often do you implement "temporary deprivation"?

Lord, help us to be wise in the way we give to our children and provide for their wants and needs. It's so easy to just go along with the crowd and do what everyone else seems to be doing. Show us how You want us to live. Amen.

BLESSED MONEY

Blessed are those…who walk in the light
of your presence, O LORD.
Psalm 89:15

orrie ten Boom told a story about her watchmaker father, Casper. The ten Boom family once prayed that God would send someone to purchase a watch that would pay all their bills. Later that day, a man did buy an expensive watch. As he paid, he complained about another Christian watchmaker who had sold him a faulty watch.

Casper asked if he could see this watch. It turned out to need only a minor repair, which Casper made, assuring the customer that the other watchmaker had sold him a good product. The amazed gentleman returned Casper's watch and got his money back. As soon as the man left, Corrie demanded an explanation for her father's actions.

"There is blessed and unblessed money," Casper replied. He said that God would not be glorified in the ruined reputation of another Christian. A few days later, another customer bought the most expensive watch in the ten Boom shop, providing funds for not only the bills, but also two years of watchmaking training for Corrie in Switzerland.

No amount of riches is worth the price of bringing dishonor to the name of God. Scripture says, "Better a little with the fear of the LORD than great wealth with turmoil" (Proverbs 15:16). Let's be sure that our financial gains can be counted as "blessed."

Before you say good night…

- How can you teach the "blessed money" concept to your children?
- Is any unblessed money coming into your family right now?
- What would you have done in Casper ten Boom's place?

Lord, You know our hearts and our motives. Our lives are wide open in Your sight. Help us to honor You and our fellow believers not only with our money, but also in the way we earn it. Amen.

GIFT OR CURSE?

If we have food and clothing, we will be content with that.

1 Timothy 6:8

*M*any parents who have been blessed financially plan to leave a large inheritance to their children. They've worked hard to achieve prosperity and naturally feel that their kids should benefit from their success. If you are among these generous moms and dads, we urge you to proceed with caution—great danger lies behind your good intentions.

We believe that giving large amounts of money to kids who haven't earned it can be extremely destructive. It can make them unhappy, greedy, and cynical. It detracts from their motivation to trust in God and provides opportunities to give in to new temptations. (A sociological study published years ago, *Rich Kids,* validated these concerns.) It's also been our observation that nothing divides siblings more quickly than money. Many loving families have been devastated over inheritances, or even by arguments about "Who gets Grandma's dining-room table?"

Some people do handle wealth gracefully, of course. But if you have been blessed with material wealth, you must decide if leaving a large inheritance is worth the risk. Do you want to remove from your children the challenges that helped you succeed—the obligation to work hard, live frugally, save, build, dream, and rely on the Lord? The best counsel is available in Scripture (Proverbs 30:8): "Give me neither poverty nor riches, but give me only my daily bread."

Before you say good night...

- Are you teaching your children to trust the Lord for their daily needs?
- What kind of inheritance do you want to leave your kids?

Thank You, Father, for the way You have provided for us through the years. Help us to trust You more and more as the days go by, that we might grow in our faith and be an example to our children. Amen.

He Owns It All

"Everything under heaven belongs to me."
Job 41:11

When I (JCD) was a four-year-old boy, my grandmother gave me a one-dollar bill. I thought I was fabulously rich. Two days later, my mother asked me if I was going to give God His "tithe" on the money. That was a new idea for me. I dutifully placed a dime in the offering plate that Sunday and learned a valuable lesson. It was the beginning of a lifelong policy of giving God a portion of every dollar I've ever earned.

Do you do the same? Have you taught your children about tithing? Do they see you give regularly? It's not that we owe 10 percent of our income to God, and the other 90 percent belongs to us. He owns the 90 percent, too, and what we do with those resources is a spiritual decision. The book of Malachi (3:8–9) tells us that a person who doesn't tithe is actually robbing God!

Tithing can be likened to exercise that stretches and strengthens our generosity. It doesn't represent the limit to our giving, but rather, a starting point that helps us grow. Paul said, "See that you also excel in this grace of giving" (2 Corinthians 8:7). Let's steward God's resources in ways that are wise and pleasing to Him.

Before you say good night...

- Do your children truly understand that God owns everything?
- Are you tithing? Could you give more? How about your kids?
- How can you best teach them to give back to the Lord?

Forgive us, Jesus, for living at times as if our money is our own and not a gift from You. We need to grow in these things, just as in every other area of our lives. Thank You for Your patience with us and for daily walking at our side. Amen.

FRINGE BENEFITS

"It is more blessed to give than to receive."
Acts 20:35

We know of a man who is the chief executive officer for a municipal services firm. He and his wife give half of their income to God's work each year. This man says, "My joy in giving comes from serving God in a way that I know He's called me to and realizing that what I give is impacting people for Christ. It just feels wonderful and fulfilling."

The more we give to God, the more we feel a sense of joy, and the more God delights in us. The Macedonian Christians understood this pleasure that comes from giving: "Out of the most severe trial, their overflowing joy and their extreme poverty welled up in rich generosity" (2 Corinthians 8:2). Though they were poor, the Macedonians "pleaded with us for the privilege of sharing" (v. 4) in order to know "overflowing joy."

The best reason for giving to God, however, is not to bring pleasure to your life today, but to reserve joy for the eternal tomorrow. Jesus advises us to "store up for yourselves treasures in heaven" (Matthew 6:20). He also instructs us to give to those less fortunate than ourselves, saying, "Although they cannot repay you, you will be repaid at the resurrection of the righteous" (Luke 14:14). We already know that heaven will be a place of rejoicing for every believer, yet those who give to God's purposes are promised even more rewards.

To put it another way, giving to God is simply a good investment for your family. The fringe benefits alone will pay eternal dividends!

SMD

Not a Moment
to Spare

A Father's Blessing

by Morgan Cryar

any a morning as a child I stumbled through the darkness to our family's truck, fell back to sleep, then was awakened by the sound of the truck sputtering to a halt in the Louisiana woods. I can remember, even when I was too young to dress myself, climbing out of that truck alongside my dad—the most important person in my life at the time—and stepping into the gray, early morning light to hunt squirrels or deer.

One morning ten years ago I was once again headed for the woods to hunt with Dad. But this time I was grown, with a family of my own. I had been touring for months and had promised to make a trip from our home in Nashville, Tennessee, to the swamps outside Lake Charles, Louisiana, where I grew up. Though I didn't know it, this would be no ordinary morning. It was the morning that I would find out that Dad approved. This morning he would give me his blessing.

When we got into Dad's old truck and he turned the ignition key, music began to pour from a cassette in the tape deck. I knew the music well and was surprised to hear it in Dad's truck. It was my most recent recording, blaring into the morning stillness! I couldn't help myself; I said, "I didn't know you even had this. Do you listen to it?"

His answer amazed me. "It's the only thing I listen to." I glanced around, and sure enough, it was the only cassette in his truck. I was dumbstruck! He said, "This is my favorite," referring to the song playing at the time. I let his words sink in as he turned down the volume to match the morning.

We drove in silence down the road toward the hunting spot, and I wondered at what had just happened. It seems now like such a small thing—a few spoken words. But there seemed to be something different in the air. I sat taller in my seat. I looked at my dad out of the corner of my eye and thought back to two turning points in our relationship.

One happened while I was in college. I remembered having it dawn on me that I had never heard my dad say that he loved me. I knew that he did, but I couldn't remember hearing him say so. That was something my dad just didn't do. For some reason it became important to me that I hear those words from his own lips. I knew, however, that he would never initiate it. So that summer, as I drove home from college, I determined to "force his hand" by telling him *first* that I loved him. Then he'd have to say it back. It would be simple. Just three little words. I anticipated a glorious new openness once I came home and said, "I love you, Dad," and then he would respond.

But simple is not always easy. The first day came and went, and I thought, *I have to tell him tomorrow!* The next day came and went. Then the next, and the next. Then twelve weeks passed, and it was the last day of my summer break. I was frustrated at not having said those three little words to my dad.

My little, beat-up car was packed and sitting on the gravel driveway. I promised myself that I would not start the engine until the deed was done. To someone with an emotionally open relationship with his own father, this may all seem a bit silly, but to me it was serious business. My palms were wet and my throat was dry. My knees grew weak as departure time came.

It had been a good summer visit. There was a general sadness in the house because I was headed back to school across the state. Finally I could wait no longer. I hugged my mom, my brother, and my sister good-bye and went back to find my dad.

I walked up to him, looked him in the eyes, and said, "I love you, Dad."

He smiled a half smile, put his arms around me, and said what I needed to hear: "I love you too, son." It seemed as though a thousand volts of electricity were in the air as we hugged each other (another thing that hadn't happened since I was a small child). It was such a little thing, but it changed everything!

From that point on, all of our conversations were signed off with: "I love you, Dad." "I love you too, son." It became commonplace to embrace when we greeted each other and when we parted. As plain as it sounds, it resulted in a new sweetness between my dad and me. The memory of it came back to me in the truck that morning on the way to the woods.

The other turning point came after college. I remembered that I had learned at a seminar about clearing my conscience with those whom I had wronged. This was entirely new to me—admitting guilt and receiving forgiveness from those I had offended.

Part of the process was to ask God to show me anyone and everyone with whom I needed to clear my conscience. Sure enough, at the top of the list was Dad.

So I sat down with my dad and started first with the worst things that I had done. I proceeded from there to the least serious offenses. I confessed everything that I knew had hurt him, even from my childhood. Then I simply asked, "Dad, will you forgive me?"

Just as I had expected, Dad was embarrassed and tried to shrug it off: "Aw, it's all right, son."

I said, "It will mean a lot to me if you will forgive me."

He looked right at me and said, "It has already been forgiven."

That was his way of saying that he had not held a grudge. And once again, everything changed. From that moment, Dad treated me with new respect. I hadn't anticipated it, but he also began to treat me like an adult—like a friend.

In the stillness of the morning, on the way to the woods, these things floated through my memory, and I rested in my dad's approval of my calling, my work, my music.

I had no way of knowing just how precious his blessing would become to me. One short week later, after my family and I had driven back to Nashville, I received the telephone call from my brother, Tommy, telling me that Dad had walked out onto the porch and had died of a heart attack. He had been young and healthy—only forty-nine years old. It was my darkest day.

Though my family and I tasted intense grief, I still had much for which to be grateful. I had enjoyed thirty years with my dad—some of them as his friend. He had given me a strong enough start that I knew I could meet the challenge of rearing my own children, including my son who was born on Father's Day six years later.

Even though my dad is gone, in the wee hours of that morning on the way to the woods, he had given me something of great value to pass along—a father's blessing.

LOOKING AHEAD...

None of us know the moment our Father will call us to join Him in heaven. We live as if our tomorrows will stretch on forever. We may have mistreated someone close to us or left a promise unfulfilled—yet we think to ourselves, *It can wait. I'll take care of it another day.*

But what if we don't have another day? What if this is our last twenty-four hours—or even twenty-four minutes—on earth? Will we enter heaven with the peace of a life lived completely, or will we carry with us an oversized package of regret because of words unspoken and deeds unfinished?

In tonight's story, God graciously allowed an adult son to experience his father's love and friendship, as well as his approval, just a week before his death. That exchange became a precious final gift. My prayer is that you won't wait to give such a gift to your own beloved children.

JCD

Faith Talk

"I have not found anyone in Israel with such great faith."
Matthew 8:10

*I*n the blink of an eye, you will be hugging your children good-bye and sending them off to college, to a first job, or even to start a family of their own. They'll bring along a few reminders of home on their new adventure—perhaps a favorite pillow or teddy bear. Will they also take a firm understanding of how faith has made a difference in your life?

It's easy for Christian parents to assume that their beliefs have been successfully passed on to their children. If the kids attend church, participate in church youth activities, and read the Bible occasionally, all appears to be well—and these are certainly good signs. But as my (JCD's) father once pointed out to me in a letter, "the greatest delusion is to suppose that our children will be devout Christians simply because their parents have been."

Have you asked your kids lately about what their faith means to them? Have you revealed specifically how Jesus has helped you through times of struggle and doubt? We urge you to talk with your children about Him, to pray for and with them, and to make these special moments a family priority. May I suggest that you do it now, while there is still time?

Before you say good night...

- What do you honestly know about your children's personal faith?
- How much time do they spend weekly in God's Word?
- Are you comfortable sharing your beliefs with your kids?

Lord, time rushes by so quickly. It always seems as though there is more to do than we could ever get done. But please, Lord, help us not to take our children's relationship with You for granted! Help us to take the time—make the time— to speak to them about what matters most for eternity. In Jesus' name, amen.

THE BLESSING

> *"I will pour out my Spirit on your offspring,*
> *and my blessing on your descendants."*
> Isaiah 44:3

uthor Bruce Wilkinson and his son, David, were sitting quietly in Bruce's living room. Suddenly David spoke up. "Dad, will you bless me?" Surprised, Bruce said, "David, you know I do bless you." "No, Dad," David said. "I want you to *really* bless me." David stood up, walked to his father's chair, and knelt in front of him.

Bruce was stunned, but also filled with a tremendous desire to answer his son's request. He put his hands on David's shoulders and began to pray—for David's mind, health, interests, and skills, for his friendships and work, for his dreams, for every part of his life. Bruce didn't stop until he was sure his son not only *was* blessed, but also *felt* blessed. Both father and son now say that moment deepened their relationship and gave David a new sense of spiritual confidence.

Some children spend their entire lives striving for the love, acceptance, and blessing of their parents. They suspect that their parents love them and are praying for them, yet they've never encountered a tangible example of this heartfelt affection and support.

Don't let your children go through life without a blessing. Kneel down with them today and pray for the Lord's abundance and mercy to be with them always.

Before you say good night...

- Do your children feel blessed by you?
- In what specific areas do your children need blessing?
- Should you establish a tradition of regularly blessing your kids?

Lord, You are the Fountain and Source of every blessing. May Your blessing upon our lives flow through us to the children You have given us. Help us bless them in a way that will bring confidence, peace, and joy to their hearts. Amen.

PROMISES, PROMISES

You are God! Your words are trustworthy.
2 Samuel 7:28

As parents, we make many promises to our children, committing to attend events or be available to help with homework or simply buy a favorite brand of cereal. When we keep our promises, we build a trust relationship with our children. But when we break our word, we damage our kids' ability to trust us, others, and God.

Ted was a father who made one promise after another, but rarely followed through. He would say to his daughter, "Samantha, we're going to get a horse for you," or comment to his son, "Bobby, just give me a little time to rest up, and I'll hit you some grounders." Ted never made time for either. When his children began drifting away, Ted finally realized that he needed to change. By then, however, they'd learned to get along without him; his words no longer carried any weight. Yet Ted was determined to regain lost ground with his family. After two years of keeping his commitments, he began to earn back their trust.

Your kids will need the ability to trust in order to form healthy relationships as adults and to establish a firm faith in God. If you are handing out empty promises at home, don't wait another minute to mend your ways. Listen instead to the words of Jesus: "Let your 'Yes' be 'Yes,' and your 'No,' 'No'" (Matthew 5:37).

Before you say good night...
- Do you keep your promises to your children?
- Do your children see you keeping promises to others?
- What promises do you need to begin to fulfill?

Heavenly Father, we know how important it is to keep our word. Let us think before we speak and act on our words, so that we can be models of integrity and trust for our families. Help us to be Your trustworthy servants. Amen.

PURE LIVES

They kept themselves pure.
Revelation 14:4

There is no question that God intends for parents to raise children that are "self-controlled and pure" (Titus 2:5). But in an age where "safe sex" is preached with evangelistic fervor by the entertainment industry, the media, and even some leaders in government, we must do everything in our power to counteract these negative influences. The stakes are too high to do otherwise.

Here's one idea you might try. Years ago, when our daughter, Danae, was a preteen, we presented her with a small gold key. It was attached to a chain worn around her neck and represented the key to her heart. She made a vow then to give that key to one man only—the one who would share her love through the remainder of her life. In a similar way, you could present a special ring to your son. These symbols provide tangible reminders of the lasting, precious gifts of abstinence until marriage and fidelity to a mate for life.

You may think of other ways to encourage your kids to live pure lives. Whatever you choose, we recommend that you act today. In our immoral society, an adolescent who receives the active support of his or her family is much more likely to succeed in living a moral life.

Before you say good night...

- How are your kids doing in resisting the immoral messages in our culture?
- What new ideas could you implement this week to counteract those messages?

Lord, help us to open our eyes to the struggles our children face, and then to find new and creative ways to help them stay pure. We pray tonight that You will grant them pure hearts and minds, protecting them from every immoral influence. Amen.

OUR PRICELESS JOY

Blessed is the man whose quiver is full of [children].
Psalm 127:5

*F*rom a financial perspective, parenting is definitely an expensive proposition. The estimated cost for a middle-income family to raise a child born in the year 2000 is $165,630—and that doesn't include paying for college, which today can run into six figures by itself (our apologies for any heart palpitations we've just caused!).

But our children are more than just another expense, aren't they? Though they require an incredible investment of our resources—time, money, energy, patience—they give back even more. Can we put a price on our pleasure in receiving a lovingly crafted gift, on the pride that fills us when our child hits all his lines in the school play, on the contentedness we feel after an extra-long bedtime hug? Can anything make us understand our heavenly Father's love for us quite like our own unconditional love for our children?

There are days when the costs and trials of parenthood add up to what seems an unbearable burden. When that happens, we urge you to turn to the pages of Scripture. The psalms remind us that children are a "heritage" and a "reward" (Psalm 127:3); they are "arrows in the hands of a warrior" (v. 4). As you read the Word of God and praise Him for your kids, you'll feel genuine appreciation returning to your heart. Sure, kids are expensive—but they are worth every penny.

Before you say good night...

- Do your children sometimes feel like a burden instead of a blessing?
- In addition to prayer and studying the Word, how can you help each other appreciate your kids?

Lord, we really do love our kids. In those moments when our frustrations build up, please move us to respond in a way that brings glory to You. Thank You for entrusting us with these precious lives. Amen.

SPECIAL OCCASIONS

No man knows when his hour will come.
Ecclesiastes 9:12

*L*inda's mother had died, and author Faith Andrews Bedford was helping her friend go through her mother's things after the funeral. Linda opened a drawer and pulled out a set of linen place mats and matching napkins still in their original box.

"Mother bought these when she and Dad went to Ireland fifteen years ago," she said, running her fingers over the embroidery. "She never used them—said they were for a special occasion."

Next, Linda opened a corner cupboard and took down a set of crystal glasses. "She never used these, either," Linda said. "She bought them in Chicago and declared that we'd all get to toast Dad and her on their fiftieth wedding anniversary. But then Dad died after their forty-eighth. They had all those years to use these lovely glasses instead of waiting for a day that would never be shared."

From her mother's closet upstairs, Linda pulled out a blue silk dress with rhinestone buttons. The price tag was still attached.

"Let me guess," Faith said. "For another special occasion?" Linda nodded sadly.

Do you ever find yourself thinking like Linda's mother, saving your very best—all the special things you'd like to say to or do with your family—for some future occasion? Have you considered the possibility that such a moment might never arrive?

Life is a precious gift from our loving Lord—yet it is also fleeting. As James the brother of Jesus wrote, each of us is "a mist that appears for a little while and then vanishes" (James 4:14). Solomon, meanwhile, advises us to find meaning in God and not to waste His gifts: "Eat your food with gladness, and drink your wine with a joyful heart, for it is now that God favors what you do. Always be clothed in white, and always anoint your head with oil. Enjoy life with your wife, whom you love" (Ecclesiastes 9:7–9).

With our hectic schedules, it's so easy for us to put off enjoying our time with those we love. Rather than waiting for "someday," I hope that you and your family will begin to treat every day as a special occasion.

SMD

Assault on Innocence

HOLDING ON TO INNOCENCE

by Dale Hanson Bourke

The sun had just risen over the Chesapeake Bay when my son shook me awake. "Time for our adventure," he announced.

I groaned, glanced at the clock, and tried to think of something that would convince him to let me sleep a little while longer.

"It's too early. The crabs are still asleep," I replied in a groggy but authoritative voice.

"But, Mom," he pleaded. It was guilt that finally drove me out of bed. I had promised him an adventure that morning, a time when he wouldn't have to share me with his little brother. I could see the excited look on his face even with only one eye half open. Sitting up in bed, I tried to quiet Chase down as I pointed to his once-sleeping father.

Pulling my clothes on, I went through a quick checklist of gear: crab net, bucket, towel, string, bait. My stomach turned at the thought of the raw chicken necks in the refrigerator. *Why are crabs attracted to such disgusting things?* I wondered. Then I laughed to myself. Part of what attracted my son to this "sport" was the chance to watch me cringe at the sight of raw chicken hanging on a string.

Walking down the hill on our way to the water, Chase chattered excitedly. "Do you think we'll catch lots and lots of them, Mom?" "Will you tell me if we catch a baby and have to throw him back?" "Can crabs jump out of the bucket and come get you?"

I listened to this little man-child with amusement. One minute he bragged about his ability to catch crabs, even though he had never gone crabbing before, and the next he was afraid. Last night at bedtime, he had prayed, "And please help me be very brave when I go to catch crabs." He clutched my hand as we walked, and I knew he was a little nervous about this unknown experience. But he trusted me, and I promised I wouldn't let any crabs "come get him."

I laid our towel out on the dock in a little ceremony meant to help him appreciate our adventure. Out of the bag came string and dripping chicken pieces ready to attract our prey. We sat on the towel, eased our lines into the water, and waited.

Less than thirty seconds had passed when Chase asked, "Should we check our lines, Mom?"

"No, Chase. You'll feel a crab pulling on the line."

Another thirty seconds passed. "You think we need to find a better spot?"

"No, Chase," I replied. "We just have to be patient."

Chase shifted on the towel and peered into the water. "I sure don't see any crabs in there."

Suddenly, his string moved. "Mom, help!" Chase yelled, nearly dropping the string. He grabbed me as I reached for the net. "We got one," he announced to the world. And then, "Careful, don't let him get us."

The net wrapped around the Maryland Blue, and I lifted him out of the water, legs thrashing, mouth still holding the chicken. He fell into our bucket with a plunk, opening and closing his claws menacingly.

Chase stood back, eyeing him suspiciously. "Are you sure he can't get out?" he questioned. I assured my son of his safety. "Maybe we should put him back now so he can breathe," Chase said.

Breathe? I wondered for a moment why this mattered—and then I understood. My son did not know that most people catch crabs in order to eat them.

We netted two more crabs before we decided to show them off, then throw them back into the bay. As we carried our bucket back to the cottage, Chase began to play one of his favorite games. "Mom, why did God make trees?" he asked.

"To give us shade and wood," I replied.

"Why did God make chickens?"

"To give us eggs and meat," I told him. "And crab bait."

"Why did God make crabs?" he asked, and I realized that he suspected the worst.

I debated over my answer as I saw the look of concern in his eyes. Then divine inspiration struck: "So we could have an adventure," I said.

My son smiled at me as he took my hand, holding on to innocence just a little while longer.

LOOKING AHEAD...

Children are born into this world as precious creations of God. They are filled with a purity and innocence that we parents should attempt to preserve whenever possible. This doesn't mean that our babies are born innately "good," as some would have us believe. Scripture reminds us that "all have sinned and fall short of the glory of God" (Romans 3:23), babies included. That is why even the youngest of children soon display tendencies toward rebellion and selfishness. Yet these youngsters are still innocent lambs entering a world filled with hungry wolves; they are absolutely dependent on their parents for protection and guidance.

When God formed Adam and Eve and placed them in the Garden of Eden, they were innocent in their nakedness and in their understanding of the world. But when Eve listened to the serpent and she and Adam ate from the tree of the knowledge of good and evil, their eyes were opened, and they covered themselves (Genesis 3:6–7). Their innocence was permanently lost.

Our culture is filled with serpents that attempt to fill the minds of our children with evil. These predators include drug pushers, unprincipled movie and television producers, sex abusers, abortion providers, heavy-metal freaks, and many who inhabit the Internet. Once our children encounter these evils, their innocence—just like Adam and Eve's—is gone forever.

We'll talk more this week about our culture's relentless assault on innocence—and about how you can preserve the simple, pure spirits of your children by heeding the words of Scripture: "I want you to be wise about what is good, and innocent about what is evil" (Romans 16:19).

JCD

NOT OF THIS WORLD

> *"In this world you will have trouble.*
> *But take heart! I have overcome the world."*
> John 16:33

*D*oes it feel like you have a tougher job raising children than your parents did, or certainly than your grandparents did? If your answer is yes, there's a good reason for it. It's probably true.

As one columnist noted, the problem for parents in this generation "isn't that they can't say no. It's that there is so much more to say no to." She went on to write that parents used to raise their children in accordance with the cultural values voiced by ministers, teachers, neighbors, and leaders. But in the 1990's the messengers were "Ninja Turtles, Madonna, rap groups, and celebrities pushing sneakers." Today it's even worse. As a result, parents face a daunting and often discouraging task.

It's not a new challenge, though. Even in biblical times, the apostle Paul advised that "the wisdom of this world is foolishness in God's sight" (1 Corinthians 3:19). Wise men and women—including fathers and mothers—have never set their hearts or hopes on the warped values of contemporary culture. Instead, they fix on the eternal values of the world above, knowing that "the man who hates his life in this world will keep it for eternal life" (John 12:25).

You *can* win the battle for your kids. A good start is to focus on the eternal goal and enlist the mighty power of God in persistent prayer.

Before you say good night...

- What parenting challenges do you face that your parents didn't?
- How can you help each other guard your family from inappropriate messages in the culture?

Heavenly Father, we do become discouraged at times in saying "no" so often on behalf of our kids. Encourage us to never waver in seeking the best for our precious children, and may we always stay fixed on the eternal goal. Amen.

No Vile Thing

Whatever is noble, whatever is right,
whatever is pure…think about such things.
Philippians 4:8

A father was watching television with his thirteen-year-old daughter. In attempting to accommodate her, they selected a drama that was popular with teenagers. The dad was shocked by what he saw and heard, but he tried hard not to turn their time of "togetherness" into a parental lecture. Finally, he couldn't take it anymore. "Honey," he said, "I just can't sit here and let this trash come into our home. This is awful. We're going to have to watch something else." To his surprise, his daughter said, "I wondered when you would finally turn it off, Dad. That program is terrible."

Our children may resist our efforts to screen out the filth that permeates their world, but they know it's right to do so. They will respect us for saying, "God gave us this home, and we're not going to insult Him by polluting it with foul programming." However, in order to make this judgment, you have to be watching *with* your children when a program comes on. You also have to keep TVs and computers out of your kids' bedrooms, where it's impossible to monitor what's being seen.

It's not a bad idea to unplug your TVs and computers altogether when your kids are young—but if you do have these devices in your home, we suggest you base your viewing policy on the words of the psalmist: "I will set before my eyes no vile thing" (Psalm 101:3).

Before you say good night...

- Do you truly know—and endorse—what your kids are watching?
- Do you have the courage and wisdom to protect your home from "vile things"?

Spirit of God, stir us to vigilance! Forgive us for allowing influences into our home that warp attitudes and rob innocence from our precious children. Help us to take whatever action we need to take to protect our little ones. Amen.

MUSICAL MADNESS

Let them...tell of his works with songs of joy.
Psalm 107:22

*J*t's been over a year since Carl, now twenty-one, walked away from a life dominated by hard rock music and drugs and rededicated his life to Christ. He is still plagued by memories of the concerts where young men groped mercilessly at girls in "mosh pits," where every type of drug was inhaled or ingested, where kids screamed, "Satan rules!" At times he has to turn on classical music, open his Bible, or simply pray to drive the lewd lyrics out of his head.

The music industry takes the prize for producing outrageous and dangerous material for kids and promoting a culture of sin. Most parents are unaware of the extent of filth and violence being marketed to their children. A CD released by rapper Eminem, for example, featured lyrics glorifying sex, drug use, and the murder of a pregnant woman. The F-word and other obscene terms were uttered repeatedly. This CD premiered at number one on the charts and sold nearly three million copies in its first month.

What a contrast to the praise-filled words sung by King David over two thousand years ago and still voiced in churches today: "O LORD, our Lord, how majestic is your name in all the earth!" (Psalm 8:1). Music has incredible influence to harm or heal the minds and spirits of our children. We pray that you will use *your* influence as parents to keep garbage out of your home—and encourage your kids to listen to music that brings honor and glory to our Maker.

Before you say good night...
- How familiar are you with the music your kids listen to?
- Does it have a godly impact on their lives and attitudes?

Lord, You have given us the beautiful gift of music. Let us never take that gift for granted or allow it to bring harmful images into our homes. May we and our children always sing songs of praise that honor Your holy name! Amen.

KILLING TIME

*The LORD examines the righteous, but the wicked
and those who love violence his soul hates.*

Psalm 11:5

One of the most disturbing trends in today's society is the increasing incidence of kids killing kids. It is frightening to realize that school shootings such as the one at Colorado's Columbine High School, where two classmates murdered a teacher and twelve of their peers, have become almost commonplace. Our culture—through television, movies, the Internet, and video games—teaches our kids to get even with or kill those who get in their way.

It's the same method that the Nazis employed before and during World War II. Recruits were required to perform disturbing tasks systematically until they were no longer shocked or revolted by them. They were desensitized to violence—as are children who observe repeated acts of brutality in the media. That's why the American Medical Association and other child development authorities recently stated what most of us have understood for a long time: "[The] effects [of violence] in the media are measurable and long lasting. Moreover, prolonged viewing of media violence can lead to emotional desensitization toward violence in real life."

Scripture describes our heavenly Father's feelings on this matter in the strongest terms: "Those who love violence his soul hates" (Psalm 11:5). Don't wait another day to shield your family from violent images. The stakes are not only your kids' emotional well-being, but their relationship with God Himself.

Before you say good night...

- Have your kids been desensitized to violence by the media?
- What can you do to protect them from negative media influences?

Lord, we must raise our children in a fallen and violent world. Sensitize our hearts and alert us to the darkness that deepens by the day. Show us what You would have us do. Amen.

SOMETHING FOR NOTHING?

The highway of the upright avoids evil.
Proverbs 16:17

When parents of a twelve-year-old Connecticut boy caught him stealing twenty dollars, they suspected he might have a problem with drugs. But they discovered their youngster was stealing from his own home to feed a different addiction: betting on basketball games. Gambling among adults, and even teens and younger children, has proliferated since our state governments began embracing lotteries as a "something for nothing" source of revenue in the early 1990s. Buying a lottery ticket has become an almost patriotic act.

Yet the apostle Paul warns what happens when we are careless with God's money: "People who want to get rich fall into temptation and a trap and into many foolish and harmful desires that plunge men into ruin and destruction" (1 Timothy 6:9). Indeed, gambling addictions have been linked to substance abuse, suicide, and child abuse, resulting in the destruction of families.

The easiest way to protect your family from the ills of gambling, of course, is to refuse to play the game. For instance, we have traveled to Las Vegas without ever putting a nickel in a slot machine, even though two rolls of coins came with our hotel reservations. As Scripture says, "Do not swerve to the right or the left; keep your foot from evil" (Proverbs 4:27). Sometimes the obvious solution is the most effective one of all.

Before you say good night...

- Do you play the lottery or dabble in other forms of gambling?
- If so, what impact do you think it has on your kids?
- How does God feel about these activities?

Dear God, we admit that we sometimes act without considering the consequences of our deeds. Grant us strength to resist foolish ways and to protect our families from the evil that surrounds us. Amen.

LION ATTACK

Idle hands are the devil's workshop.
Proverbs 16:27, TLB

*T*here's no doubt that our culture's assault on innocence is being engineered by Satan. The apostle Peter says that the devil "prowls around like a roaring lion looking for someone to devour" (1 Peter 5:8). If you have a strong-willed teen under your roof, he or she could very well be Satan's next target.

When a lion approaches a buffalo herd with the intent to kill, he typically avoids the healthiest members of the herd; rather, he spends his time scouting for a sick, injured, or elderly member to attack. Your strong-willed teen is like a vulnerable buffalo in some ways. Those who suffer from low self-esteem are more likely to fall under the influence of peers than their more confident siblings. Like the lion, the devil may very well single out your vulnerable son or daughter to attack with weapons such as drugs, alcohol, or sexual temptation.

To hold back the enemy, we suggest that you keep your strong-willed teen involved in healthy activities. Though constant busyness and over-stimulation are equally harmful to any child, large quantities of unstructured time can be devastating for the naturally rebellious teen. Get him or her involved in the best church youth program you can find, and encourage participation in athletics, music, part-time work, and other activities. Scripture warns that "Idle hands are the devil's workshop." That can certainly apply to your strong-willed son or daughter.

Approach your kids' adolescent years as a wonderful and exciting time to be enjoyed, but also recognize that it poses many risks and challenges to their spiritual and physical health. Do whatever you can during this brief period to get them through the minefield of evil through which they must walk. There is greater safety in the early twenties, when judgment and confidence will develop in your kids. Until then, invest yourselves in their welfare, and above all—stay on your knees!

SMD

Protect Them from Evil

DOUBLE LIFE

by Michael Fitzpatrick

For five years I had been struggling with an addiction to pornography—a battle I was losing. I had become a Christian two years before, but my addiction changed my relationship with my family and took even my love of God hostage. It's not that I didn't pray. I did—usually while looking at porn sites on the Internet. Lust consumed me, and I felt powerless to change.

One Sunday morning, I sat in the sanctuary half-listening to the sermon. My thoughts were on a verse from Psalm 121: "I lift up my eyes to the hills—where does my help come from? My help comes from the LORD, the Maker of heaven and earth."

I wanted to believe that God could rescue me, but there I was, sitting in church yet living a double life. *People at church think I'm a strong teen role model,* I thought. *My family thinks I'm a devoted Christian. The truth is that I'm neither. I lift up my eyes to the hills, but help comes from nowhere.*

Seconds later, my attention was riveted to the words spoken from the pulpit. "The LORD detests men of perverse heart but he delights in those whose ways are blameless" (Proverbs 11:20).

God detests me? The thought shocked and horrified me. But why wouldn't He? I was a hypocrite and a liar. I was a failure in my faith. My ways were far from blameless. For the first time I saw my sin the way God saw it. I bowed my head and sent an urgent prayer to heaven. *God, if You are listening to me, hear my plea. I am a sinner and a slave to my sin. God, save me! I believe that You can, yet I'm still shackled. Relieve me of this burden—please. I have no other options.*

I hurried out of the church, avoiding everyone I knew from my youth group. At home, I fell on my bed and stared into space for half an hour until my mom knocked on the door.

"Honey," she said, "I just got a call from the church. One of the kids can't go to camp, and the camp fee is nonrefundable. They want to know if you'll go in his place. Interested?"

I need to get away from that computer and think about something else.
"Yeah, I'll go…"

"Are you all right?"

"Yes, but Mom, could you leave, please? I need some time alone." My mom left my room.

God, I'm in a black pit and can't see light in any direction. How do I break these bonds? How do I break this addiction? I pray and pray, yet You don't seem to hear my cry. The Israelites waited four hundred years before You released them from bondage in Egypt. How long do I have to wait? Why won't You answer me?

A few hours later I left my room and discovered that I had the house to myself. Immediately my mouth went dry, and I looked at the computer sitting there, luring me.

Nobody will see.

I booted up and connected to the Internet. A Christian home page came up, and I stared at it for a minute. Then, hating myself for doing it, I logged on to the Playboy site. I swallowed hard as lewd photos filled the screen. A few minutes later, I switched back to the Christian web site. Five words stared at me:

Jesus watches where you surf.

A pair of eyes followed my cursor as I moved it across the screen. The words…the eyes…it was all too much. I fell across the keyboard, sobbing. "I'm a Christian who looks at porn sites! Lord, forgive me and change me—I need a miracle! Work something awesome in my life!"

The words on that screen still burned in my mind as I walked up the hill at church camp a few days later. I saw three girls playing Ping-Pong and introduced myself to them. As we talked, I noticed that a light seemed to radiate from them. Their smiles, their attitudes, their words— it was the glow of Jesus in them. At that moment, a warmth and love filled and satisfied me more than any lewd images ever had.

With sudden clarity I understood that pornography had controlled me because I'd tried to use it to fill a void for real love—the kind that only

Jesus could fill. I found a spot alone and rededicated my life to Him. Once again I asked God to forgive my sin and give me the strength to resist.

When I got home from camp, the first thing I saw when I walked in the house was the computer. Cold fear gripped me—my mouth went dry; my hands felt clammy. It was time to confront the monster in my life. Romans 6:17 came to my mind: "But thanks be to God that, though you used to be slaves to sin, you wholeheartedly obeyed the form of teaching to which you were entrusted." I prayed, turned, and walked away.

That wasn't the only time I had to resist temptation. In the months that followed, every time I turned on the computer I had to resist it. More months passed, but finally, with God's help, the day came when it wasn't a struggle anymore. The Lord had given me the power to defeat my addiction. I was free! My double life was over—and my relationships with my family and with God were back where they belonged.

LOOKING AHEAD...

The dangers of this world are truly terrifying for moms and dads trying to safely guide their kids through the minefield of childhood. Pornography, drugs, sex, and violence are just some of the weapons that Satan uses in an attempt to gain control of your daughters and sons in their most vulnerable moments. But as Michael Fitzpatrick reminds us, we *will* prevail if we keep turning to the original source of truth and power.

Jesus, on the night He was betrayed, gathered His disciples in a vineyard and prayed eloquently for them, saying, "I have given them your word and the world has hated them, for they are not of the world any more than I am of the world. My prayer is not that you take them out of the world but that you protect them from the evil one" (John 17:14–15).

In the same way, the world hates your children if they belong to God. Though we might wish that the precious little ones in our care could be spared from the evil influences in our immoral society, God has a purpose for their lives on this earth, and we must yield to His plan. Our task is to pray for our kids, to teach them the ways of God, and to protect them as long as we have breath in our bodies.

Last week we discussed the "assault on innocence." This week we'll take a look at more threats to your family—and how, by resting in God's grace and mighty authority, you can successfully deliver your children into the joy of eternity.

JCD

SEPARATED FROM GOD

> *Your iniquities have separated you from your God.*
> Isaiah 59:2

Last night's story by Michael Fitzpatrick illustrates the depth and pain caused by pornography. It reminds me (JCD) of the interview I had with Ted Bundy in Florida just hours before he was executed for killing three girls. Bundy told me that as a thirteen-year-old, he discovered pornographic materials at a dump. The images excited him and started him on a path that eventually led to murder.

Certainly not every adolescent who reads pornographic magazines or watches obscene videos will grow up to be a killer. But many will develop addictions that will cause terrible damage to their lives and those they love. The threat is genuine, particularly since these disturbing images are now available on the Internet with just the click of a mouse—perhaps at the local library, or even in your own home.

The psalmist asks, "How long will you love delusions and seek false gods?" (Psalm 4:2). The greatest evil of pornography is that it separates the addict from God. To prevent that from happening to your kids, be careful about exposing them to sexual imagery and monitor closely what they see on the Internet. By shielding your sons and daughters from the scourge of pornography, you'll enable them to "draw near to God with a sincere heart" (Hebrews 10:22).

Before you say good night...

- Are your kids at risk for viewing pornography? Why or why not?
- How could you better shield them from objectionable images?
- Have they seen *you* toying with obscenity?

Dear God, we understand that obscene images pose an awesome threat to our children. Protect our family, Lord! Give us the wisdom and energy we need to build a hedge around our kids so that they may always draw near to You. Amen.

KEEPING WATCH

"May the LORD keep watch between you and me."
Genesis 31:49

*J*oel, a high school senior, had everything going his way—a college scholarship, a first-place award in his school's talent contest, popularity among his peers. Lately, however, he'd tired of his "goody-goody" image; at the urging of some new friends, he began experimenting with drugs. When police stopped his car one night, Joel swallowed a bag of crack to avoid arrest. Later that night, he went into convulsions. His parents rushed him to the hospital, but Joel was dead by morning.

Many parents would say, "That only happens to other families." But with the easy availability of illegal substances in today's schools, the temptation to "just give it a try" is great. Satan will use peers to try to entice your son or daughter into sin: "They promise them freedom, while they themselves are slaves of depravity" (2 Peter 2:19).

What can parents do to protect their kids? It is a daunting question. In the early years of adolescence, boys and girls will do *anything* demanded by their peer group. Get to know your kids' friends, and watch for these warning signs: 1) inflammation of eyelids and nose, pupils very wide or small; 2) extremes of energy; 3) extremes in appetite; 4) sudden personality changes; 5) lack of cleanliness; 6) physical deterioration; 7) needle marks (may appear as sores and boils); 8) a shift in moral values. Finally, pray daily for your children while adopting this Scripture: "Keep watch over yourselves and all the flock" (Acts 20:28).

Before you say good night...

* Do your kids show any of the warning signs listed above?
* Do they have a strong faith that will help them resist peer pressure?

Heavenly Father, we are saddened to think about the many lives that are corrupted by the temptations of the evil one. We ask that You keep sin far away from our children. Help us to be ever vigilant on behalf of our family. Amen.

THE REAL MORAL AUTHORITY

Christ…is the head over every power and authority.
Colossians 2:10

*P*arents already have a tough enough task in teaching kids to be moral; now government-subsidized programs and leaders take them in the opposite direction. In Minnesota, Planned Parenthood distributed "Prom Survival Kits" to teens that included three condoms and a coupon for a visit to a Planned Parenthood clinic. Meanwhile, in a recent television appearance, Secretary of State Colin Powell recommended that kids use condoms. He said, "It's lives of young people that are put at risk by unsafe sex, and therefore, protect yourself." What the secretary didn't mention is that the Centers for Disease Control and Prevention and the National Institutes of Health said in 2001 that there is no evidence that condoms protect against most sexually transmitted diseases.

Today's culture is at war with your family over the hearts and minds of your kids—but you *can* win this battle. Start by reminding your children that right and wrong derive not from program leaders or governments, but from the mighty Creator of the universe. His moral laws are as inflexible as physical laws. If a man jumps from a twenty-story building, he will die; similarly, violating God's commandments brings on disastrous consequences: "The wages of sin is death" (Romans 6:23). An adolescent who understands this truth is much more likely to live a righteous life in a society that celebrates sinful behavior.

Before you say good night…

- What do you think about the concept of "safe sex"?
- Do your kids fully understand the consequences of sin?

Lord, we sometimes grow weary of the struggle against our immoral culture. Infuse our children with Your truths, remind them of Your authority and power, and grant them the determination to live a righteous life. Amen.

MTV MADNESS

Do not love the world or anything in the world.
1 John 2:15

*S*cripture says that "everything in the world—the cravings of sinful man, the lust of his eyes and the boasting of what he has and does—comes not from the Father but from the world" (1 John 2:16). That is why we are instructed, "Do not love the world or anything in the world" (v. 15).

Of course, millions of young people who lack a strong faith are very much influenced by the world and its values. MTV, the twenty-year-old cable broadcast, is one of the most dangerous institutions among the young. It is the world's most-watched cable channel among viewers between ages twelve and twenty-four; more than 300 million people watch it daily. As one of its corporate ads recently proclaimed, "[MTV] is a cultural force…MTV has affected the way an entire generation thinks, talks, dresses, and buys." That's a scary thought, considering that MTV and programs like it will do almost anything to attract an audience. One of its "stars," for instance, was videotaped while being sloshed around upside down in a portable toilet; he ate a live goldfish and then vomited it into a bowl. Sex and violence are its stock-in-trade.

It's sobering to realize that your kids are the targets of these outrageous programs. That's why it's more important than ever to teach them to love God and obey His commands, "for everyone born of God overcomes the world" (1 John 5:4). While you're at it, you might turn off your TV, too.

Before you say good night...

- How much are your kids influenced by worldly values?
- Have you "locked out" MTV and similar filth from your home?
- Do your kids know the difference between worldly and godly values?

Father, we so want our children to focus not on the values of the world, but on Your perfect ways. Help us to put distance between our family and those who would try to manipulate us with evil intent. Amen.

Godless Chatter

Turn away from godless chatter.
1 Timothy 6:20

*I*n the past two weeks we have talked about cultural dangers facing your family today. One of the roots of these troubles is a philosophy called postmodernism, also known as moral relativism, which teaches that truth is unknowable. *Nothing* is right or wrong. *Nothing* is good or evil. The postmodernist is convinced that God, or anything resembling ultimate values, simply doesn't exist. One of the foremost proponents of this philosophy is Peter Singer, a tenured professor and "bioethicist" at Princeton University. Singer wrote, "Very often it is not wrong at all [to kill a child once it has left the womb]. Simply killing an infant is never equivalent to killing a person." This is where the postmodernists are taking us—to an almost total disregard for the value of human life.

We point out these disturbing developments to emphasize the influence of ideas on your kids and their behavior. Scripture says, "As [a man] thinks in his heart, so is he" (Proverbs 23:7, NKJV). If your children begin to believe that they are the result of nothing more than happenstance, it undermines their motivation to be moral, lawful, respectful, and thankful—and to trust in an all-knowing, merciful God.

The apostle Paul urged Timothy to "turn away from godless chatter and the opposing ideas of what is falsely called knowledge" (1 Timothy 6:20). That is good advice for families, too.

Before you say good night...

- Have you taught your kids that right and wrong exist and are defined not by the culture, but by the King of the universe?
- How can you keep "godless chatter" from influencing your kids?

Almighty God, we unequivocally affirm Your place as the only authority on truth! Thank You that Your unchanging Word transcends the conflicted and evil concepts that dominate our day. Show us how to teach our children to reject any ideas that do not come from You. Amen.

THE RIGHT RESPONSE

"To him who knocks, the door will be opened."
Matthew 7:8

*W*e've spent the last two weeks talking about serious threats to the physical and spiritual health of your children. Any one of these terrible "weeds," given the chance to fully mature, has the potential to overwhelm your precious son or daughter. If you are feeling a little disheartened tonight, I don't blame you!

That's why I want to encourage you. As parents, we don't have to throw our hands up in despair over the culture's attacks on our kids. We can respond in the way God always wants us to respond in times of trouble—by falling to our knees in prayer. The Lord not only wants us to pray for our children, but also instructs us on how we should ask for that help:

Ask in Jesus' name. Jesus told His disciples, "Until now you have not asked for anything in my name. Ask and you will receive, and your joy will be complete" (John 16:24). Jesus grants us the authority to make a petition on His behalf. We can come before God on the merits of Christ, not our own qualifications.

Ask while abiding in Jesus. Christ said, "If you abide in Me, and My words abide in you, you will ask what you desire, and it shall be done for you" (John 15:7, NKJV). When we seek a close relationship with Jesus, our prayers for our children naturally align with the heart of Christ.

Ask according to God's will. Jesus taught us to pray, "Your will be done on earth as it is in heaven" (Matthew 6:10). We please God when we recognize His will for our kids, and for us as parents, and pray accordingly.

Ask in faith. There is *power* in faithful prayer. Likewise, a lack of faith limits your effectiveness in praying for your family. Scripture makes this clear: "When he asks, he must believe and not doubt, because he who doubts is like a wave of the sea, blown and tossed by the wind" (James 1:6).

Ask with thanksgiving. "By prayer and petition," Paul says, "with thanksgiving, present your requests to God" (Philippians 4:6). This thanksgiving is the inevitable result of our faith in God's answers to our prayers and our faith in God's loving control over every aspect of our lives and family.

Your prayers will make a difference—perhaps even be *the* critical influence—in protecting your children from harm. No problem is too great for God to handle. Put your worries, and the threats facing your kids, in His hands. He will hear, and He will answer.

SMD

Know Your Kids

SWEET DREAMS

by Jeannette Clift George

*M*y mother was a gifted pianist. Music never left her fingers, her heart, or her home. Even though she gave up a concert career when she married my father, she loved to play the piano and she thought I would feel the same.

I practiced obediently, if not skillfully, doing endless scales or one-note melodies punctuated by chords repeated with little variation. My assigned music was in a large and floppy collection that kept sliding off the piano as though it, too, wanted to leave the room. I was *not* a gifted student. At a piano recital, I took twelve emotion-packed minutes to introduce my piece, which I forgot the moment I sat down to play it.

One afternoon I was laboring joylessly over "The Happy Farmer," and Mother was out in the backyard laboring with *great* joy over her day lilies. As I played, Mother called from the yard, "No, it's F-sharp, honey, F-sharp!"

I struck every note my two hands could reach and began to cry. Mother hurried in to me. "What's the matter?" she asked.

"How did you know it was wrong?" I cried. "You were out in the yard and I was here with the music. What I played sounded just fine to me!"

Mother looked at me in dismay. She had not intended to discourage me. "Besides," I said, still spattering tears upon the keyboard, "I'm only doing this to please you."

My mother stared at me in astonishment. Never in her life had she imagined that anyone did not *want* to play the piano. All her dreams of handing down the joy of music to her daughter melted in the glare of my outburst. And in one instant, she accepted the painful revelation.

She came to me, smiling, and hugged me. She brushed away my tears and said, "Well, honey, you don't have to do it. We'll find something that pleases you."

Now I wish I had learned to play the piano, but I think back to that moment in awed awareness of my mother's instant understanding. She looked into my heart and realized that I would not be happy living out *her* dream. She freed me to pursue my own dream: theater.

My mother and father attended every performance of mine in the Houston area. No matter how demanding the role or how critical the production, my mother would always say, "Sugar, you can do it. I know you can." And something in me deeper than fear and doubt believed her. Even in the wearying long hours of rehearsals and performances my mother's creative encouragement was a joy.

One night after a late performance that had been further lengthened by a picture call, I came home after Mother had gone to bed. There was a light on in the kitchen and downstairs hallway. Tiptoeing, I climbed the stairs to my room. I was very tired, and in that moment stumbled upon the deep loneliness that seems to haunt the actor after working hours. As I moved to turn off the light, I glanced down the stairwell.

A large chrysanthemum plant was on a table in the hallway. That night it bloomed with greetings from my mother. She had cut out tissue paper faces and placed them in the center of each blossom and had printed messages on the border of each face... "Good Night, Jeannette...Sweet Dreams." No bouquet ever meant more to me or has stayed so fresh in my memory. When I think of how God has gifted all of us with our own unique creativity, I think of those flowers, and I thank God for my mother.

LOOKING AHEAD...

It can be easy for us as parents to place expectations on our children, nurturing our own dreams rather than allowing theirs to blossom and grow. Much more difficult is the challenge of getting behind the eyes of your child, seeing what he sees and feeling what he feels. When he is lonely, he needs your company. When he is defiant, he needs your help in controlling his impulses. When he is afraid, he needs the security of your embrace. When he is curious, he needs your patient instruction. When he is happy, he needs to share his laughter and joy with those he loves.

If you truly *know* your child, you'll be in a much better position to respond to the ups and downs of parenting—and while you're at it, to actually enjoy the process! We'll talk more in the next few days about how to become "wise and understanding people" (Deuteronomy 4:6, NKJV) and gain an intimate understanding of our children.

JCD

Song of the Stone

"Speak, for your servant is listening."
1 Samuel 3:10

*S*imon Verity is a master stone carver who honed his craft restoring thirteenth-century cathedrals in Great Britain. With each careful blow of his chisel, Verity listened closely to the song of the stone. A solid strike indicated that all was well. But a higher-pitched *ping* meant that a chunk of rock might be ready to break off. He constantly adjusted the angle of his blows and the force of his mallet to the pitch, pausing frequently to run his hand over the freshly carved surface. Verity knew that one wrong move could cause irreparable damage to his work of art. His success depended on his ability to read the signals being sung by his stones.

In a similar way, parents need to listen to the "music" of their children, especially during times of confrontation and correction. It takes patience and sensitivity to discern how your child is responding. If you listen carefully, your boys and girls will tell you what they're thinking and feeling.

Scripture says, "Let the wise listen and add to their learning" (Proverbs 1:5). By listening and honing your craft, you too can become a master carver who creates a beautiful work of art in your children.

Before you say good night...

- How well do you listen to the "music" of your children?
- Do you usually know what they are thinking and feeling?
- What more can you do to create a beautiful work of art in your kids?

Dear Lord, as parents we seek to overcome our flaws and inexperience to become master "carvers" of our children. Give us the ears to listen for every note in the lives of our kids, and grant us the wisdom to adjust as we help shape these precious beings into the people You want them to be. Amen.

AWARDS ASSEMBLY

He who seeks good finds goodwill.
Proverbs 11:27

For years, Roger had poked and prodded Gordon, his oldest son, to be a better student. Roger was always a little disappointed in Gordon and his B-average grades. He never quite measured up to Roger's expectations.

When Gordon was a senior in high school, Roger was puzzled by an invitation to a student awards assembly. He couldn't imagine any awards that Gordon would win. Roger went to the event anyway, but grew increasingly annoyed at watching other students march up the aisle for applause. Why was he here? Why was his son so mediocre? Finally, the principal came to the last presentation—a new award for an exceptional student. Roger was astonished to hear Gordon's name announced, followed by a long description of his son's fine character, kindness, trustworthiness, and quiet leadership. The principal finished by thanking Gordon, saying, "No one who has really gotten to know you will ever be quite the same again."

Roger had never gotten to know his son, much less appreciate him for who he was. In his efforts to teach and "improve" Gordon, Roger became blind to his son's best qualities. It reminds us of this Proverb: "He who seeks good finds goodwill, but evil comes to him who searches for it" (11:27). Teach your children, but remember also to seek out and acknowledge their positive traits. You'll discover a son or daughter to be proud of.

Before you say good night...

- Are you overlooking any of your children's positive traits?
- How might you change the way you "value" your kids?

Heavenly Father, teach us to value our children for who they are, rather than who we wish them to be. Help us to know their thoughts and dreams, their strengths and weaknesses, their fears and failures. Enable us to love them unequivocally, just as You love us. Amen.

GOD'S LAMP

The LORD will guide you always.
Isaiah 58:11

*T*rying to talk with an unresponsive older teenager is like insert-ing dollar bills into a broken change machine—your words go in, but nothing comes back out! Yet it's vital that you stay in touch with your sons and daughters preparing to leave the nest. At a moment when you least expect it, they may ask for your advice on life's "big questions": "I want to follow Jesus, but will He tell me what to do?" Or, "I think God is calling me to the ministry, but how can I support a family on a pastor's salary?"

These are the times to gently put your arms around your kids and remind them of God's infinite love: "As a father has compassion on his children, so the LORD has compassion on those who fear him" (Psalm 103:13). God, the ultimate parent, will never abandon any of us or ignore a request for guidance. His Word is "a lamp to my feet and a light for my path" (Psalm 119:105). That doesn't mean He gives us a three-hundred-watt beam that reveals the entire landscape. But the Lord will illuminate our next step, and we must trust Him to lead us through the darkness beyond.

Your teen won't be ready to discuss these deep scriptural insights every day. But if you stay close to your son or daughter, you'll know just the right moment to drop in a few wise words from the Lord.

Before you say good night...

- What "big questions" are on your kids' minds right now?
- What advice do you want to give them? Is it based on Scripture?
- Are your kids trusting God to light their paths, one step at a time?

Father, we pray right now that You would grant us divine discernment. Help us to know our children as You know us, to see beyond their resistance and facades. Give us words of love and wisdom as we respond to their greatest struggles. Amen.

CHANGING WITH THE TIMES

Blessed is the man...who gains understanding.
Proverbs 3:13

The summer after I graduated from high school, I (JCD) traveled fifteen hundred miles from home and entered a college in California. I will never forget the exhilarating feeling of freedom that swept over me. I felt accountable for my life and did not have to explain my actions to anyone. The following December, my parents and I met for Christmas vacation at the home of relatives. Suddenly, I found myself in conflict with my mother. She was responding as she had when I was still in high school, asking when I would be coming in at night, urging me to drive safely, and watching what I ate. My mother had failed to notice that I had changed, and I was eager for her to get with the program.

In a similar way, when Mary and Joseph discovered that their twelve-year-old, Jesus, was not with their party on its way out of Jerusalem, they did not know where to look for Him. They eventually found Him in the temple courts, listening and asking questions. They didn't realize how far Jesus had grown in comprehending His unique relationship with His heavenly Father: "Didn't you know I had to be in my Father's house?" (Luke 2:41–50).

Scripture instructs us to "walk in the way of understanding" (Proverbs 9:6). When we seek to understand and adapt to the changes in our children, we'll find we appreciate them all the more—and vice versa.

Before you say good night...

- How have your children changed in the last few months?
- Are you treating them with new "understanding" as a result?

Heavenly Father, we ask You to guide our relationships with our children. Help us to recognize their growth and maturity and to encourage them even as they change to draw nearer to You. Thank You for showing us how to "walk in the way of understanding." Amen.

SURPRISE!

The man who thinks he knows something
does not yet know as he ought to know.
1 Corinthians 8:2

We've been encouraging you this week to seek a better understanding of your children. We readily admit, however, that no matter how hard you try, your kids will still surprise you. I (JCD) remember calling home years ago from an out-of-state speaking engagement. Danae, who was then thirteen, informed me that she was going to be running in the 880-yard race at a track meet that Saturday. I gasped. "Danae," I said, "that is a very grueling race. Have you ever run that far before?" She admitted that she hadn't, even in practice. Though I advised against it, she decided to run in the race anyway.

Well, you can guess what happened—she won the race. The following year, she triumphed in the 880 again, setting a school record in the process. Now I began to get excited. *The kid has talent,* I thought. *She'll be a great runner someday.* Wrong again. Danae ran three more races, winning two of them, and then lost interest in track. So much for fatherly wisdom.

Even if you dedicate yourself to knowing and understanding your children, you won't always succeed. God has designed our ever-changing sons and daughters as complex, unique human beings. Parents must take to heart the Scripture that says "A patient man has great understanding" (Proverbs 14:29). Your ability to recognize who your children are—and who they will become—will only occur with generous measures of patience and reliance on the Lord.

Before you say good night...
- How often do your kids surprise you?
- Are you patient in seeking to understand your kids?

Heavenly Father, we know we must rely on You as we seek to know our children. Grant us patience when our understanding seems inadequate. Enable us to enjoy even the surprising moments with our precious children. Amen.

THE POWER OF WORDS

*Whoever would love life and see good days
must keep his tongue from evil.*
1 Peter 3:10

Our words are an incredibly important tool for understanding and communicating with our kids. What we say, and how we convey what we say, can make the difference between drawing closer to the hearts of our sons and daughters and hurting them with an insensitive or inappropriate remark.

I thought about the impact of our words when I read a story by former First Lady Hillary Rodham Clinton, whose father never affirmed her as a child. When she was in high school, she brought home a report card with an A grade in every subject. She proudly showed it to her dad, hoping for approval or praise. Instead he said, "Well, you must be attending an easy school." Thirty-five years later, that thoughtless remark is still etched in Mrs. Clinton's mind. That father may have considered it a casual quip, but it created a point of pain for his daughter that has endured to this day.

If you doubt the power of words, remember what John the disciple wrote under divine inspiration. He said, "In the beginning was the Word, and the Word was with God, and the Word was God" (John 1:1). John was describing Jesus, the Son of God, who was identified personally with words. Can a better case be made than that? Matthew, Mark, and Luke each describe a related prophetic statement made by Jesus that confirms the eternal nature of His teachings. He said, "Heaven and earth will pass away, but my words will never pass away" (Matthew 24:35). We remember what Christ said to this hour, more than two thousand years later.

Words are a mighty instrument with lasting power to enlighten, encourage, and heal—or, when used carelessly, to wound and destroy. How we use them has eternal impact: "Your words now reflect your fate then: either you will be justified by them or you will be condemned" (Matthew 12:37, TLB). As parents, let's choose words that always benefit our kids and bring glory to God.

SMD

Lessons along the Way

CHASE AND THE BEANSTALK

by Dale Hanson Bourke

*S*omething about the look on my son's face made me suspicious. "Did you have a nice day at school?" I asked. He nodded, then looked at the floor.

"Did anything extra special happen today?"

"No, not really," he replied.

"How's your bean plant doing?" Chase's face brightened. The kindergartners were growing bean plants, and for some reason his had shot up above all the others. For days, Chase had been the envy of his friends as his plant towered over the other little sprouts.

"It's still growing," he said excitedly. "Pretty soon it's going to go to the ceiling!"

I noticed that Chase gestured with one hand while the other remained in his pocket. Suspicious, I asked if he had brought anything home from school.

"Not really," he answered, once again looking at the floor.

"What's in your pocket?"

The look of surprise and obvious guilt on my son's face almost made me smile. My son is too young to act, too innocent to hide his feelings. But I could see he was struggling with something that he knew was wrong.

Slowly, carefully, he pulled the treasure from his pocket. Opening his fist, he displayed a wrinkled bean.

I tried to catch Chase's eye, but he looked away. I could not imagine what was causing such a struggle. "Where did you get the bean?" I questioned gently.

"At school," he responded softly, shuffling his feet.

"Did your teacher give it to you?"

"Not really," Chase whispered. "It was just an extra one."

"Did you steal it?"

My words sounded harsh, but from the look on Chase's face I knew he understood. It wasn't just an extra bean. It was something he wanted and took without permission. Taking the bean was a great wrong, and Chase knew it.

"I guess so." My son seemed almost relieved by his confession. "I just wanted to grow another bean plant at home like the one I have at school."

There was more to this story, I realized. Chase's bean plant had put him on top among his peers. He had been king of the kindergarten every morning when class began and his friends saw his plant, bigger than the rest. Chase stole the bean because he loved the feeling of being ahead. It was a deeper problem than a five-year-old could understand.

I didn't want to minimize the wrong, or overwhelm him with guilt. But this was not just about a bean. If Chase didn't understand that, it would be easier for him to cross over the line the next time.

"I know you love your bean plant at school, and I can understand why you wanted to grow another one," I told my son. "But taking something that isn't yours is wrong. It's stealing. You have to give it back."

Tears formed in Chase's eyes. "Please, Mommy, can't I keep it?"

"No, Chase," I said firmly, wondering if I was being too hard on my son. "You must take it back tomorrow. And you must tell your teacher that you are sorry that you took it without permission."

The next day, Chase took the bean back to school. His teacher later told me that he solemnly presented it with the confession: "I'm sorry I stolded this bean."

When Chase returned home that afternoon, he seemed back to his old self. "Did you give the bean back?" I asked.

"Yes, Mom."

"Then I have a surprise for you." I pulled out a package of bean seeds and watched his eyes grow wide.

"Can we plant them now?" he begged.

As we planted the beans in our window garden, I felt as though I was participating in a sacrament. Every time a bean went into the dirt, I thought of the times I had cut corners or justified wrongs in the spirit of getting ahead. I wanted people to envy me, too. I wanted to be the best, the brightest, among my friends. Sometimes it was easy for me to think, *It was just a slight exaggeration.* But each bean reminded me of the enormous price I pay whenever my desire for approval overwhelms my commitment to obedience.

Chase's act of contrition humbled me, too. As our bean plants grow in the window, they remind me that even the smallest wrong draws us away from God…while a tiny step back toward what's right brings healing and a new closeness to Him.

LOOKING AHEAD…

Beginning in kindergarten (if not before), our children learn many lessons in the classroom—how to spell, to count, to write. But the most important instruction has nothing to do with books and paper. Rather, it is the lessons our kids absorb in everyday experiences that reinforce the principles of Scripture.

As parents, we must be discerning in the instruction we give and the wisdom we seek to impart, always being aware of the awesome responsibility before us. We need look no further for inspiration than Christ, who said, "You call me 'Teacher' and 'Lord,' and rightly so, for that is what I am" (John 13:13).

With Jesus as our example, we'll talk more this week about how to teach our children godly lessons as we prepare them to walk in step with Him.

JCD

HEARTS OF COMPASSION

Clothe yourselves with compassion.
Colossians 3:12

t was a cold December in Philadelphia. Eleven-year-old Trevor Ferrell was watching TV in his comfortable home when images of street people flashed on the screen. Trevor's heart was touched—he had to do something. He grabbed a blanket and pillow from his closet and begged his parents to take him downtown. They resisted at first—it could be dangerous, after all—but eventually relented. Soon, Trevor was handing the blanket and pillow to a grateful homeless man.

That night marked the first of many visits by the Ferrell family to Philadelphia's street people. Trevor's friends started joining him, others began donating items to hand out, and a ministry was born. Trevor's Campaign for the Homeless attracted national interest and inspired chapters across the country. An abandoned Philadelphia hotel was turned into Trevor's Place, a home for street people, and an adjacent building was transformed into Trevor's Next Door, a residential living and service center.

Hundreds of people found help and hope because a fifth-grader remembered the words of Jesus: "Whatever you did for one of the least of these brothers of mine, you did for me" (Matthew 25:40). Christ had incredible compassion for the down-and-outers of the world, touching even lepers who were likely shunned by others (Luke 5:12–13). When you encourage your children to help those in need, you move them that much closer to the compassionate heart of Christ.

Before you say good night...

- How are you encouraging your kids to show compassion to others?
- What could you do this week for the "least of these" in your town?

Lord Jesus, may we all have ears to hear the cries for help around us. Show us how to respond as You would, bringing Your compassion to our family and to our world. Amen.

GOD'S JUSTICE

Blessed are all who fear the LORD, who walk in his ways.

Psalm 128:1

*T*here are times when parents should allow their children to experience the unpleasant consequences of sin. Our kids need to understand that those painful consequences come by God's design. Children have a right to know that our merciful God of love is also a God of righteous wrath.

When I was nine years old, my (JCD's) mother read me the story of Samson (Judges 13–16). I heard that after this mighty warrior fell into sin, the Philistines put out his eyes and held him as a common slave. Samson repented before God and was forgiven, but he never regained his eyesight or his freedom. "There are terrible consequences to sin," my mother told me. "Even if you repent and are forgiven, you will still suffer for breaking the laws of God." I am thankful today that my mother had the courage to acquaint me with this "warning note" in Scripture. The knowledge that I would one day stand accountable before God led me to moral decisions at times when I could have easily chosen otherwise.

As you teach your children about the Christian faith, be sure to communicate that we serve a God not only of love, but of justice: "The LORD is known by his justice" (Psalm 9:16). To reveal only one side of the coin is to distort one of Scripture's most significant truths.

Before you say good night...

- Are you teaching your kids equally about God's love and justice?
- Do your kids understand that there are inevitable consequences to breaking moral laws?

Heavenly Father, may we be bold enough to believe in justice and honor as much as we believe in love and grace. Give us the courage to teach our children who You truly are, an infinitely powerful God whose every interaction with us has eternal meaning. Amen.

AN APPLE A DAY

> *"Love your enemies, do good to those who hate you."*
> Luke 6:27

Carole, as class monitor, was forced to report that one of her seventh-grade classmates had been acting up during their teacher's absence. Joyce, an explosive brunet, threatened to clobber Carole at afternoon recess. Scared and miserable, Carole fled home for lunch and poured out her tale of woe to her mother. "Carole, take her an apple," said her mother calmly. "Take her an apple!" wailed Carole. "What good will that do? She's ready to pull out my hair!" "I know," said her mother. "But the Bible says to do good to those who are spiteful to you. It also says that a soft answer turns away wrath. Try it!"

After lunch, Carole reluctantly placed a shiny red apple on Joyce's desk and mumbled, "I'm sorry you are so angry." Joyce was speechless. Finally she stammered, "Well...well...I guess I deserved it." The situation was defused, and Carole and Joyce eventually became friends.

It can be difficult for children (as well as their parents!) to wholeheartedly embrace Jesus' instruction to "do good to those who hate you, bless those who curse you, pray for those who mistreat you" (Luke 6:27–28). They feel that their adversaries deserve a different response. But Christ is unequivocal in His direction. We are to follow the Lord's example, who offers us love that *we* don't deserve: "Be merciful, just as your Father is merciful" (Luke 6:36).

Before you say good night...

- Do you pray for your "enemies" in the presence of your children?
- What would happen if your family tried a "soft answer" in the face of wrath?

Almighty God, Your ways are the best ways for the living of our days. Help us to teach our children about Your mercy and to model it ourselves. May we respond to others with love and compassion, just as You do toward us. Amen.

THE GIFT OF SEX

You father's blessings are greater than the
blessings of the ancient mountains.
Genesis 49:26

he Lord gave us the holy gift of physical intimacy as a means for expressing love between husband and wife. We are told that when a man and wife unite in marriage, they become "one flesh" (Genesis 2:24). Solomon's Song of Songs clearly celebrates sexual pleasure between married lovers. In today's immoral culture, however, that purpose has been twisted. Sexual "freedom" is preached with evangelistic fervor. A motel marquee suggests to its patrons, "Have your next affair with us." Premarital virginity and marital fidelity are portrayed as outdated concepts. In this warped atmosphere, how can parents instill healthy attitudes toward the gift of sexual intimacy?

You can start by taking a leadership role. Gradually introduce your kids to God's plan for sex, beginning at age three or four and ending shortly before puberty. Let your kids' questions be a guide to how much you should reveal. And if they don't ask, don't wait for someone else to fill in the blanks. When our son, Ryan, showed no interest in the subject of sex, I (JCD) finally took him on a fishing trip and suggested we discuss "how babies are made and all that." Ryan said, "What if I don't wanna know?" I dragged him kicking and screaming into the world of adult sexuality.

We are told to "Train a child in the way he should go" (Proverbs 22:6). That means we are to teach our children about *all* of God's gifts and truths—including His wonderful gift of sex—when the timing is right.

Before you say good night...
- How much do your children know about sex?
- What are you doing to counteract immoral sexual messages?

Heavenly Father, we ask You to help us raise our children with the love You inspire, the reverence You intend, and the attitudes You desire for each of us toward the unique blessing of sexual intimacy. Amen.

GOD'S RULES

"Be careful to obey my laws, and you will live safely."
Leviticus 25:18

James was driving his three young children over a snowy mountain pass. Suddenly their van hit a patch of black ice. James felt a sickening sensation as the van veered across the oncoming lane, smashed into a snowbank, and skidded on its side for thirty yards before finally coming to a stop. Shaken and fearing the worst, James looked behind him—and was relieved to see all three children still strapped snugly in their seat belts, none the worse for their rough ride. He was so thankful he'd followed the rules for seat belts that day.

God has rules for our journey through life, too. They're called the Ten Commandments (Exodus 20:3–17). Each bears truth and wisdom designed by the Creator to guide and protect you and your children from harm. They are: 1) Worship no other gods than the Lord. 2) Do not make idols for yourselves. 3) Do not misuse the name of the Lord. 4) Observe the Sabbath as a holy day. 5) Honor your father and mother. 6) Do not murder. 7) Do not commit adultery. 8) Do not steal. 9) Do not give false testimony against your neighbor. 10) Do not covet anything that belongs to your neighbor.

You will pass on thousands of lessons to your kids over the course of childhood. If you keep these ten at the top of the list, your family will feel the touch of God's hand: "He who respects the commandment will be rewarded" (Proverbs 13:13, RSV).

Before you say good night...

- How well do you and your children know the Ten Commandments?
- Is your family living by each of them?

Dear Lord, we are so grateful for Your holy instruction. Thank You for laws that show Your eternal love for each member of our family. May we persevere in passing on all of Your commandments to our children. Amen.

STILL LEARNING

[The righteous] are always generous and lend freely.
Psalm 37:26

*W*e *do* want to be effective parents. There is so much to teach our kids, and so little time. But as we struggle and strain to bestow wisdom on the next generation, we might also pause to consider how much our children can teach us.

I recall a story by a woman named Elizabeth Cobb about a mother who wanted to show her children how to be more generous. After a tornado had touched down nearby, the mother taped a newspaper picture of a now-homeless family on their refrigerator. The photo included the image of a tiny girl, her eyes wide with confusion and fear. The mother explained this family's plight to her seven-year-old twin boys and three-year-old daughter, Meghan. Then, as the mother sorted out old clothes, she encouraged her boys to select a few of their least-favorite toys to donate.

While the boys brought out unwanted playthings from their rooms, Meghan slipped quietly into her own room and returned hugging something tightly to her chest. It was Lucy, her faded, frazzled, and much-loved rag doll. Meghan paused in front of a pile of discarded toys, pressed her round little face against Lucy's for a final kiss, then laid the doll gently on top.

"Oh, honey," the mother said. "You don't have to give away Lucy. You love her so much." Meghan nodded solemnly, eyes glistening with held-back tears. "Lucy makes me happy, Mommy," she said. "Maybe she'll make that other little girl happy, too."

The twins stared openmouthed at their baby sister. Then, as if on cue, they wordlessly walked to their rooms and returned not with castoffs, but with some of their prized toy cars and action figures. The mother, now almost in tears herself, removed a frayed coat from the pile of clothes and replaced it with a just-purchased hunter green jacket. The parent who had wanted to teach her kids about generosity had instead been taught.

Meghan intuitively knew that her beloved rag doll was not hers to keep forever. Though she could not have explained it, she understood the meaning of the Scripture that says, "Naked a man comes from his mother's womb, and as he comes, so he departs. He takes nothing from his labor that he can carry in his hand" (Ecclesiastes 5:15). When Meghan realized that another little girl needed Lucy more than she did, she willingly gave up her cherished toy.

God wants us to use our possessions, our wealth, our talents, and our very lives to bring glory to Him. As the apostle Paul says, "You will be made rich in every way so that you can be generous on every occasion" (2 Corinthians 9:11). As you strive to incorporate that lesson into your family, you might start with the example of your own children.

SMD

Are We Doing Anything Right?

I Wasn't Prepared for a Prodigal
by Gigi Graham Tchividjian

flood of gratitude engulfed me as I sat in church behind my handsome young son. His arm draped around the shoulders of Kim, his beautiful fiancée, as they listened to the words of the song "The Keeper." He, too, was having a difficult time holding back the tears.

Just five years before I had wondered if I would see this beloved son again. Tullian was our prodigal. His father, Stephan, and I had given him all we could. We loved him dearly, but he chose to disregard his teaching and training and turned his back on all that we offered. We had no choice but to let him go—at sixteen.

I'll never forget the day he left home. I stood in the doorway, watching my son walk slowly down the driveway and out into the street. Then, with a heart that felt heavy as lead, I reluctantly turned away.

I forced myself to go through the motions of fixing dinner and doing the evening chores. When I finally crawled into bed, I lay awake, crying and wondering. Where was he? Had he eaten supper? Did he have a place to sleep? Could we have done things differently? *Would he ever come home again?*

I thought back on the months before that day. The ups and downs, the emotions, the harsh words, the frustrations, the disobedience, the dishonesty, the questions, the long nights…sitting and waiting, wondering, worrying, asking, "Why?" Why was our son choosing to rebel? He could have a warm, loving home, physical comfort, an education, a godly heritage. We had wanted him, prayed for him, and had been overjoyed at his arrival. Tullian had been such a fun-loving, happy child. We called him our "sunshine."

Unable to control the tears, I thought about all the chances we had given our son. We had taken him back again and again only to have him abuse our trust and disrupt our family life.

I wasn't prepared for a prodigal. I never imagined I would one night lie in bed, wondering where my son was. But once you love, you are never free again, and the Lord caused this heartbreaking situation to teach me many things. I had to cope with overwhelming sadness that at times almost engulfed me. But as painful as it was, Stephan and I also realized we could not allow the behavior of this one child to consume us. At times we had to purposefully put our prodigal out of our minds. It simply wasn't fair to focus all our attention and emotional energy on him at the expense of the other members of the family.

I also had to deal with guilt. I wondered: Could I have brought him up differently? Had I been too strict—or not strict enough? Had I shown enough love? Had I truly gone the extra mile?

I even found it difficult at times to trust the Lord. Eventually, when I accepted the fact that God loved my son even more than I did, I was able to surrender Tullian to Him. But as the years came and went, I still found myself discouraged. My hopes would build, only to come crashing down in bitter disappointment. I was tempted again and again to try to do God's job for Him. Then I would cry the words of the old hymn, "Oh for grace to trust Him more!" And in response I would hear a still, small voice deep within my heart saying, "Love and patience…love and patience."

I didn't have a problem with the love part. After all, I'm a mother. But I had a lot of trouble with the patience. My mother reminded me that in dealing with an all-knowing, all-loving, all-powerful God, I had to pray not only with persistence, but with patience.

More years passed. Then, totally unexpectedly, Tullian took his girl-friend by the hand one Sunday, and from high in the balcony of our church, they went forward to give their lives to Jesus Christ.

I was overwhelmed with joy—but also a bit skeptical. I didn't want to have my hopes dashed again. I waited and watched. As the weeks turned into months, we saw this young man grow and mature into a sincere, dedicated child of God.

Recently he wrote these words to an older Christian friend:

Things went real raw after I last saw you. My whole life went down the tubes. I really fell far from the Lord. Drugs, alcohol, sex, the whole nine yards. I dropped out of school, got kicked out of my house; things couldn't have gotten much worse.

But I don't want to go on about the bad stuff. I want to tell you about what the Lord has done for me. After leading a very empty, up-and-down lifestyle, I gave the Lord total control of my life. What a change. Things I used to live for don't even matter anymore. Things I used to run away from, I'm hungry for.

Isn't God good? He has been so patient with me. He never gave up on me. For the first time in my life I feel peace and contentment. I don't worry about anything. I am a totally different person.

Yes, our prodigal had returned.

I smiled in the church that day as I reflected on all these things. My mind drifted back to the present. The song was coming to a close. With thanksgiving in my heart I glanced again at Tullian and Kim sitting in front of me. I, too, was feeling peace and contentment when snatches of a favorite psalm floated into my mind: *Truly, the Lord is thy keeper…He does not slumber…He shall preserve thy going out and thy coming in.*

LOOKING AHEAD…

Parenthood is one of the greatest blessings in life—yet it can also bring on the greatest anguish. Can anything compare to the pain of watching beloved daughters or sons walk away, turning their backs on the love, values, and faith you have so carefully nurtured over many years? Is there a higher torment than seeing your precious children suffer or needlessly abuse themselves? Far too many mothers and fathers wake up to this agonizing reality, and you have my utmost sympathy if you are facing this situation tonight.

Nearly as distressing for many moms and dads is the *fear* that they will lose their children as we have just described. These parents are tortured daily by doubt and guilt. They ask themselves: Do I know what I'm doing? Am I turning my children into monsters? Have I doomed them to eternal damnation by the mistakes I've already made?

Fortunately, there is hope in all of these circumstances. As Gigi Tchividjian has shown us, God does sometimes answer our fervent prayers in this life for our wayward offspring, though it may be years later. And even if we don't live to see our prodigals return on earth, we still have the great hope of a "homecoming after we are gone."

We'll offer further encouragement this week to parents who are plagued by doubt and guilt. Like the psalmist, you too can cry out, "May your unfailing love be my comfort" (Psalm 119:76). Your heavenly Father will hear and respond—you can depend on it.

JCD

PARENTAL DOUBT

An anxious heart weighs a man down.
Proverbs 12:25

few years ago, Focus on the Family conducted a survey on the most common frustrations of parenting. The majority of mothers and fathers did not criticize their children, but said they were troubled by their *own* inadequacies. Comments such as "I've lost confidence in my ability to parent" and "I've failed my children" revealed just how deep this mind-set reaches in today's society.

It was not always so. Parents of previous generations worried about economic depression, world wars, and later the cold war with Russia. Mothers and fathers didn't invest much effort in hand-wringing over their children, at least not until a problem developed. When I (JCD) asked my dad if he worried about all the things that could go wrong in raising a child, he smiled sheepishly and said, "Honestly, Bo (his pet name for me), I never really gave that a thought."

The self-doubt that plagues so many parents today is largely a cultural phenomenon. If you are among these parents, we suggest you turn away from the world's whispers and focus on the comfort and truth that come from our heavenly Father: "Cast your cares on the LORD and he will sustain you" (Psalm 55:22). You can no more be a perfect parent than you can be a perfect human being. Lean on the Lord to make up the difference—and don't let anxiety and guilt steal the joy of parenting.

Before you say good night...
- Are you ruled by self-doubt as parents?
- What attitude does God want you to have toward parenting?

Heavenly Father, we ask You for the faith to believe in Your love and Your power totally. We know that faith is a gift from You, and we ask for a faith strong enough to banish all doubt and establish all trust. Amen.

SPACE FLIGHT

"The righteous will live by faith."
Romans 1:17

The early days of the American space program were thrilling times. John Glenn and other astronauts would blast off from Florida's Cape Canaveral into the "last frontier." Their return voyages were especially dangerous. When a spacecraft reentered earth's atmosphere, only a heat shield on the bottom of the capsule protected it from temperatures exceeding one thousand degrees Fahrenheit. During this phase, communication with earth was blacked out for approximately seven minutes. The world would wait anxiously until a reassuring voice finally announced, "This is Mission Control. Everything is A-OK."

Your kids are a bit like those early astronauts. They one day climb aboard a capsule called adolescence and lift off into uncharted regions of space. Soon you as parents are going through the scariest experience of your lives—you've lost all contact with the "capsule." The same kid who used to talk nonstop has now reduced his vocabulary to "I dunno," "Maybe," and "I forget." It's a period of great apprehension for those on the ground!

This is the time to remember the words of the apostle Paul: "We live by faith, not by sight" (2 Corinthians 5:7). You haven't failed as a parent; your child is simply going through the social and hormonal turbulence of adolescence. If you have raised your kids by God's principles, your teaching and patience *will* be rewarded. When the time is right—perhaps in your son or daughter's early twenties—you will likely reestablish communication and discover that everything is indeed A-OK.

Before you say good night...

- Do you feel like a failure because your child is in a "blackout" period?
- How can you help each other stay confident in your roles as parents?

Father, please forgive us when we forget that You are in control of the lives of our kids. Help us to have a firm faith in You, in Your Word, in the roles You have given us as parents, and in our children. Amen.

THE GREAT LIE

"I am clear of my responsibility."
Acts 18:6

M ary Alice and her husband dedicated themselves to raising their three daughters by Christian principles. Two turned out wonderfully; the third caused continual grief before running off at the age of eighteen with a thrice-married ex-convict. As a result, Mary Alice came face-to-face with one of the most painful emotions in human experience: guilt. In her words, "I thought I would go around forever with FAILURE branded on my forehead. My husband and I had long discussions about whether we should drop out of the church and not attempt to minister to others because of our failure."

These are the words of parents who believed the great lie. In their minds, they had destroyed their precious daughter. They were convinced that even God could not forgive so great a sin. Guilt sometimes *is* valid and represents the displeasure of God Himself. When that is the case, we must seek the Lord's forgiveness, and then rest in the knowledge that our parental transgressions and failures are removed from us "as far as the east is from the west" (Psalm 103:12).

At other times, however, our guilt is entirely of our own creation. If this is your situation, you might follow the example of the apostle Paul. Despite his devoted efforts to preach the gospel to the Jews in Macedonia, they became abusive and forced him to leave. His response? "I am clear of my responsibility" (Acts 18:6). Likewise, you are clear of your responsibility when you have given your very best to your children.

Before you say good night...

- Do you feel guilt over your parenting efforts? Is it valid?
- What does God want you to do about your guilt?

Father, even as You build our faith in You, we ask You to build up our confidence in the rightness of our own actions as parents. Please take away our doubts and our guilt, and let us focus on Your infinite sufficiency. Amen.

SHARING GUILT

"The soul who sins is the one who will die."
Ezekiel 18:20

A pastor sat in his study, utterly devastated. He'd just learned that his twenty-one-year-old son had impregnated his girlfriend at the Christian college campus he attended. The pastor felt as guilty as if he personally had been caught in an adulterous affair. *What did I do wrong? How could it have happened?* Remembering the words of Scripture—"An elder must be…a man whose children…are not open to the charge of being wild and disobedient" (Titus 1:6), the pastor saw no choice. Though he was an effective and popular leader, he would resign immediately.

Was this anguished servant overreacting in his decision to resign? We think so. We believe the Scripture above refers to younger children. In Paul's day, males and females were considered grown much earlier, marrying at fourteen or sixteen years of age. The Lord appears to settle the matter in the book of Ezekiel: "The son will not share the guilt of the father, nor will the father share the guilt of the son. The righteousness of the righteous man will be credited to him, and the wickedness of the wicked will be charged against him" (18:20). Remember, too, that the father of the Prodigal Son was not blamed for the young man's wickedness (Luke 15:11–32).

For mothers and fathers of grown children, it may be a comfort to realize that each adult is responsible only for his own behavior. Instead of taking on the sins of our grown kids, let's respond by bathing them in continual, loving prayer.

Before you say good night…

- How do you think you would respond to a grown child's sin?
- How does the Lord want you to respond in such situations?

Heavenly Father, how easy it can be for us to entwine our lives with that of our children. Give us discernment to understand Your Word as we apply it to our family, and help us to come to You in prayer for every circumstance. Amen.

HE IS STILL THERE

I call on the LORD in my distress, and he answers me.
Psalm 120:1

We've talked this week about some of the most difficult aspects of parenting, but there is a special anguish that comes with the death of a beloved child. I (JCD) will never forget the boys and girls I came to know during my years on the Attending Staff at Children's Hospital in Los Angeles. Most of these kids suffered from terminal illnesses. Some were under ten years of age, yet their faith in Jesus Christ was unshakable. Their parents had successfully passed on the wonderful message of salvation. What a reception these boys and girls must have received when they met Him who said, "Let the little children come to me" (Mark 10:14).

To the mom or dad who has recently lost a child, let me offer this word of encouragement: your Father has not lost track of your circumstances, even though they seem to be swirling out of control. He is there. Hold on to your faith in the midst of these unanswered questions. Lay claim to the words of the psalmist: "My soul is weary with sorrow; strengthen me according to your word" (Psalm 119:28). Someday God's purposes will be known, and you will have an eternity to talk it over. In the meantime, I pray with all my being that the Lord will help you through the heartbreaking loss of—or should I say temporary separation from—your precious son or daughter.

Before you say good night...

- Do you struggle with trusting God during times of heartache?
- How can you help each other renew a "childlike faith"?

Father, sometimes it is so hard to understand Your ways. We cry out to You at such times! Give us comfort, give us peace, give us understanding as we live to remain faithful to You even in the midst of our sorrows. Amen.

CONFIDENT PARENTS

"Blessed is the man…whose confidence is in [the LORD]."
Jeremiah 17:7

*M*att, visiting his parents with his wife and two young sons, was in a reflective mood. While taking a walk with his father, he remarked, "You know, Dad, while I was growing up, I sort of had the feeling that you didn't have a clue about this parenting stuff. But now that I'm a dad myself, I'm starting to change my mind. You're getting smarter every year!"

Raising healthy, educated, self-disciplined children who love God and their fellow human beings may very well be the most challenging responsibility in living. It's an unbelievably complex assignment. And of course, the job is even tougher in a culture that tries to undermine everything we do at home. Yet too many moms and dads today are complicating the task by taking on unnecessary guilt, fear, and self-doubt. I don't believe that is what God has in mind!

The Scriptures clearly tell us that children are to be considered a blessing from God (Psalm 127:3–5), and that the privilege of raising them should be a wonderful, joyful experience. He has granted parents the authority to raise their sons and daughters: "Children, obey your parents in the Lord, for this is right" (Ephesians 6:1). And when parents depend on Him to teach and lead their families, they can act with confidence: "Such confidence as this is ours through Christ before God. Not that we are competent in ourselves to claim anything for ourselves, but our competence comes from God" (2 Corinthians 3:4–5).

We will make mistakes in bringing up our kids. Fortunately, however, we are not asked to do everything perfectly as moms and dads. Our children usually manage to survive our mistakes and failures and turn out better than we have any right to boast about. They may even figure out that we *did* know what we were doing most of the time!

When problems flare up in your family, I know how easy it is to second-guess your parenting decisions. But God did not entrust you with this job by accident. As long as you choose to obey the Lord and dedicate yourselves to raising your children according to the principles outlined in Scripture, no one can better fill the role of parent for your wonderful sons and daughters than you. When you are confident in Him (Jeremiah 17:7), you can be confident parents.

SMD

Character Counts

YERR OUT!

by Clark Cothern

My father gave me a great example of character when I was a boy watching a church-league softball game.

Dad was forty-three at the time and very active. Though he wasn't known for hitting grand slams, he was good at placing the ball and beating the throw. Singles and doubles were his specialty, and he did the best he could with what he had.

This particular dusty, hot Phoenix evening, Dad poked a good one right over the second baseman's head, and the center fielder flubbed the snag and let the ball bloop between his legs.

My dad saw this as he rounded first base, so he poured on the steam. He was five feet ten inches, 160 pounds, and very fast. He figured that if he sprinted for third and slid, he could beat the throw.

Everyone was cheering as he sent two of his teammates over home plate. The center fielder finally got his feet under him and his fingers around the ball as Dad headed toward third. The throw came as hard and fast as the outfielder could fire it, and Dad started a long slide on that sun-baked infield. Dust flew everywhere.

The ball slammed into the third baseman's glove but on the other side of Dad—the outfield side—away from a clear view by the ump, who was still at home plate. Our team's dugout was on the third base side of the diamond, and every one of the players had a clear view of the play.

Dad's foot slammed into third base a solid second before the ball arrived and before the third baseman tagged his leg. But much to the amazement—and then dismay—and then anger—of the team, the umpire, who hesitated slightly before making his call, yelled, "Yerr out!"

Instantly, every member of Dad's team poured onto the field and started shouting at once—Dad's teammates were intent on only one purpose: They wanted to win, and by golly, they knew they were right!

The two runners who had crossed home plate before Dad was called out had brought the score to within one. If Dad was out—and we all knew he wasn't—his team was potentially robbed of a run.

With only one inning left, this one bad call could cost them the game.

But just as the fracas threatened to boil over into a miniriot, Dad silenced the crowd. As the dust settled around him, he held up a hand. "Guys, stop!" he yelled. And then more gently, "There's more at stake here than being right. There's something more important here than winning a game. If the ump says I'm out, I'm out."

And with that, he dusted himself off, limped to the bench to get his glove (his leg was bruised from the slide), and walked back into left field all by himself, ready to begin the last inning. One by one, the guys on his team gave up the argument, picked up their own gloves, and walked out to their positions on the field.

I've got to tell you, I was both bewildered and proud that night. My dad may have been dusty, but I saw a sparkling diamond out there standing under the lights, a diamond more valuable than all the runs his team might have scored.

For a few minutes that evening I was a rich kid, basking in my father's decision to be a man, to hold his tongue instead of wagging it, to settle the dust instead of settling a score. I knew what he showed me at that selfless moment was worth more than all the gold-toned plastic trophies you could buy.

Dad held court that night, and everyone on the field and in the crowd was a member of the jury. When the verdict came in, their decision was unanimous: This was a man of character.

LOOKING AHEAD...

Webster's dictionary defines a person of character as possessing "moral excellence and firmness." Words such as *integrity, honor,* and *honesty* also come to mind. There is something intangible about these qualities in a man or woman, yet we know character when we see it. A little boy saw it in his father in the story above. Your children see it when you apologize after an angry remark, or turn off a lewd television show, or resign from a company involved in questionable practices.

We are reminded repeatedly in Scripture that the way we conduct ourselves is important to the Lord: "The man of integrity walks securely" (Proverbs 10:9); "Set an example for the believers in speech, in life, in love, in faith and in purity" (1 Timothy 4:12); "Live holy and godly lives" (2 Peter 3:11). It is vital that we pass this biblical truth on to our children.

Does character count in your family? Let's talk more about it in the days ahead.

JCD

FATHER'S DAY GIFT

When you are tempted, he will also provide a
way out so that you can stand up under it.
1 Corinthians 10:13

I
t was the day before Father's Day. Hank, a ten-year-old, and his dad were in a store together, but in different aisles. Hank was penniless and still hadn't figured out what to give his father the next day. His eyes found a display of golf balls—his father's favorite brand. Hank knew his father would love those balls! Quickly, he hid a box of three balls under his shirt. Almost immediately, though, Hank was uncomfortable. He realized he'd done wrong. Reluctantly, he returned the box to the shelf and walked away.

Years later, Hank admitted to his dad that he still felt awful about the Father's Day he didn't give a card or gift. His father replied, "Son, I remember that year. I watched you take those balls off the shelf that day in the store. I suspected you were about to steal them for me, and I felt so sad. But then you put them back. You probably thought I was hurt that you didn't give me a present, but watching you return those balls was the best Father's Day present I ever received."

This tale of Hank and his father, inspired by an anonymous story in *God's Little Devotional Book for Dads,* serves as an important reminder of God's promise to always provide a "way out" of temptation. Tomorrow, why don't you share 1 Corinthians 10:13—along with the story of Hank and the golf balls—with your kids?

Before you say good night...

• What are the biggest temptations facing your family right now?
• How can you help each other find the "way out" God promises?

Dear God, sometimes it is so hard to resist the allures that surround us. Thank You for the promise of a way out of every tempting situation. We humbly ask that You show our children the way out when they too are tempted. Amen.

LEARNING THE HARD WAY

Righteousness guards the man of integrity.
Proverbs 13:6

Many kids feel pressure to earn good grades at school; some resort to dishonest means to get them. I (JCD) once succumbed to this temptation. When I was in the eighth grade, I was required to read a certain number of great books during the first semester. Unfortunately, I hadn't even started as we approached the end of the term—so I selected the thickest, heaviest books in the library and told my teacher I had read them all. Consequently, she gave me an A on my report card. My mom was impressed, my dad was proud, and I was as guilty as sin.

In a moment of true confession, I admitted to my mother that I had cheated. Instead of getting mad or grounding me for six years, she simply said with quiet intensity, "Well, you'll just have to read the books." "But, Mom," I said, "how can I read the collected works of William Shakespeare, *Ben Hur,* and about ten other huge books?" "I don't know," she replied, "but you're gonna do it." I spent the rest of that school year poring over the classics while my friends played football and talked to girls. No one ever paid more dearly for a little dishonesty.

My wise mother's response taught me a priceless lesson. She understood that God is "pleased with integrity" (1 Chronicles 29:17)…and she made sure that I never forgot that truth.

Before you say good night...

- Have your kids ever cheated at home or school? How did you respond?
- How can you encourage godly integrity in your family?

Father, we want to come before You as people of righteousness and integrity. Help us to avoid sinful shortcuts in our lives, and show us how to respond with wisdom when our own children fall short of Your perfect ways. Amen.

Never Too Late

Make every effort to be found spotless,
blameless and at peace with him.
2 Peter 3:14

Lucille Lind Arnell tells a story about her mother, who raised nine children in Chicago during the thirties and forties. To get her family out of the house, "Mama" often took them on streetcar trips. When they lined up to get on board, the conductor sometimes let kids pass who were old enough to pay. Mama, who knew she could use every penny, never objected.

Years later, Mama began thinking about all those times her kids rode free on the trolley. She decided she'd been wrong to not pay their fares. So she sat down and composed a letter to the Chicago Transit Authority, then mailed it along with a ten-dollar bill (this was 1951, when ten dollars could have fed her family for two weeks). The transit authority responded with a note thanking Mama for her honesty. That letter, a tribute to one woman's sense of integrity, now hangs in a place of honor in the home of one of her daughters.

Another aspect of character is the fervent desire to be found "blameless" before God. Though no one else may be aware of our transgressions, He knows where we stand—and He is always ready to forgive. Let's show our children that it is never too late to do what is right.

Before you say good night...

- Do you think "Mama" was right to confess her dishonesty?
- Do you need to take any "forgotten" sins to the Lord?
- Do your kids understand that it's never too late to correct a wrong?

Heavenly Father, we so desire to be found blameless before You. Search our hearts and reveal any lingering sin, and help us to bring that to You in repentance. Let us be the examples of integrity for our children that You call us to be. Amen.

CHARACTER VACATION

*Whatever happens, conduct yourselves in
a manner worthy of the gospel of Christ.*
Philippians 1:27

*I*t's easy for moms and dads to come up with reasons for taking a "character vacation." You may think, for instance, *Everyone else cheats on their taxes, so why shouldn't I?* Or, *No one will care if I take a few things from the office (or factory) to use at home.* But once you start your slide into the pit of rationalization, it's very difficult to climb back out—and equally tough to keep your children from joining you.

In the first days of the Christian church, a man named Ananias and his wife, Sapphira, thought they could fool God by appearing to be generous. First they sold a piece of property. Then Ananias, with his wife's knowledge, kept some of the money and presented the rest to the apostles, pretending that it was the full amount from the sale. Peter confronted him: "What made you think of doing such a thing? You have not lied to men but to God." Ananias immediately fell down and died. When Sapphira arrived later, also pretending that they had given the full amount, she too died at Peter's feet (Acts 5:1–10).

Our kids are watching our character closely. God is watching, too. He knows when our actions are forthright and when we distort the truth: "The integrity of the upright guides them, but the unfaithful are destroyed by their duplicity" (Proverbs 11:3). We must remember—and teach our children—that God's desire for us is to keep our character intact.

Before you say good night...
* Are there times when you take a "character vacation"?
* Are you modeling godly character to your children?

Gracious Lord, we too often allow troubles and our own priorities to pull us away from You. Let us cling to You and Your eternal Word, no matter what the circumstances. Build our trust as we stay ever faithful to You. Amen.

BAD COMPANY

Do not be misled: "Bad company corrupts good character."
1 Corinthians 15:33

very parent is under terrible pressure in today's fast-paced culture. The demands of jobs, maintaining a house, keeping up with financial commitments, church responsibilities, and trying to raise a family keep us running at breakneck speed. As a result, too many kids are regularly left at home to care for themselves (41 percent of children ages twelve to fourteen, according to the U.S. Census Bureau). It's no wonder that we are sometimes barely aware of what our kids are doing day to day. In an immoral culture, that can be disastrous.

Lonely and energetic adolescents in this situation are especially vulnerable to the worldly influence of peers. Their need for acceptance by friends at this time is overwhelming. To protect your children from these potential dangers, we urge you to stay close to them. Know who their friends are; have them over for dinner or a family activity. Talk to your kids about your spiritual beliefs and values. Explain the impact of peer pressure and how difficult it can be to go against the wishes of the group. Then remind them of God's position in Romans 12:2: "Do not conform any longer to the pattern of this world, but be transformed by the renewing of your mind."

Your encouragement at this critical time can help assure good character in your kids—no mater what company they keep.

Before you say good night...
- How well do you know your children's friends?
- How can you initiate conversations to get to know them?
- How much unsupervised time do your kids have each week?

O God, we want to encourage our children as they enter the difficult years of adolescence. Grant us the wisdom to guide and lead them with eternity's values in mind, and to show that Your acceptance is all we ever need. Amen.

TRUTHFUL LIPS

Truthful lips endure forever,
but a lying tongue lasts only a moment.
Proverbs 12:19

I never fully comprehended the significance of lying when I was growing up. I knew that being untruthful was wrong, but I never came to terms with the moral implications. I can recall many instances when boys asked me for dates and I lied to them because I didn't want to go. I often lied to my mother when I was about to be caught for something I had done. The implications of this sin did not come home to me until several years after I was married.

I went into the kitchen one day to fix Jim a tuna sandwich. Though he *hated* mayonnaise, I snuck a small amount into the tuna to hold it together and make it (from my perspective!) better. Jim's first question when I served the sandwich was, "Did you put mayonnaise in the tuna?" Caught red-handed, I lied. I said, "I know you don't like mayonnaise. Of course I didn't put it in your sandwich." Jim ate his lunch without noticing a thing, but the incident bothered my conscience for days. Finally, I confessed.

Not surprisingly, Jim was very disappointed. He told me, "Marriage must be built on mutual trust. If a husband and wife are honest with each other about the little things, they will not deceive each other about the big things." We had a long talk about our relationship and committed to each other that lying would not be part of it. I have attempted to live by a higher standard from that moment.

Of the seven things we're told are detestable to the Lord in Proverbs 6:16–19, two relate to untruthfulness—"a lying tongue" and "a false witness who pours out lies." Clearly, this is a serious matter in His eyes. Unless a child is too young to understand the difference between fantasy and truth, parents should teach their children with great emphasis that truth be told in all situations.

Of course, honesty will come to your kids most easily if you practice it yourself, especially in your interactions at home. It took me a while to figure that out, but I'm so glad I did. You will be, too.

SMD

Tough Times

It Is Well with My Soul

by Jennifer Rothschild

I began my sophomore year of high school experiencing all the usual teenage changes.

But there had also been one very unusual one.

Near the end of junior high, I began to realize that my eyesight was deteriorating.

As I picked my way carefully through the packed hallways of Glades Junior High, I was amazed at how my classmates streamed through the crowd with such ease—even in dark stairwells. How could they do that without bumping into schoolmates or lockers? When we played softball in P.E., I couldn't understand how my teammates could catch the ball so easily. I would stand out in right field, glove in hand, and stare intently at the ground, trying to see the shadow of the approaching ball. Then I'd listen to where it landed and hope I could find it.

Difficult as it was to admit…I began to realize that it wasn't normal for me not to be able to see a softball in the air or the stairs in a stairwell. As a result, I began to feel more awkward and self-conscious. At last I became so concerned that I told my mother, who (as you might imagine) immediately took me to an ophthalmologist.

The eye doctor tried to remedy my failing sight with prescriptions for stronger glasses, but they didn't help. Eventually, he referred me to an eye hospital. After several days of testing, the doctors met with my folks and me. They told us that I had retinitis pigmentosa, a degenerative disease that slowly eats away the retina of the eye.

There was no cure and no way to correct damage already done.

The doctors said I had lost so much vision that, at fifteen, I was already legally blind. And they told us that my retinas would continue to deteriorate until I was totally blind.

Blind…totally blind.

The words sounded so final. So certain. So cold. I felt a chill inside that I'd never felt before.

Nothing else was said. Silence fell upon us like shadows fall just before night, and it shrouded us as we left the hospital, walked across the parking lot, got in the car, and journeyed home.

I have often thought that it was probably much harder for my parents that day than it was for me. Yes, my eyes were being robbed of sight, but their hearts were being crushed. Can you imagine their heartache? Can you hear the sound of that door slamming in their souls? Surely one of life's greatest sorrows must be to watch your child suffer…and to feel helpless to prevent it.

My dad gripped the steering wheel tightly as he piloted us home through the spidery Miami streets. I could only imagine the prayers he must have been praying. He had always been my source of wisdom, my counselor, my comforter, my rescuer, and the one man I trusted completely. I wonder if he was thinking, *Dear Lord, how can I fix this?*

Yet on the ride home he was silent.

My mother sat next to him in the front seat. I could feel her broken heart. A mother's heart is so tender. I wonder what her prayers were like on that day. My mom was my standard, my cheerleader, my encourager, my mentor, and my friend. I think she must have been wondering, *Will she be safe?*

Yet on the ride home, she too, was silent.

I had always been strong-willed, trusting, sensitive, and talkative. Yet, sitting in the backseat, I also kept silent. I remember the reasons for my silence as if it were yesterday. My heart was swelling with emotion, and my mind was racing with questions and thoughts. *How will I finish high school? Will I ever go away to college? How will I know what I look like? Will I ever get a date or a boyfriend? Will I ever get married?* I remember feeling my fingertips and wondering how in the world people read Braille.

And then it hit me.

I would never be able to drive a car.

Like most teenagers, I thought that having wheels was just like having wings. I couldn't wait to drive! That was a step toward independence to which nothing else compared. But now it was a rite of passage I would never experience, and I was crushed.

After forty-five long minutes, we arrived home. Once inside, I went immediately to the living room and sat down at our piano. It was old and stately and had a warm, comforting sound. For me it was a place of refuge.

By then I had played the piano for several years. In fact, I'd had almost five years of lessons. The funny thing about my lessons, though, was that I'd managed to stretch them out over an eight-year period. I was one of those kids who would beg my mother to let me take piano lessons—and then after about six months beg her to let me quit! Three or four months later we'd start the whole routine over again.

I barely muddled through my lessons, and I'm sure it wasn't pleasant for the listener to hear me practice. Let's just say that I was a little short on natural talent! I did, however, practice diligently every night after dinner. That's because if I did, I was excused from clearing the table and washing the dishes.

But this time was different.

I wasn't seeking refuge from chores, and I didn't play the few songs I'd memorized. Instead, I began to play by ear, and the melody that filled the living room that afternoon belonged to a song I'd never played before. My fingers followed a pattern along the keyboard that was new to me, yet…somehow familiar.

The song I played was "It Is Well with My Soul."

I think God guided my heart and hands to play that hymn. Some people have told me it was a miracle that I could sit down at the piano that day and begin to play by ear for the first time. Perhaps it was. Who knows? But to me, there was a bigger miracle that dark day.

The miracle was not that I played "It Is Well with My Soul," but that it actually *was* well with my soul.

Now, more than twenty years later, I look back and wonder at all that has happened. I still can't see, of course, and I know well the hardships that blindness brings. Yet I have been blessed with a wonderful husband and two sons, as well as a meaningful speaking ministry. God has been good to me.

On that day so long ago—in the hospital, on the ride home, and at the piano—even as I mourned my loss, I looked into the heart of my Teacher. I knew His Word and His character, and they were what allowed me to say then—and still say today—"Whatever my lot...it is well with my soul."

LOOKING AHEAD...

There are times when we as parents are not able to shield the children we love from troubles, disappointment, and heartache. Rejection by friends, failure, injuries, and illness are, for the most part, matters over which we have little control. When these trials occur, we end up feeling as helpless as Jennifer Rothschild's parents on the day they learned that their daughter was going blind.

Two thousand years ago, Jesus warned us that life on earth would not be easy: "In this world you will have trouble" (John 16:33). Yet we know that one reason the Lord allows trials in our lives is to create opportunities to draw near to Him. He understands how easy it is for us to fall away from daily prayer, worship, and study of His Word when times are good. It is why the apostle Peter said, "Do not be surprised at the painful trial you are suffering, as though something strange were happening to you. But rejoice that you participate in the sufferings of Christ, so that you may be overjoyed when his glory is revealed" (1 Peter 4:12–13).

It can be terribly difficult to rejoice in the midst of hardship or crisis, especially when our own children are involved. Yet these are the times, more than ever, that your family needs to know that God remains in control and is still the source of all love, comfort, and strength. We'll talk more about this important truth in the days ahead: Even when it is not well with our circumstances, it *can* be well with our souls.

JCD

THE ROLLER COASTER OF LIFE

Though you have made me see troubles,
many and bitter, you will restore my life.
Psalm 71:20

Mark Twain once said that life is just one darn thing after another. No matter how tranquil our days, we can be sure that an upheaval is just around the corner. Even Jesus experienced this roller-coaster aspect of human existence. His ministry began at the Jordan River, where He was baptized by John. Then God spoke to Him from heaven, saying that He was "well pleased" (Matthew 3:17). What an exhilarating moment!

What followed this incredible event, however, was one of the most terrible ordeals Jesus would encounter—a forty-day battle with Satan in the desert. After this difficult period, the pendulum swung back again. Jesus became tremendously popular as people learned that a "prophet" was in their midst. But then the chief priests and Pharisees began plotting to kill Him. And so it went. Eventually, the darkest day in human history—the crucifixion—was followed by the most wonderful news ever given to mankind, the resurrection of our Savior.

Our point is that there is no stability or predictability in this imperfect world. You must expect troubles, hardships, and heartache. The only anchor for you and your family in this topsy-turvy world is the unchanging, everlasting Lord. Even when you're surrounded by tragedy, you can rest in this truth: His promises never fail, and His love never ends.

Before you say good night...

- Do your kids understand that we all must go through trials?
- Have you taught them to depend only on God for their security?

Our Father, how wonderful it is to have You as our God! Thank You for Your faithful, consistent love during the topsy-turvy moments of life. We pray that each member of our family will learn to always depend on You. Amen.

THE ADVERSITY PRINCIPLE

*After you have suffered a little while, [God] will himself
restore you and make you strong, firm and steadfast.*
1 Peter 5:10

As strange as it seems, easy living and a stress-free existence can be disadvantageous for animals and for us humans. Think about the big male lion lying in a cage at the zoo. All his needs are met, and his hunting skills are useless. His muscles turn flabby, and he yawns his way through the day. Meanwhile, the lion that's roaming free on the plains of Africa, stalking and competing for his next meal, remains fit and strong because of the challenges and dangers he faces.

Within limits, adversity is beneficial to you and your children, too. Troubles that require comforting leave you better able to comfort others (2 Corinthians 1:3–4). Physical suffering, when endured in the name of Christ, makes it easier for you to say no to sin (1 Peter 4:1). Hardships due to your faith lead to restoration and strength (1 Peter 5:9–10). Trials also produce perseverance, character, and hope (Romans 5:3). There are many other examples of this "adversity principle" at work in Scripture.

Human beings who have survived hard times are tougher, more resilient, and more compassionate than those who have never faced difficulty or pain. You might remember that the next time your family is battling adversity in the jungle of life.

Before you say good night...

- Do you try, out of love, to sweep aside every hurdle and difficulty encountered by your children?
- Do you fight their battles for them?
- Are you helping or handicapping them by this assistance?

Lord, it is so difficult to watch our children struggle—and so tempting to fight their battles for them. Please grant us wisdom and restraint when You are using adversity to shape and strengthen our sons and daughters. Amen.

HOLD ON TO FAITH

"We must go through many hardships to enter the kingdom of God."
Acts 14:22

We talked last night about several benefits to facing adversity. One, however, rises above the rest: Trials strengthen our faith and bring us closer to the Lord.

A steadfast faith ranks at the top of God's system of priorities. Without it, He says, it is impossible to please Him (Hebrews 11:6). I (JCD) am reminded of a woman named Marian Benedict Manwell, whose brain was damaged permanently by a broken spring that penetrated her head as a baby. She was crippled for life. Other kids taunted her and mocked her deformity. When Marian was ten, her mother died of cancer. Despite—or more likely because of—these difficulties, Marian developed a deep faith in Christ. She eventually married a wonderful Christian husband and was blessed with eight children, all of whom grew up serving the Lord.

I'm not suggesting it's easy to welcome misfortune into your life. I grieve for those who are confronting the loss of a loved one or some other terrible situation tonight. I can only say that it *is* God's will for us to be thankful in all circumstances and that He understands our pain: "Blessed are you who weep now, for you will laugh" (Luke 6:21). Hold on to your faith, teach your children to do the same, and He will sustain you and your family.

Before you say good night...

- Is your faith strong enough to endure adversity?
- Are your children developing an unshakable dependence on God?

Lord, how can we teach faith to our children if we don't show it when troubles or hardships crash into our world? Help us to cling to You every day—with all our hearts—so that our kids will learn what it means to grow in faith. Amen.

HELP AT HOME

You are the helper of the fatherless.
Psalm 10:14

When Kathy's husband died, her sons were seventeen and twenty. Both boys missed their dad terribly. When they encountered difficulties that Kathy's husband normally would have handled, she felt inadequate. The issues they faced at that age were not ones she could "kiss and make better." So Kathy laid the situation at God's feet through prayer, knowing that she needed help to deal wisely with her boys.

The Lord responded. When one son faced losing his job because he didn't have a vehicle that would make it over snowy roads, a friend unexpectedly offered the use of his four-wheel-drive rig. When the other son hit a coyote with the used car he'd just purchased, a friend was there to offer advice and arrange for repairs. And when Kathy saw that her eldest son needed spiritual grounding and guidance, a mentor was provided in the form of his Christian boss at the fire station where he was interning.

Single parents can't do it all for their kids, especially in times of hardship or crisis. They need assistance from friends, relatives, neighbors, and fellow believers who heed the call of Scripture: "Defend the cause of the fatherless, plead the case of the widow" (Isaiah 1:17). Most of all, they need to take their needs in prayer to their loving Lord, the "helper of the fatherless" (Psalm 10:14).

Before you say good night...

- Do you need to put your parenting issues before the Lord in prayer?
- Do you know a single parent you could reach out to this week?

Lord Jesus, be our strength when we are overwhelmed, our hope when we are discouraged, and our confidence when we feel alone or afraid. May Your grace and power shine out of our weakness, for the sake of our children, and for the sake of all those who look to us for strength. Amen.

LIVING IN THE PRESENT

We are hard pressed on every side, but not crushed;
perplexed, but not in despair.
2 Corinthians 4:8

uthor Donna Partow writes that her unemployed husband, Cameron, began a job search with high hopes. But the "Aha!" of finding a new job never came. Cameron networked; he knocked on doors; he circled want ads. He even dialed job hot lines until midnight each evening. Then he began to bog down emotionally. He and Donna would tell their daughter, "Well, honey, I wish we could do such and such, but we'll just have to wait until Daddy gets a job."

Suddenly Cameron and Donna realized that they had put life on hold, freeze-framing every fun moment until their hard times passed. They resolved that day to live in the present regardless of their situation. They began going out for fast food like other families, although they'd buy only one item each. They maintained a busy social life and did inexpensive but meaningful activities together as a family. Most importantly, they refused to give in to despair and depression.

Such measures, of course, don't bring employment or relieve financial strain—but they sure beat self-pity and despondency. The apostle Paul encouraged new believers with a reminder of when they "joyfully accepted the confiscation of your property" because of their faith (Hebrews 10:34). Likewise, let's remember the joy we always have in Christ—no matter what the circumstances.

Before you say good night...

- Are you putting parts of your lives "on hold" because of hard times?
- How can you help your family enjoy life despite any current trials?

Father, we thank You for Your provision for our needs and for forgiveness of sins. Grant us Your joy and peace, no matter what our daily challenges, and help us to always place our trust in You. Amen.

LET GOD BE GOD

In God I trust; I will not be afraid.
Psalm 56:4

*D*r. Jim Conway was a guest on a Focus on the Family radio broadcast to relate the story of his daughter, Becki. When Becki was fifteen, she began having trouble with one of her knees. For the next eighteen months, doctors ran tests and took biopsies. Finally, a doctor came to the Conway home and delivered the distressing verdict—Becki had a malignancy and her leg would have to be amputated.

Dr. Conway, a pastor, refused to believe it. He was convinced that God was about to perform a miracle. His church began a twenty-four-hour vigil of fasting and prayer. On the morning of the scheduled surgery, he asked the surgeon to verify that Becki's cancer had been healed. But it hadn't. Becki's leg was lost—as was the faith of a crushed, angry, and confused father.

Over the next several weeks, Dr. Conway battled his feelings over Becki's amputation. He eventually realized that he had two choices: continue along a path of anger and despair over the loss of Becky's leg or put the matter in God's hands and choose to believe that He knew what He was doing. He decided, in his words, to "let God be God" and trust Him to turn tragedy into triumph. The struggles with his emotions didn't completely disappear. But like Job, Dr. Conway chose to draw on the wisdom and love of our sovereign Creator: "Though he slay me, yet will I hope in him" (Job 13:15).

There are times that God simply doesn't make sense. When He allows tragedy to strike your family, a sense of abandonment or despair can be overwhelming. But in your hour of crisis, I urge you not to lean on your own ability to understand. Don't demand explanations. You will find peace only when you choose to "let God be God," rest in His wisdom and protection, and heed the words of David in Psalm 52:8: "I trust in God's unfailing love for ever and ever."

SMD

Keeping Perspective

INFAMY ON ICE

by Phil Callaway

*M*y dream as a kid was to be a hockey player. I couldn't wait for Saturday evenings. After my bath, I would hurry to the living room, sit down next to the big Philco radio, and listen to hockey night in Canada.

Ah, how I loved the roar of the crowd. The tension of overtime. Players' names that brought visions of grandeur: Gordie Howe, Frank Mahovolich, Bobby Orr, Phil Callaway. It's true. I imagined the announcer, his voice rushed with excitement: "It's Callaway, blazing down the ice...splitting the defense...he shoots...he scores! Oh my, I have not seen anything this exciting since the Allies invaded Normandy!"

Certain that hockey was my calling, I pursued my dream with everything I had. Before long I was playing with real teams in real arenas, with a real helmet to protect my really hard head. Our teams were never very good, but that didn't lessen my enthusiasm. I couldn't wait to turn professional so I could fly Mom and Dad to the games. I'd buy them front-row seats right behind the players. They could help the coach make important decisions.

In tenth grade we posted our first winning season. It was a milestone year for me. In fact, something occurred that year that changed my dream for good.

It happened like this.

Late March. The championship game. An event of such magnitude in our small town that a crowd of millions, or at least a few hundred, packed our small arena to watch the stars come out. Peering in nervous anticipation through a crack in the locker room door, I had the distinct feeling that this would be *my* night. The years of stickhandling were about to pay off. Those who had paid the scalpers twenty-five cents would not be disappointed.

But as the game progressed, my dream began to fade. In fact, as the clock ran down to the final minute, the dream had all the makings of a nightmare. We were behind 3–2 as I climbed over the boards. The final buzzer was about to sound. The fat lady was about to sing. We needed a miracle. We needed Phil Callaway.

And so I took a pass from the corner and skillfully rifled the puck past a sprawling goalie. The red light came on. The girls went wild. The game was tied. And I was a hero. I had scored the goal of my dreams.

Only one goal could top it. The overtime goal.

As I sat in the dressing room waiting for the ice to be cleared, I eased open the locker room door for another peek at the crowd. *Prepare yourselves, you lucky people. Tonight destiny is on my side. Tonight will be* my *night. You will remember me for years to come. Last week when I missed the open net, you chanted my name reassuringly:*

> *That's all right, that's okay.*
> *We still love you Callaway.*

But not tonight. No need for sympathy, thank you. Only applause. Wild, exuberant, adoring applause.

And, sure enough, about five minutes into overtime I scored the winning goal. It is a moment that is forever available to me on instant replay and sometimes in slow motion. As the puck slid toward the open net, I dove, trying desperately to forge its direction. As the crowd rose to its feet, I swatted the puck across the goal line.

The red light lit.

The girls screamed.

But they were not cheering for me.

I had just scored into my own net.

I don't remember much that happened after that. In fact, the next number of years are a bit of a blur. I do remember making a beeline for the locker room, where I sat down and threw a white towel over my head. And I recall the comments of my fellow teammates: "Don't worry about it, Callaway. Anyone coulda done that…if he was totally uncoordinated."

I pulled the towel around my ears to muffle the laughter. Then I unlaced my skates. And hung them up. For good.

Upon arriving home, I headed straight for my room. A bad case of the flu had kept Dad from the game.

"How did it go?" he asked, standing in the doorway, studying my pale face and knowing part of the answer.

"Aw, Dad," I said, hanging my head. "I can't tell you. You're sick enough."

Flopping onto my bed, I put my hands behind my head and stared at the stucco ceiling. Dad entered my room and sat beside me, saying nothing.

"Did you ever do something so stupid you wished for all the world you could go back twenty-four hours and start the day again?" I asked.

"Well," said Dad, "there was the time I shot out Old Man Henderson's headlights with my .22…and then there was—"

I interrupted him for the first time in years. Then sat up. Buried my head in my fists. And told him everything: The shock of the crowd. The shame of the dressing room. My play that would live in infamy. I didn't dare look at his face. The face of a proud dad. A dad who had dreams of his own for his youngest son.

There was silence for a minute. Then Dad put his hand on my knee and did the most unexpected thing in the world.

He began to laugh.

And I couldn't believe I was doing it…but I joined him.

It was the last thing either of us expected. It was the very best thing.

More than twenty years have passed since the night Dad and I sat on the edge of my bed laughing together. I remember it as the night I determined to skate again. In fact, I'm still skating. I've even managed to score a few goals over the years. Into the right net. But no goal will ever be as memorable as that overtime goal.

For several years after I'd wake up in a cold sweat reliving that awful moment, but when I'd remember Dad's hand on my knee…I'd smile from ear to ear. You see, that was the night I discovered something that makes the heaviest burdens seem a whole lot lighter.

There on my bed, my father gave me a glimpse into the face of my heavenly Father. A face full of compassion, forgiveness, and grace.

A smiling face.

The face of One who laughs with us.

LOOKING AHEAD...

Sometimes life gets so bad that there is only one thing left to do: laugh. When your dishwasher floods the kitchen, when you accidentally delete a day's work on the computer, or when you score the winning goal for the wrong team, you'll find the situation much easier to handle if you can respond to it with a smile instead of a scream.

As we hurry through our days, it's easy to let life's problems and stresses distort our perspective. That may be one of the reasons why God gave us laughter…and sunsets…and ice cream…and music…and children.

The child-raising years are filled with some of life's biggest challenges, yet they pass by so quickly. Soon, by God's grace, your family will be together in a new, eternal home—a joyous place called heaven. That knowledge should help you keep the temporary pitfalls of daily life in proper perspective.

JCD

A LIFESTYLE OF WORSHIP

Worship the LORD in the splendor of his holiness.
1 Chronicles 16:29

*N*othing puts parenting, or life itself, in perspective quite like time spent praising our glorious God. The act of worship brings pleasure to our Maker (Proverbs 15:8) while increasing our determination to do what is right. Praising Him is not simply an obligation to cross off our "to do" list every Sunday morning, but a continuing lifestyle: "I will sing of the LORD's great love forever" (Psalm 89:1).

Judy's family practiced that daily adoration when she was a girl. Even on vacation in a California wilderness, she remembers her family gathering in their small cabin after breakfast for the purpose of honoring God. Her older sister, Ruth, would open this time with a prayer. Then her brother, Jim, would lead the family in songs of praise on his guitar. Finally, Judy's mother would read from the Bible and her father would talk about the meaning of the Scripture. "On many of those mornings, all I wanted to do was go out and play," Judy says. "But it always set just the right tone for the rest of our day together. And today those worship times are among my sweetest memories."

We have a Savior who is preparing a place for each of us in His kingdom (John 14:2). That's *always* a reason for rejoicing and worship! Let's gather our children around us every day to pray, study, and glorify God. As King David wrote, "I will praise you, O Lord my God, with all my heart" (Psalm 86:12).

Before you say good night...

• Does the act of worship change *your* perspective on parenting?
• How might an increase in times of praise benefit your family?

Father, You are a mighty and glorious God! Even as we sing praises to You, we tremble before Your name. Help us to set aside time as a family to honor You, that we may renew our perspective as Your beloved children. Amen.

Wonders to Remember

Many, O LORD, my God, are the wonders you have done.
Psalm 40:5

bby surveyed her house and shuddered. Toys were strewn across the floor; dishes were stacked high in the sink and on the kitchen counter; piles of laundry were everywhere. She sighed and asked herself, *Why exactly did I decide to be a mother?*

Suddenly her three-year-old, Kyle, dashed in from the backyard and grabbed her hand. "Mama, come see! Come see!" Obediently, Abby stumbled after her excited son. They reached a brick walkway, where Kyle proudly pointed to a green and yellow caterpillar. Together, mother and son squatted down for a closer look. Abby marveled at the caterpillar's fine black stripes and wiggly antennae. She turned to let the sun's rays bathe her shoulders in warmth and spotted the delicate strands of an intricate spiderweb still under construction in her camellia bush. She pointed out the web to her son. "Wow," he whispered. Side by side they watched the spider complete the beautiful design. *Thank You, God,* Abby breathed. *Now I remember why.*

It's easy to let the burden of parenthood steal our appreciation for God's amazing creation. Yet Scripture says that "He has caused his wonders to be remembered" (Psalm 111:4). We *will* remember—and discover a more spiritual perspective on the mundane side of life—if we only take the time to look. Sometimes our kids will be the ones to lead us there.

Before you say good night...

- How often do you and your family stop to admire God's creation?
- How does it change your perspective—and that of your kids—when you do?

Awesome God, we can barely comprehend the splendors You have created for our enjoyment. Thank You for incredible blessings and for the ability to appreciate them. Let our family always remember Your amazing wonders. Amen.

TIMES TO LAUGH

*"God has brought me laughter,
and everyone who hears about this will laugh with me."*
Genesis 21:6

ids are a wellspring of humor if you look for it. For instance, there was the mother who was making phone calls in the family room while her three-year-old daughter and five-month-old son played together. Suddenly the mother realized that the kids were gone. Panic-stricken, she raced down the hall and around the corner, where she found them playing cheerfully. Relieved but upset, she shouted, "Adrianne, you know you are not allowed to carry Nathan! He is too little—you could hurt him if he fell!"

Startled, Adrianne answered, "I didn't, Mommy." Knowing that Nathan couldn't crawl, the mother demanded, "Well, then, how did he get all the way into your room?" Confident of her mother's approval, Adrianne smiled and said proudly, "I rolled him!"

This story reminds us that when King Solomon began his quest to discover the meaning of life, he believed that laughter was "foolish" (Ecclesiastes 2:2). But when he investigated further, he realized that God orders all things according to His purposes—that there is "a season for every activity under heaven" (3:1), including "a time to laugh" (v. 4). On those days when your toddler rolls your youngest offspring down the hall, you may discover that the most godly response is not one of anger or disapproval. You've entered a new season—a time to laugh.

Before you say good night...
* Are you usually lighthearted or serious around your kids?
* Do you approach life with a sense of humor? If not, why?

Thank You, Lord, for those lighter moments along life's road. Please don't let us become so intense and tightly wound that we can't let loose with a good, long laugh now and then at ourselves, our children, and our circumstances. Amen.

FAMILY JUSTICE

The end of a matter is better than its beginning.
Ecclesiastes 7:8

A couple of decades ago, twelve-year-old Jeff and his ten-year-old brother, Scott, argued daily. Shouts of "Give it back! It's my turn!" frequently filled the house. Their mother and father, when he was home, intervened often and did their best to maintain peace between their young warriors. Though it often felt like a losing battle, they generally kept a positive attitude about their roles as mediators. This faithful mom and dad understood that the Scripture "Blessed are they who maintain justice" (Psalm 106:3) certainly included parents. God's Word helped them keep the worst of the child-rearing wars in perspective.

Sibling rivalry has been known to drive even the most patient and reasonable of parents crazy. It was responsible for the first murder on record, when Cain killed his brother Abel. Though a degree of antagonism between your children may be inevitable, you can minimize these conflicts by avoiding comparisons between your kids, by establishing and enforcing clear boundaries between them, and especially by instilling an equitable system of justice at home. Someone has said, "Strong families make good neighbors." It is true. Solomon told us why: "When justice is done, it brings joy to the righteous" (Proverbs 21:15). While you can't eliminate sibling rivalry altogether, you can insist on civility at home. Over time, that can lead to lasting friendships.

Before you say good night...

- Is sibling rivalry a problem in your home? What do you think is its cause?
- Do you "maintain justice" as taught in Scripture?

Heavenly Father, it can be so painful to watch our children fight. We ask for Your guidance for our response to these moments. Help us to be fair at all times, and give us wisdom to maintain justice in our family. Amen.

GET 'EM THROUGH IT

If you find [wisdom], there is a future hope for you.
Proverbs 24:14

waitress once recognized me (JCD) when I came into the restaurant where she worked. She was a single mother and wanted to talk about her twelve-year-old daughter, who had been a struggle to raise. "We have fought tooth and nail for this entire year," she said. "We argue nearly every night, and most of our fights are over the same issue. She wants to shave her legs, but I feel she's too young." My response? "Lady, buy your daughter a razor!"

That twelve-year-old was paddling into a time of life that would rock her canoe. As a single parent, this mother would soon be trying to keep her rebellious adolescent away from drugs, alcohol, sex and pregnancy, early marriage, school failure, and the possibility of running away. In that setting, it seemed unwise to make a big deal over such a small issue as shaving. While I agreed with the mother that adolescence should not be brought on prematurely, there were higher priorities to consider.

Scripture says that "By wisdom a house is built, and through understanding it is established" (Proverbs 24:3). Those same qualities should be applied to raising families. It takes both wisdom and understanding to know when to tighten your grip and when to loosen it. In the case of hardheaded kids floating toward the rapids in the teenage years, the wisest approach may be to simply get 'em through it.

Before you say good night...

- Are you focusing on the matters that most affect your kids' welfare?
- Do you always seek God for wisdom and understanding in your parental decisions?

Father, may we keep our focus on those things that are most important to the well-being of our children. May our discernment be equal to the task. Most of all, help both of us to keep our eyes upon You. Amen.

THE SAND MAN

*Sing psalms, hymns and spiritual songs with
gratitude in your hearts to God.*
Colossians 3:16

*I*t's easy enough to express our gratitude to God when He graciously blesses us with many good things. But on those days when everything seems to go wrong, a grateful heart is harder to come by.

I'm reminded of a story by Gigi Graham Tchividjian about the time she decided to fix up the large family sandbox for her six energetic children. She called the local sand company, and a truck soon arrived. To Gigi's dismay, the truck began making deep trenches in the grass. The ground was soft from recent heavy rain. As the driver maneuvered, the truck also broke off several branches from overhanging trees.

Then it happened. The sand truck got stuck. The more the driver accelerated, the deeper he sank, until the truck began sliding down the hill, plowing a gaping hole. An hour later, a tow truck arrived. This driver backed around and hooked up to the first truck, leaving more black trenches. He tugged and pulled, breaking sprinkler pipes, splintering branches, and uprooting small trees in the process. It was no use. Both trucks were stuck. Eventually, truck number three arrived—the cab of an eighteen-wheeler.

That night, after five-and-a-half hours of mass destruction, the three trucks departed. Gigi was left with a yard that looked like a war zone and bills for five tons of sand and two tow trucks. The day had been a disaster. But when she tucked in her eight-year-old for the night, she was astonished at his prayer: "And thank You, Lord, for the exciting day and all the entertainment we had!"

There are times when we feel we could do with a little less "excitement" and "entertainment" in our lives. But the Lord knows best, and He directs us to "give thanks in all circumstances, for this is God's will for you in Christ Jesus" (1 Thessalonians 5:18). That's a godly perspective worth remembering—on the bad days as well as the good.

SMD

I Do Have Value

PERCEPTIVE

by Gary Smalley and John Trent

*S*ixth grade hadn't been a banner year for Eric. Never very confident in school, he had a particular dread of mathematics. "A mental block," one of the school's counselors had told him.

Then, as if a mental math block wasn't enough for an eleven-year-old kid to deal with, he came down with measles in the fall and had to stay out of school for two weeks. By the time he got back, his classmates were multiplying fractions. Eric was still trying to figure out what you got when you put a half pie with three-quarters of a pie...besides a lot of pie.

Eric's teacher, Mrs. Gunther—loud, overweight, terrifying, and a year away from retirement—was unsympathetic. For the rest of the year she called him "Measly" in honor of his untimely spots and hounded him ceaselessly with makeup assignments. When his mental block prevented his progress in fractions, she would thunder at him in front of the class, "I don't give a Continental for your excuses! You'd better straighten up, Measly. Them ain't wings I hear flappin'!"

The mental block, once the size of a backyard fence, now loomed like the Great Wall of China. Eric despaired of ever catching up and even fell behind in subjects he'd been good at.

Then came a remarkable moment.

It happened in the middle of Mrs. Warwick's ninth grade English class. To this day, some twenty-five years later, Eric still lights up as he recalls The Moment.

The fifth period class had been yawning through Mrs. Warwick's attempts to spark discussion about a Mark Twain story. At some point in the lecture, something clicked in Eric's mind. It was probably crazy, but it suddenly seemed like he understood something Twain had been driving at—something a little below the surface. Despite his fear of sounding foolish, Eric raised his hand and ventured an observation.

That led to the moment when Mrs. Warwick looked straight into

Eric's eyes, beamed with pleasure, and said, "Why, Eric…that was *very* perceptive of you!"

Perceptive. Perceptive? Perceptive!

The word echoed in Eric's thoughts for the rest of the day—and then for the rest of his life. *Perceptive? Me? Well, yeah. I guess that* was *perceptive. Maybe I am perceptive.*

One word, one little positive word dropped at the right moment somehow tipped the balance in a teenager's view of himself—and possibly changed the course of his life (even though he still can't multiply fractions).

Eric went on to pursue a career in journalism and eventually became a book editor, working successfully with some of the top authors in America. His newfound confidence placed him on a path he might otherwise have never discovered and enjoyed.

All it took was a kind word at the right moment—and a teacher who was a bit perceptive herself.

LOOKING AHEAD…

The world can be a forbidding place for children, especially if they feel that they somehow don't measure up. A relatively minor difficulty—such as Eric's "mental block" with math—can easily develop into a crisis of confidence, particularly when a child must listen to constant reminders of his or her deficiencies.

I still recall my own thirteenth and fourteenth years, which were the most painful of my life. I found myself in a social cross fire that gave rise to intense feelings of inferiority and doubt. Yet I survived this period, and even gained several positive qualities from the experience. I was sustained, though I wasn't fully conscious of it at the time, by the faith I had developed through my parents' teaching and example. I believed in a loving God who valued me for the person I was, who—even though I was unworthy—sent His Son to die for me (John 3:16).

If your children understand in their hearts that the Creator of the universe loves them personally and has sacrificed His own Son on their behalf, they will enjoy a much healthier self-concept and be far better equipped to take on the trials of adolescence. We'll talk more this week about the relationship between self-worth and your family's faith.

JCD

COUNTERING CRUELTY

You created my inmost being;
you knit me together in my mother's womb.
Psalm 139:13

Psychologist Clyde Narramore once told about a second-grade teacher who wanted to demonstrate the relative meaning of the words *large* and *small* to her class. She selected a girl and boy and had them come to the front of the room. The teacher then put her hand on the girl's head and said, "Large, large, Sharon is large." Sharon, now self-conscious, was indeed the tallest girl in the class and was sensitive about it. Then the teacher said, "Small, small, David is small." Poor David was humiliated. The last thing any boy wants is to be known as the smallest and most powerless child in his class. The teacher was oblivious to the pain she was causing Sharon and David.

As your children grow, any deviation from the norm—in height, weight, hairstyle, skin color, voice, et cetera—will be pointed out by their peers and used to embarrass them. Sometimes even adults who should know better will play this cruel game. It's your job as parents to counteract these hurtful comments with love. Encourage your children. Remind them of their strong qualities and abilities. And above all, employ Scripture passages such as Luke 16:15 to teach your kids that the misguided values of man are often the very opposite of the values of God: "For what is highly esteemed among men is an abomination in the sight of God" (NKJV).

Before you say good night...

- Do you ever tease your children in ways that hurt?
- How can you help your kids feel positive about their unique characteristics?

O Lord, if only we could see into hearts as You do. If only we could see the wounds and burdens in our child's spirit. Your eyes miss nothing, Lord. Grant us wisdom so that we might comfort and encourage even as You do. Amen.

LOVE AND RESPECT

Show proper respect to everyone.
1 Peter 2:17

*L*ove is an important means to building a healthy self-concept in your children, but it is only half of the equation. Respect is equally vital—and it's entirely possible to show one without the other. For example, when your son starts to speak to another adult, you may cut him off in midsentence and explain what he's trying to say. Or you lecture your daughter before she leaves for a weekend at a friend's house on how to avoid making a fool of herself.

A child is perfectly capable of understanding that he or she fails to measure up in the eyes of Mom or Dad. "Sure, they love me because they're my parents. I can see that I'm important to them, but they're not really proud of me as a person. I'm a disappointment to them." The first step in building a sense of worth in your children is to be careful about what you say and do in their presence. Then, rather than focusing only on their problems, be sure to communicate your respect for them and the wise choices they *do* make. When the apostle Peter instructed believers to "show proper respect to everyone," he certainly meant it to include the impressionable members of their own families. As you display an attitude of respect *and* love toward your children, you'll establish a home in step with the heart of God.

Before you say good night...

- Do you show your children respect as well as love? How?
- Are you sometimes disrespectful to your kids? In what ways?
- Which of your kids' traits and accomplishments are worthy of your respect and praise?

Father, by the restraining power of Your own Spirit, keep us from damaging home and family with careless, critical words. Help us to focus on building up one another. We seek Your strength to accomplish this. Amen.

A CHRISTLIKE HEART

The LORD does not look at the things man looks at.

1 Samuel 16:7

*L*ori Salierno, in her book *Designed for Excellence,* relates that she developed a terrible case of acne when she was in high school. Everything she tried failed. She even heard girls at school whispering about her face. One night her will to cope copped out. Sobbing, she threw herself on her bed. Eventually her father came in to comfort her. "Lori," he said, "I'm sorry. I know it's tough, but you can overcome this. You need to forget about your face and start to work on your inner qualities."

Lori wasn't too sure her father knew what he was talking about, but she thought it was worth a try. She decided to focus on the Lord's command to "Love your neighbor as yourself" (Matthew 22:39). She began visiting a nearby nursing home, telling residents about herself and listening to their stories. The more Lori learned about the hearts and concerns of these senior citizens, the more her own pain seemed to diminish. One day, when a resident told Lori that she was "beautiful," Lori realized that she truly *felt* beautiful. Her trips to the nursing home boosted her self-image and made it easier for her to face her schoolmates.

Scripture says that "Man looks at the outward appearance, but the LORD looks at the heart" (1 Samuel 16:7). When we teach our children to know and follow the Word of the Lord, they will move ever closer to the heart of Jesus—and develop a healthy self-concept in the process.

Before you say good night...

- Are your kids most concerned about their outer or inner qualities?
- Have you ever talked about 1 Samuel 16:7 with your kids, explaining what God values most in His children?

Dear God, we find it so easy to place great significance on matters that mean little in Your eyes. Thank You for clear instruction on what has lasting value and what will bring us closer to Your heart and will for our family. Amen.

BETTER THAN WORMS

I am fearfully and wonderfully made;
your works are wonderful.
Psalm 139:14

I (JCD) had just finished addressing an audience on the importance of self-confidence in children when a woman approached me. My comments had contradicted her theology. "God wants me to think of myself as being no better than a worm," she said, apparently referring to David's analogy in Psalm 22:6. "I would like to respect myself, but God could not approve of that kind of pride, could He?"

It's true that the Bible condemns the concept of human pride. God seems to hold a special disdain for this particular sin. In Proverbs 6:16–19, a "proud look" (KJV) is listed first among God's seven most despised sins. But language is dynamic; the meaning of words shifts with time. I don't believe that the Lord is displeased with a parent's pride in a son who succeeds at school or daughter who wins a race. The biblical meaning of *pride*—better translated today as *haughty*—is the case of a person who is too pompous to bow humbly before God, confessing sins and submitting to a life of service to others.

Your children should never be taught that they are worthless. Jesus did not leave His throne in heaven to die for the "worms" of the world. He loves us as members of the family of God, calling us "brothers and sisters." I call that cause for genuine self-esteem.

Before you say good night...

- Do your kids understand the biblical meaning of *pride?* Do you?
- Do any of your kids exhibit attitudes of haughtiness or worthlessness?
- If so, what can you do to help them develop godly self-esteem?

Lord, we are so grateful to be brothers and sisters in Your holy family. Help us to avoid the kind of pride that so clearly offends You, and enable us to respect ourselves in a manner that is pleasing to You. Amen.

HIGH SCHOOL REUNION

A heart at peace gives life to the body, but envy rots the bones.
Proverbs 14:30

*I*sabel Wolseley writes in *Daily Guideposts, 2002* that she felt inadequate and envious during her senior year of high school. Her classmates seemed to "have it all." They had the right clothes, friends galore, top grades, and self-assurance. They were the ones chosen for school plays, as class officers, for special projects. Now, of course, they were receiving all the end-of-the-year awards. Isabel, who lived on a farm and whose family was less well-off than many of her classmates, had never even been nominated for an award.

It was decades later that Isabel finally got the nerve to attend a high school reunion. When she arrived and began talking to her old classmates, Isabel made a shocking discovery—she wasn't the only one who felt inadequate back then. As one friend put it, "You lived on a farm! You had a Shetland pony to ride. A haymow to play in. Now you're a writer and you travel all the time. I've always envied you!"

It is said that comparison is the root of all feelings of inadequacy. We will *always* come up short when we weigh our most embarrassing shortcomings against someone else's greatest assets. We parents need to help our kids understand this concept. Scripture warns that "envy rots the bones" (Proverbs 14:30). Let's encourage our children, instead of dwelling on others who "have it all," to give thanks to God for loving us and preparing a place for each of us as members of His holy family.

Before you say good night...

- Is envy robbing your children of self-confidence?
- What can you do to prevent envy from seeping into your family?

O great Creator, thank You for every blessing You have bestowed on our family. Help us to avoid the trap of envy, and to guide our children to an attitude of gratitude and confidence in Your plans for their lives. Amen.

TRUE VALUES

We are God's workmanship,
created in Christ Jesus to do good works.
Ephesians 2:10

My daughter, Danae, was a beautiful child even at fifteen months of age. Our family and friends, as well as complete strangers, loved to hold her in their arms, or tease her, or give her candy. Everyone, it seemed, wanted to shower her with affection.

That all changed, however, on the day of Danae's encounter with a table in our living room. She was just learning how to run on little legs, and Jim was playfully chasing her through the house. Suddenly, Danae lost her balance and fell into the sharp edge of a table, driving a front baby tooth completely into her gums. It was an awful moment for all of us!

Although there was no permanent damage, Danae's head-on collision with the furniture temporarily distorted the shape of her mouth. All her babyish appeal was now gone. When Jim took her to the store the next evening, he immediately noticed a change in how others responded to our little darling. Instead of offering her smiles and tenderness, they tended to stare or turn away. These strangers were not intentionally mean, but they were demonstrating one of our most flawed values: We often reserve our love for the most attractive among us.

This kind of unjust thinking can be particularly devastating to a youngster with an already shaky self-concept. That's why it's so important for us to teach our children the true values that come from God. He wants us to live with humble reverence for Him and for every member of His human family. The Lord of lords and King of kings has created me and you and each of our children with unique talents and temperaments. He loves each of us just as we are and has a meaningful plan for our lives.

When you explain the depth of Christ's great love to your son or daughter—that He gave His very life for him or her—you'll put the matter of self-worth in its proper perspective. That's an important message for your kids…and for Mom and Dad, too.

SMD

The Power of
Perseverance

NEIGHBORHOOD SECRETS

by Sandra Byrd

I peeked at her every day, holding the slats on my miniblinds just right so the viewing space would be imperceptible. Certain as the morning paper, at 10 A.M. she'd shepherd two dapper preschoolers into a clean minivan. They looked Sunday-school neat every day.

I envied her gauzy dresses, loosely catching a whispered breeze. I wanted to feel pretty and feminine and put together again. I probably wouldn't wear wide-brimmed hats woven of sun-bleached straw and cinched with a strawberry ribbon, but I might like to try. My car wouldn't need to be spotless—but lately there were so many coffee cups rolling about on the floor, they were talking of starting a union.

After a few minutes, I'd leave my post and go back to the television, and back to the baby who was crying once more. I went into the kitchen to warm some tea, disgusted with the mess on the countertops—again.

Could every woman in the world except me juggle all these balls?

One day, more out of anger than curiosity, I pulled my hair into a ponytail and set the baby in her stroller. I made sure I was at my neighbor's step at ten. "Oh, hello!" I said, blushing slightly.

"How are you?" she responded, her lovely British lilt reflecting genuine pleasure.

"Fine, fine…" I stumbled. "By the way, um, how do you guys always get out here so early looking great?" It blurted out. She knew what I meant.

"When Lizzie was born, I never got out the door until *Reading Rainbow* was over, and even then my house was a wreck," she chuckled. Hmm, I mused, *Reading Rainbow* was over at eleven. I was ready around noon, but at least I was within the hour. Encouraged, I pressed on.

"And you always look so pretty." I gestured at her outfit.

"I started buying these dresses after I had the kids. Loose fit and all, you know," she pulled at the waistband and let it snap, showing me the stretch.

"What about your house?" I pressed, though my brain was screaming, "Let it die!"

"Now that I have more energy, it's not so hard to keep up." She saw my droopy eyes. "But the baby was at least six months old before I kept enough dishes clean to eat the next meal."

We chatted for a few more minutes, and she left for wherever mothers of older children trundle off to on a peaceful summer morning. The baby and I strolled a bit and went home.

Later that evening, Michael stayed with the baby and I went out to buy a crinkly, gauzy dress. When I returned, I saw he'd made the kitchen sparkle. A sliver of hope penetrated my foggy brain: *Maybe I can do this after all.*

The seasons passed and another summer arrived. One day my nattily dressed child and I visited a different neighbor, on the kitty-corner side of my street. We cooed at her new baby. This neighbor and I had often chatted in the past, but I hadn't seen her since her baby had come. Her graying roots needed color, as did her complexion. She finally blurted out, "How come I'm the only woman that can't keep it all together?"

"Let's sit down on the grass," I said. "I'll tell you a neighborhood secret."

L O O K I N G   A H E A D ...
Sometimes those calm and orderly days before you had children seem a distant memory, don't they? You may be giving all you've got to your family, yet the dishes are piled higher than the Eiffel Tower, the grass looks

like a jungle, and the kids seem unable to grasp even the most basic forms of civilized conduct. It's enough to make any mother and father throw their hands up and shout, "I give up!"

But don't do it. Don't give up or give in to the feeling that it's hopeless. As you persist in your efforts to be a godly spouse and parent, you will experience small victories along the way—and over time, those little successes will turn into much larger ones. I've seen it happen often, in my own family and in countless others.

Remember, the Lord is watching: "I know your deeds, your love and faith, your service and perseverance, and that you are now doing more than you did at first" (Revelation 2:19). He *will* honor your persistent dedication to walking in the ways of Scripture.

We'll talk about the power of perseverance in the days ahead. My prayer for you is the same as the apostle Paul's: "May the Lord direct your hearts into God's love and Christ's perseverance" (2 Thessalonians 3:5).

JCD

KIDS AND COCKLEBURS

Watch your life and doctrine closely. Persevere in them.
1 Timothy 4:16

*H*ave you ever had the experience of walking through an open field in late summer and feeling the sting of cockleburs in your shoes and around your ankles? These thin, brown weeds are armed with dozens of sharp spines that grab your socks and eventually work their way into the skin. They're terribly annoying.

Cockleburs are remarkable in another way, however. Inside their prickly seedpods are not just one, but several seeds, and they germinate in different years. If the first seed fails to sprout one year due to poor conditions, the second is still waiting in the ground. When the next season rolls around, it begins to open and grow. And if that one doesn't take root, there is still a third seed waiting for the year after that.

Cockleburs can tell us something about parenting. When the "seeds" of your diligent instruction on life and faith fail to germinate, the effort seems in vain. Yet if you persist in your teaching and in setting a godly example, your endeavors are likely to be rewarded (1 Timothy 4:16). Like a cocklebur seed that lies dormant for a decade or more, the lessons you plant now may one day break through and blossom in the hearts and minds of your children.

Before you say good night...

- Have you seen examples in your kids of lessons that blossomed years after they were planted?
- What "seeds" are you planting in your children today?
- How can you help each other to be patient as you wait for your seeds to sprout?

Father, we need Your strength to "keep on keeping on." Lift our hearts when we become discouraged. Help us to persevere in sowing good seeds in the lives of our children, leaving the results—and the harvest—to You. Amen.

EMPTY SHELLS

I know your deeds…your service and perseverance.
Revelation 2:19

Elmer Bendiner flew on numerous bombing runs over Germany during World War II. He never forgot one of those missions.

Bendiner's B-17 was hit especially hard by enemy antiaircraft guns; eleven shells pierced the fuel tank. If even one of those shells had exploded, the plane would have been blown out of the sky. Incredibly, however, all remained intact. As Bendiner wrote in his book, *The Fall of Fortresses,* he eventually learned the explanation for this miracle. When demolition experts opened up the shells, they found no explosive charge. All were empty—but one. That shell contained a small note, apparently from a factory munitions worker, written in Czech. Translated, it read: "This is all we can do for you now."

Scripture says that God notices our persistent acts of faith: "I know your deeds, your love and faith, your service and perseverance" (Revelation 2:19). That includes our small efforts as well as the great ones. When you are discouraged by the evils threatening your children and feel that your "insignificant" attempts to shield them make no difference, remember that the Lord is watching—and when it is within the wisdom of His divine plan, He will honor even the smallest endeavor: "Blessed is the man who makes the LORD his trust" (Psalm 40:4).

Before you say good night…

- Do you believe that God notices your efforts to protect your children (see Revelation 2:19)?
- How has God blessed even small efforts in the past?

Lord, we thank You that tomorrow is a new day. We ask that You would meet us in the morning with fresh strength and power so that we can make the most of each opportunity You place in our paths. Amen.

PRAYING FOR KEEPS

"Ask and you will receive, and your joy will be complete."
John 16:24

y (JCD's) grandmother prayed for her six children throughout their formative years, but her youngest son—my father—was a particularly headstrong young man. For seven years following his high school graduation he rejected the teachings of the church. Yet my grandmother never stopped praying.

One evening my Uncle Willis, who loved Jesus passionately, went looking for my dad (who was visiting his parents' home) as the family prepared to go to church. "Jim," he said, "aren't you going with us to the service tonight?" "No, Willis," my dad said. "I'm through with all of that. I don't plan to ever go back again." Willis said nothing. But as my father sat looking at the floor, he saw big tears splashing on his brother's shoes. *I'll go,* my dad thought, *just because it means that much to him.*

At the service that evening, James Dobson Sr. invited Jesus Christ into his heart—a decision he never wavered from the rest of his life. God answered the prayers of my grandmother by placing a key person at a critical crossroads. If you pray with persistence and confidence, He will do as much for your children, too.

Before you say good night...

- Do you pray for your kids with persistence and confidence?
- How have your prayers already changed the lives of your children?
- How can you help each other to keep praying even when you're tired or discouraged?

Lord Jesus, You have taught us to "pray always and not give up." Strengthen us, Lord, to do this for our children. As long as You give us breath, help us to pray for the special lives You have entrusted us with, and to never give up or let up until we are all together in Your presence. Amen.

PATIENT ENDURANCE

This calls for patient endurance on the part of the saints.
Revelation 14:12

*A*re you facing a parenting challenge that just won't go away? Is it your daughter's health? Your son's irresponsibility? Your child's disinterest in God? Is it simply a lack of energy to keep up with rambunctious toddlers or rowdy teens?

We know how hard it can be to maintain optimism and confidence in the face of a never-changing trial. We're told in Scripture that Abraham and Sarah faced such a challenge. God had promised Abraham that he would become the father of a great nation. That was wonderful news to an aging man and his barren wife. What followed, however, were years of continued infertility.

After more than two decades passed, Abraham was even more confused. He and his wife were simply too old to have children. Yet he still believed in God's power: "He did not waver through unbelief regarding the promise of God, but was strengthened in his faith" (Romans 4:20). Abraham's faith was later rewarded with the birth of Isaac (Genesis 21:2).

Isn't that a wonderful example of faith under fire? It should give you courage to retain spiritual confidence even when the pieces don't fit. Your "patient endurance" will not go unnoticed by your heavenly Father. Even when it appears nothing is happening, God is at work in the lives of each member of your family.

Before you say good night...

- What situations in your lives could use some "Abraham-like" faith?
- In what ways have you already seen the rewards of your faith?
- How well do you demonstrate "patient endurance" to your family?

Father, we need to walk by faith, not by sight. What we see of our situation so often causes us to lose heart. Open our eyes, God, to see Your great power and mighty hand in our lives. Encourage us tonight, for Jesus' sake. Amen.

IF AT FIRST YOU DON'T SUCCEED...

We consider blessed those who have persevered.
James 5:11

Whether we ultimately fail or succeed sometimes depends on our own tenacity. We've all heard stories about people who beat the odds and achieved where others tried and failed. But we seldom stop to think about the many times those same people fell flat on their faces before realizing their goals.

Thomas Edison, for instance, reportedly built and tested more than one thousand lightbulbs before finally getting one to work. Michael Jordan was cut from his high school varsity basketball team. Louis L'Amour received several hundred rejection slips before his first short story was published. After Elvis Presley's first performance at the Grand Ole Opry, the manager advised the young singer to go back to truck driving.

Satan wants us to give up after a defeat. That's why the author of Hebrews urged Jewish Christians to "throw off everything that hinders and the sin that so easily entangles, and let us run with perseverance the race marked out for us" (Hebrews 12:1). That's a valuable lesson for your children...and a good one for mom and dad to remember, too.

Before you say good night...

- What have you accomplished that required great perseverance?
- How can you encourage persistence in your children?
- Do you believe that success can follow repeated failure?

Lord Jesus, it's difficult for us to get beyond our defeats and failures. Help us to get back on the right path and to keep putting one foot in front of another. We're so thankful that even when this business of parenting seems over our heads, You still walk right beside us. Amen.

A DILIGENT MOTHER

You need to persevere so that…
you will receive what he has promised.
Hebrews 10:36

R uth Bell Graham was a diligent mother. With a husband frequently on the road preaching the gospel and five children at home, she had to be. Her eldest son, Franklin, was the child who required the most diligence. He smoked, drank, stayed out late at night, and showed little interest in spiritual matters.

Many nights Ruth couldn't sleep from thinking about her son. So she turned to God in prayer. "Every time I pray especially for him," she later wrote, "God says: 'Love him…' which seems odd because I love every bone of him. But God means show it. Let him in on the fact. Enjoy him. You think he's the greatest, let him know you think so." Though she didn't approve of Franklin's behavior, she consistently displayed her love for her wayward son.

Ruth's diligence was rewarded in 1974, when Franklin poured out his heart to God, confessed his sin, and turned away from his former life. Today he is president of the Christian relief organization Samaritan's Purse and is the president and CEO of his father's ministry, the Billy Graham Evangelistic Association.

The Lord will respond to our diligent prayers for our family in His timing, not ours—but when we persevere in doing the will of God (Hebrews 10:36), we can count on His promises for a hope and a future with Him.

SMD

Letting Go

OUR GIRL

by Max Lucado

*J*enna, wake up. It's time to go to school."

She will hear those words a thousand times in her life. But she heard them for the first time this morning.

I sat on the edge of the bed for a while before I said them to her. To tell the truth, I didn't want to say them. I didn't want to wake her. A queer hesitancy hung over me as I sat in the early morning blackness. As I sat in silence, I realized that my words would awaken her to a new world.

For four lightning-fast years she'd been ours, and ours alone. And now that was all going to change.

We put her to bed last night as "our girl"—exclusive property of Mommy and Daddy. Mommy and Daddy read to her, taught her, listened to her. But beginning today, someone else would, too.

Until today, it was Mommy and Daddy who wiped away the tears and put on the Band-Aids. But beginning today, someone else would, too.

I didn't want to wake her.

Until today, her life was essentially us—Mom, Dad, and baby sister Andrea. Today that life would grow—new friends, a teacher. Her world was this house—her room, her toys, her swing set. Today her world would expand. She would enter the winding halls of education—painting, reading, calculating…becoming.

I didn't want to wake her. Not because of the school. It's a fine one. Not because I don't want her to learn. Heaven knows I want her to grow, to read, to mature. Not because she doesn't want to go. School has been all she could talk about for the last week!

No, I didn't want to wake her up because I didn't want to give her up.

But I woke her up anyway. I interrupted her childhood with the inevitable proclamation, "Jenna, wake up—it's time to go to school."

It took me forever to get dressed. My wife, Denalyn, saw me moping around and heard me humming "Sunrise, Sunset" and said, "You'll never make it through the wedding." She's right.

We drove two cars to Jenna's school so that I could go directly to work. I asked Jenna to ride with me. I thought I should give her a bit of fatherly assurance. As it turned out, I was the one needing assurance.

For one dedicated to the craft of words, I found very few to share with her. I told her to enjoy herself. I told her to obey her teacher. I told her, "If you get lonely or afraid, tell your teacher to call me and I'll come and get you." "Okay," she said, and smiled. Then she asked if she could listen to a tape with kids' music. "Okay," I said.

So while she sang songs, I swallowed lumps. I watched her as she sang. She looked big. Her little neck stretched as high as it could to look over the dash. Her eyes were hungry and bright. Her hands were folded in her lap. Her feet, wearing brand-new turquoise and pink tennis shoes, barely extended over the seat.

What is she thinking? I wondered. *Does she know how tall this ladder of education is that she will begin to climb this morning?*

No, she didn't. But I did. How many chalkboards will those eyes see? How many books will those hands hold? How many teachers will those feet follow and—gulp—imitate?

Were it within my power, I would have, at that very instant, assembled all the hundreds of teachers, instructors, coaches, and tutors that she would have over the next eighteen years and announced, "This is no normal student. This is my child. Be careful with her!"

As I parked and turned off the engine, my big girl became small again. But it was the voice of a very little girl that broke the silence. "Daddy, I don't want to get out."

I looked at her. The eyes that had been bright were now fearful. The lips that had been singing were now trembling.

I fought a Herculean urge to grant her request. Everything within me wanted to say, "Okay, let's forget it and get out of here." For a brief, eternal moment I considered kidnapping my own daughters, grabbing my wife, and escaping these horrid paws of progress to live forever in the Himalayas.

But I knew better. I knew it was time. I knew it was right. And I knew she would be fine. But I never knew it would be so hard to say, "Honey, you'll be all right. Come on, I'll carry you."

And she *was* all right. One step into the classroom and the cat of curiosity pounced on her. And I walked away. I gave her up. Not much. And not as much as I will have to in the future. But I gave her up as much as I could today.

LOOKING AHEAD...

I'm convinced that mothers and fathers in North America are among the best in the world. We care passionately about our kids and will do anything to meet their needs. But we are among the worst when it comes to letting go of our sons and daughters. In fact, those two characteristics are linked.

The same commitment that leads us to do so well when the children are small (dedication, love, concern, involvement) also causes us to hold too tightly as they grow up. We forget that the process of releasing our children must be a gradual one. With each stage, we let go just a little more. And when the time comes for your grown children to leave the shelter of home, you must let go completely. Your role after that point is to continue to pray every day, holding up your son or daughter before the Lord as he or she makes those first halting steps into adulthood, and to be available when asked for advice. But your son or daughter will *own* his or her decisions in the future.

I will admit to my own difficulties in this area. Before our kids were born, I understood that I would one day need to turn them loose. I wrote extensively on the subject while they were still young. But when the time came to open my hand and let the birds fly, I struggled mightily! I loved the experience of fatherhood and was not ready to give it up.

As your children mature, you too will be challenged to open your hand. It is a matter of trusing them—and of trusting God: "Trust in the

LORD forever, for the LORD, the LORD, is the Rock eternal" (Isaiah 26:4). It may not be easy, but when we release our children into the care of our loving Father, we allow them to fulfill His perfect plan for the rest of their days.

JCD

An Open Hand

> *A man will leave his father and mother*
> *and be united to his wife.*
> Genesis 2:24

hen I (JCD) was seventeen years old, my parents went on a two-week trip and left me behind. They loaned me the family car and gave me permission to invite my (male) friends to spend the fourteen nights at our home. I remember being surprised by this move and the obvious risks my parents were taking. I could have thrown fourteen wild parties, wrecked the car, and destroyed our residence (though I didn't).

Years later, I asked my mother why she risked leaving me unsupervised those two weeks. She smiled and replied, "Because I knew that in about one year you would have complete freedom with no one to tell you how to behave. I wanted to expose you to that freedom while you were still under my influence."

My mother understood that one day soon I would be following the path laid out in Scripture: "A man will leave his father and mother and be united to his wife" (Genesis 2:24). She was preparing me for independence and for one day accepting the responsibility that would accompany marriage. For moms and dads with teenagers who are close to leaving the nest, the most effective parenting approach is to hold on with an open hand.

Before you say good night...

- Are you holding on to your kids with an open hand?
- Do your kids feel that you trust them? Should they? Should you?

Father, truly You hold us with an open hand. You allow us to choose, but You are always there to warn, to guide, to counsel, to encourage. And when we fall, You are quick to pick us up and set us back on the path. Show us how to parent as we have been parented by You. Amen.

A MATURE FAITH

We will in all things grow up into
him who is the Head, that is, Christ.
Ephesians 4:15

*J*udy did everything she could to ensure the spiritual well-being of her son Kevin. She taught him the Word, took him to church, and prayed for him regularly. But when Kevin reached his teens, Judy despaired as she realized that he was turning away from God. Then, two months before his high school graduation, she learned he was hooked on drugs. Kevin soon moved to another state. It was a desperate period for Judy. She was forced to let go of her son at a time when every fiber of her being demanded that she step in and "fix" his faltering faith. Instead, she resolved to love and pray for her son from a distance.

Though you must do everything possible to encourage a living faith in the Lord during your children's youth, it is important not to push your children too hard spiritually once they reach the latter years of adolescence. They must develop their own personal belief in God to achieve the mature faith described by the apostle Paul: "We will no longer be infants.... We will in all things grow up into him who is the Head, that is, Christ" (Ephesians 4:14–15).

Judy's prayers for her son were answered after two years. Kevin entered a Christian drug rehab program and recommitted his life to the Lord. Our hope is that when you let go of your sons and daughters, your prayers for faithful children will be answered, too.

Before you say good night...
- Are you placing enough emphasis on spiritual matters at home? Are you pushing too hard?
- Are you willing to put the faith of your older children in God's hands?

Father, thank You that You love my children even more than I do. Because of Your trustworthiness, I know You will be faithful to work in their lives. Help me to depend on You to establish my children in their faith. Amen.

293

ONE STEP AT A TIME

Let us…go on to maturity.
Hebrews 6:1

Our teenage daughter had taken the proper course work, passed the state driver's test, and was already a responsible young lady. Yet the first time Danae drove off in our car alone, it was still a frightening moment for Mom and Dad! There is no sweeter sound than hearing your teen come to a complete, controlled stop in the driveway after her first solo trip in the family car.

By the teen years, however, parents should already be used to the idea of granting new responsibilities and freedoms to their kids. That vital process should begin at a pace consistent with their age and maturity during the preschool years. When your child can tie his shoes, let him. When he can choose his own clothes within reason, allow him to make his own selections. When he can walk safely to school, grant him that privilege. If responsibility and freedom are meted out gradually throughout childhood, the final release in early adulthood will be much smoother for you and your kids.

David became the king of Israel, but the Lord prepared him for the responsibility of leading His people in stages—first as a shepherd boy, then in battle against Goliath, then as a commander of soldiers in the army of Saul (1 Samuel 16:11; 17:49; 18:13). Likewise, we must prepare our sons and daughters for the responsibilities of adulthood one step at a time. A sudden transfer of power can be disastrous for both generations.

Before you say good night…

- Are you gradually granting responsibility and freedom to your kids?
- What should be the next step in this process for each of your children?

Great God and King, we ask for Your grace and wisdom as we seek to prepare our children for life as adults. Show us how to grant responsibility and freedom in appropriate measure, always depending on Your guidance for choosing the right path. Amen.

INDEPENDENCE DAY

It is for freedom that Christ has set us free.
Galatians 5:1

The act of releasing a grown child into the world is often challenging for parents, but we should keep in mind that the prospect of leaving home can be equally daunting for your son or daughter. Sometimes they will need a gentle push out the door.

You're probably familiar with the story of the Prodigal Son, who demanded his share of his father's estate, set off on his own, and squandered his fortune in wild living (Luke 15:11–13). This strong-willed child couldn't wait to sever his family ties. His older brother, however, was the hard-working and responsible member of the clan. He remained with his father, laboring for years on the family farm.

We don't know for sure how the older son felt about his life at home, but he clearly resented the homecoming lavished on his brother upon his return (vv. 28–30). Compliant children such as this eldest son often have a more difficult time disengaging from the nest. Because there is little conflict with their parents, they've developed a close, secure bond that is hard to give up. Yet God did not intend for adult children to maintain the same relationship with their parents as they did when they were small. That's why every family should anticipate an "independence day" that is a passage into freedom—not only for the grown child, but also for the parents.

Before you say good night...

- Do you have "compliant" kids that may struggle when the time comes to leave home?
- Do you talk with your kids about the future, helping them anticipate an "independence day"?

Lord, we so enjoy close relationships with our children—yet we don't want to hold them back from the plans You have for them. Open our eyes, Lord, to see how we can best release them into the world and into Your care. Amen.

YOUR SOARING KITE

There is a proper time and procedure for every matter.
Ecclesiastes 8:6

T he apostle Paul reminds us that childhood is a temporary state: "When I became a man, I put childish ways behind me" (1 Corinthians 13:11). Even with proper preparation and forethought, the task of releasing your grown children is never easy.

The late Erma Bombeck likened the parenting responsibility to flying a kite. You start by trying to get the little craft off the ground. You're running down the road as fast as you can with this awkward kite flapping in the wind behind you. Sometimes it crashes to the ground, so you tie on a longer tail and try again. Your heart pounds when it catches a gust of wind and flies dangerously close to the power lines. Then, without warning, the kite tugs on the string and ascends into the sky. You release your grip little by little until you come to the end of the twine. You stand on tiptoe holding the last inch between your thumb and forefinger. Then, reluctantly, you let go, permitting the kite to soar unfettered and independent in God's blue heaven. It's an exhilarating and terrifying moment, one ordained from the day of your child's birth. Your task as a parent is finished. The kite is free and, for the first time in twenty years, so are you.

We urge you to keep this final event of parenting in mind. Your goal is to instill the necessary components of character and self-control so that your young adult is equipped to stand alone. The centerpiece of that assignment, as we have seen, is to give your sons and daughters an unshakable faith in Jesus Christ that will see them through life's twists and turns.

Before you say good night...

- Do you have a clear fix on the ultimate goal of your parenting years?
- Are you on target in meeting that objective?

O Lord, how difficult it seems to get this right! Help us to stay focused on our first priority as parents—delivering our children safely into Your hands. Amen.

GOOD-BYE, MRS. SNAIL

Sing to the LORD a new song,
for he has done marvelous things.
Psalm 98:1

Our now-grown daughter, Danae, loved every aspect of childhood and was reluctant to leave it. As a small child, she would place her dolls on a shelf and role-play with her teddy bears, stuffed rabbits, and kittens. Each one had a special name and would take its turn sleeping with her.

I earned my own special name during that time. I had decided to give Danae and her friends a tea party. We set out the good china, cookies, and napkins. Then Danae helped me create pretend names for all her friends. We had Mrs. Perry, Mrs. White, and Mrs. Green, and I was Mrs. Snail (I didn't ask any questions!). The names stuck, and every time we put on a tea party after that morning, I was Mrs. Snail.

I thoroughly enjoyed being "Mom" in those days and wished they could have gone on forever. And I think Danae felt the same way. Her stuffed animals and old phonograph records and other toys were cherished possessions throughout her grade school years.

But kids do grow up. When Danae turned thirteen, her interests began to change. The stuffed animals went untouched in their various "homes," and the familiar records began collecting dust. About a year later, Danae went through her toys and possessions, stacking them neatly and leaving them in front of Ryan's bedroom door. I discovered them there with a note that brought tears to my eyes. It read:

Dear Ryan,
These are yours now.
Take good care of them like I have.
Love,
Danae

That brief message made me realize that Danae had left childhood behind. She was now a young woman entering an exciting new phase of learning and maturing. And as she changed, I needed to change my approach to her as a parent.

By God's holy wisdom, transitions are part of His plan for each of us. Nothing remains the same. The Lord presents us with new challenges and opportunities in every stage of this life. That's not a bad thing! When we acknowledge that God is in control of our lives and our families, it becomes easier for us to embrace change. After all, the Author of change has blessed us by establishing the greatest transition of all: "If anyone is in Christ, he is a new creation; the old has gone, the new has come!" (2 Corinthians 5:17).

SMD

The Reward

SEASON OF THE EMPTY NEST

by Joan Mills

Remember when the children built blanket tents to sleep in? And then scrambled by moonlight to their own beds, where they'd be safe from bears? And how proud and eager they were to be starting kindergarten? But only up to the minute they got there? And the time they packed cardboard suitcases in such a huff? "You won't see us again!" they hollered. Then they turned back at the end of the yard because they'd forgotten to go to the bathroom.

It's the same thing when they're twenty or twenty-two, starting to make their own way in the grown-up world. Bravado, pangs, false starts, and pratfalls. They're half in, half out. "Good-bye, good-bye! Don't worry, Mom!" They're back the first weekend to borrow the paint roller and a fuse and a broom. Prowling the attic, they seize the quilt the dog ate and the terrible old sofa cushions that smell like dead mice. "Just what I need!" they cheer, loading the car.

"Good-bye, good-bye!" implying forever. But they show up without notice at suppertimes, sighing soulfully to see the familiar laden plates. They go away again, further secured by four bags of groceries, the electric frying pan, and a cookbook.

They call home collect, but not as often as parents need to hear. And their news makes fast-graying hair stand on end:

"…so he forgot to set the brake, and he says my car rolled three blocks backward down the hill before it was totaled!"

"…simple case of last hired, first fired, no big deal. I sold the stereo, and…"

"Mom! Everybody in the city has them! There's this roach stuff you put under the sink. It's…"

I gripped the phone with both hands in those days, wishing I could bribe my children back with everything they'd ever wanted—drum lessons, a junk-food charge account, anything. I struggled with an unbecoming urge to tell them once more about hot breakfasts and crossing streets and dry socks on wet days.

"I'm so impressed by how you cope!" I said instead.

The children scatter, and parents draw together, remembering sweet-shaped infants heavy in their arms, patched jeans, chicken pox, the night the accident happened, the rituals of Christmases and proms. With wistful pride and a feeling for the comic, they watch over their progeny from an effortfully kept distance. It is the season of the empty nest.

Slowly, slowly, there are changes. Something wonderful seems to hover then, faintly heard, glimpsed in illumined moments. Visiting the children, the parents are almost sure of it.

A son spreads a towel on the table and efficiently irons a perfect crease into his best pants. (*Ironing board,* his mother thinks, adding to a mental shopping list.) "I'm taking you to a French restaurant for dinner," the young man announces. "I've made reservations."

"Am I properly dressed?" his mother asks, suddenly shy. He walks her through city streets within the aura of his assurance. His arm lies lightly around her shoulders.

Or a daughter offers her honored guest the only two chairs she has and settles into a harem heap of floor pillows. She has raised plants from cuttings, framed a wall full of prints herself, and spent three weekends refinishing the little dresser that glows in a square of sun.

Her parents regard her with astonished love. The room has been enchanted by her touch. "Everything's charming," they tell her honestly. "It's a real home."

Now? Is it now? Yes. The something wonderful descends. The generations smile at one another, as if exchanging congratulations. The children are no longer children. The parents are awed to discover adults.

It is wonderful, in ways my imagination had not begun to dream of. How could I have guessed—how could they?—that of my three, the shy one would pluck a dazzling array of competencies out of the air and turn up, chatting with total poise, on TV shows? That the one who turned his adolescence into World War III would find his role in arduous, sensitive human service? Or that the unbookish, antic one, torment of his teachers, would evolve into a scholar, tolerating a student's poverty and writing into the night?

I hadn't suspected that my own young adults would be so ebulliently funny one minute, and so tellingly introspective the next: so openhearted and unguarded. Or that growing up would inspire them to buy life insurance and three-piece suits and lend money to the siblings they'd once robbed of lollipops. Or that walking into their houses, I'd hear Mozart on the tape player and find books laid out for me to borrow.

Once, long ago, I waited nine months at a time to see who they would be, babes newly formed and wondrous. "Oh, look!" I said, and I fell in love. Now my children are wondrously new to me in a different way. I am in love again.

My daughter and I freely share the complex world of our inner selves, and all the other worlds we know. Touched, I notice how her rhythms and gestures are reminding of her grandmother's or mine. We are linked by unconscious mysteries and benignly watched by ghosts. I turn my head to gaze at her. She meets my look and smiles.

A son flies the width of the country for his one vacation in a whole long year. He follows me around the kitchen, tasting from the pots, handing down the dishes.

We brown in the sun. Read books in silent synchrony.

He jogs. I tend the flowers. We walk at the unfurled edge of great waves. We talk and talk, and later play cribbage past midnight. I'm utterly happy.

"But it's your vacation!" I remind him. "What shall we do that's special?"

"This," he says. "Exactly this."

When my children first ventured out and away, I felt they were in flight to outer space, following a curve of light and time to such unknowns that my heart would surely go faint with trying to follow. I thought this would be the end of parenting. Not what it is—the best part; the final, firmest bonding; the goal and the reward.

LOOKING AHEAD...

Isn't that a wonderful thought given to us by Joan Mills? After years of sharing struggles and joys with your kids, of celebrating every triumph and agonizing over every disappointment, the best part of parenting is yet to come. Scripture tells us that "Sons are a heritage from the LORD, children a reward from him" (Psalm 127:3). Part of that reward is the experience of watching your boys and girls grow up. Yes, it's tough at times, yet I would give anything now to relive a few of those golden days. Most parents of grown kids would say the same thing.

But another part of the reward of parenting—and according to Joan Mills in the story above, the best part—is what happens after your children mature and strike out on their own. Though your relationship with your kids changes when they reach adulthood, you may indeed find yourself falling in love with them all over again.

For our last week together, let's talk about the rewards of parenting.

JCD

JOYFUL HARVEST

Let us not become weary in doing good,
for at the proper time we will reap a harvest.
Galatians 6:9

Gigi Graham Tchividjian and her husband, Stephan, are experts on the trials and joys of parenthood—they had seven children. Not surprisingly, considering the twenty-year span between their oldest and youngest kids, they often struggled with family activities such as devotions. It was a constant challenge to present material that held the attention of the older children and was also understandable to the younger ones. Sometimes it was a battle just to get them all into the same room!

Yet Gigi and Stephan persisted. They knew that family devotions often led children to a deep love for God's Word. And years later, they began to see the fruits of their efforts. Stephan, for instance, ran into one of his sons walking in town with his fiancée. The son remarked, "We've just finished having our devotions together in the car." Another son related to Gigi over lunch how much their family devotional times had meant to him. They'd shown him that the Christian life was a daily, workable reality. Gigi realized then that the years of struggle had been worth it.

You, too, may wonder if you'll ever see the fruits of your parenting efforts. We believe that if you persevere, then at the "proper time" you will indeed reap a joyful harvest.

Before you say good night...

- Are you persevering in your spiritual goals for your children?
- In what areas did you struggle most when your kids were small, and what solutions did you find?
- How can you help each other "not become weary" as parents?

Dear Father, sometimes we become so bogged down in the daily battles that we lose sight of where we're going. Help us, Father. Empower us to make the most of our opportunities today...to love, to counsel, to warn, and to teach. Amen.

ENDINGS AND BEGINNINGS

"I am making everything new!"
Revelation 21:5

The end of formal parenting is the passing of an era, yet it also presents an exciting opportunity—the chance to develop a wonderful new relationship with your adult children. Mike and Margi Klausmeier of Colorado Springs are enjoying their kids more than ever now that they're grown. Twin sons Matthew and David have both worked with their parents in the evangelistic organization Youth With A Mission. Daughter Katie traveled with her mother on a recent missions trip to India and will soon join her mother and one brother on a journey to Cambodia. Mike says that "Our relationship with our boys has become one of adult Christian to adult Christian. We drew much closer as we shared our faith with them and they shared their walk with us." Margi adds that partnering with her daughter in missions work "pulled us together in an incredible way."

The Lord Himself said, "See, I am doing a new thing! Now it springs up; do you not perceive it?" (Isaiah 43:19). God is still at work in your grown kids. In this next phase of life, we encourage you to embrace your children as adults, and to offer them friendship as well as parental support. Then watch and see what God does. You may find that your relationship with your sons and daughters is only just beginning.

Before you say good night...

- How can you offer greater friendship to your grown kids?
- What new adventures would you like to experience with them?
- How would you like your relationship with your kids to change when they are grown?

Lord, the eras of our life seem to rush by. Thank You for Your faithful love and care through the years of our lives. Help us to develop new relationships with our adult children that draw us closer to them and bring glory to You. Amen.

REFRIGERATOR ART

> *A voice came from heaven: "You are my Son,*
> *whom I love; with you I am well pleased."*
> Mark 1:11

*E*llen, a thirty-four-year-old mother of three, enrolled in an art class at a local community college. One day her instructor announced that the assignment completed on the first day of class would be included in a notebook that was to be a major part of her grade. "May I do another project?" Ellen asked the instructor in an anxious voice. "I don't have the first one anymore." The instructor asked what had happened to the earlier work. Ellen replied with a trace of pride in her voice, "It's on my mother's fridge."

Though your relationships with your children naturally change when they become adults, it doesn't mean that you stop being parents. You can still look for ways to honor the achievements of your grown kids, to affirm their positive choices, to show your pride in the men and women they've become. When you do, you'll find yourself developing new levels of mutual appreciation and respect with your maturing sons and daughters.

If our heavenly Father chooses to part the heavens to announce His pleasure in His Son (Mark 1:10–11), we can certainly make the effort to celebrate the accomplishments of our own children. You might start with that empty space on your refrigerator door.

Before you say good night...
- How will you show your grown kids that you're *still* proud of them?
- In what ways have your parents affirmed you as an adult?
- How did those affirmations make you feel?

Father, critical, dishonoring words seem to slip so easily from our lips. By the power of Your indwelling Spirit, help us by our words and deeds to build up, encourage, and celebrate our children…and each other, too, as husband and wife. Amen.

The Blessing of Grandchildren

From generation to generation we will recount your praise.
Psalm 79:13

The book of Proverbs says that "Children's children are a crown to the aged" (17:6). In biblical times, to live to see one's grandchildren was considered a great blessing. It is still a blessing today. There is a profound joy that accompanies watching your children usher a new generation into the world. Those precious lives are a part of you, a connection between the past and the future.

The blessing of grandchildren also comes with responsibility. God is handing you the opportunity to deliver a spiritual heritage to your progeny. My (JCD's) own grandmother, called Little Mother because she weighed only ninety pounds, was the delight of my early life. She talked often about how wonderful heaven was going to be, which made me want to go there. My father told me how when he was a little boy, Little Mother would gather her six kids around her for Bible reading and prayer. Then she would talk about the importance of knowing and obeying Jesus. Many times she said, "If I lose a single one of you to the faith, it would have been better that I were never born."

If you have grandchildren, I urge you to get to know them. Ask about their interests; play games and read with them; tell them stories about your own life. Above all, teach them about Jesus. Helping to secure their faith is the only way to assure that you will be with them *throughout* eternity.

Before you say good night...

- What do you see as your role as a grandparent?
- How could you help strengthen the faith of your grandchildren?

Dear Lord, we do look forward to the blessing of grandchildren if that is part of Your plan for our family. Show us how to make the most of every moment with our grandkids, and lead us to effective prayer for our own children as they pass along our spiritual heritage to the next generation. Amen.

THE HOLY PRIZE

The gift of God is eternal life in Christ Jesus our Lord.
Romans 6:23

others and fathers who build close relationships with their adult children experience one of the great satisfactions in life. As a son, I (JCD) have many fond memories of special moments with my parents during my adult years, and as a father, I cherish more than ever the times I'm with Danae and Ryan now that they're grown. Yet there is an even greater reward for parents. Our days on this earth will eventually end—perhaps much sooner than we think. The real goal for moms and dads, then, is to enjoy their children not just in this temporary existence, but also in the eternal life to come.

It is the nature of God's loving design for families that parents and children be separated for a time, then permanently reunited in heaven. When the Lord calls me across the threshold, I know that my father and mother will be waiting with open arms to welcome me. And one day not so long after (if probabilities prove accurate), I will be doing the same for my own kids. What glorious moments those will be!

This is the reward that surpasses all others—a joyous family reunion that lasts forever. I pray that you will continually nurture your children's relationship with Jesus so that your family achieves the "crown of righteousness" (2 Timothy 4:8) promised to the faithful.

Before you say good night...

- Do you and your children look forward to eternity together in heaven?
- Do you agree that achieving eternal life through Jesus is *the* most important objective for us and our children?

Fill our hearts, O Lord, with this wondrous vision...forever with You, forever with each other in the place You have prepared for us. Whatever else this life may hold for us—wealth or honor, trials or suffering—nothing compares with the thought of a family reunion in heaven. May it be so for all of us, we pray. Amen.

STAGES OF LIFE

There is a time for everything,
and a season for every activity under heaven.
Ecclesiastes 3:1

Let me conclude my contribution to this book by sharing a final thought for women, especially those of you who are full-time moms. You may well have questions about your identity in a culture that devalues motherhood. This was an issue that troubled me when my children were young. I remember saying to my husband, "I *know* who you are, but tell me again who *I* am."

Jim very patiently talked me through those times by reminding me that God had given me the primary responsibility for the care of our two children and our home. "When that brief time is over," he said, "He will have new challenges for you to accept. You'll see." With that, I felt affirmed in my commitment to my family and cherished the experience of raising our kids. I gave priority to them during the brief window when their need was greatest, and am thankful today for what the Lord accomplished with that effort. I would not change a single day if I had life to live over.

As it turned out, Jim's words proved to be more prophetic than even he knew. As soon as our youngest child went off to college, the Lord laid on my shoulders the responsibility of calling the nation to its knees by serving as chairman of the National Day of Prayer Task Force. As a result of our work, more than fifty thousand prayer gatherings are held around the country every year. It would have been impossible for me to handle this heavy assignment while our children were young. But now that my task as a mother and caregiver is completed, God is using me in another fulfilling way.

If you are raising small children, either as a full-time mom or as an "employed mother," I hope you are not seduced by the popular culture that tells you that you're wasting your time. It is a lie. There is no greater responsibility in living than bringing new little human beings into the world and ultimately introducing them to Jesus Christ. This era will pass in the blink of an eye, yielding to yet another stage of life. As Solomon wrote,

> There is a time for everything,
>   and a season for every activity under heaven:
> a time to be born and a time to die,
>   a time to plant and a time to uproot,
> a time to kill and a time to heal,
>   a time to tear down and a time to build,
> a time to weep and a time to laugh,
>   a time to mourn and a time to dance,
> a time to scatter stones and a time to gather them,
>   a time to embrace and a time to refrain,
> a time to search and a time to give up,
>   a time to keep and a time to throw away,
> a time to tear and a time to mend,
>   a time to be silent and a time to speak,
> a time to love and a time to hate,
>   a time for war and a time for peace.
>   Ecclesiastes 3:1–8

This season for child-rearing will end before you know it, and your life will change dramatically. Be content with the assignment God has given you for now, and do it well! You have the rest of your years to give priority to your other talents in service of the Lord. An entirely new identity will await you in the next phase. But while your boys and girls are small, give them the best you have. You will never regret it!

SMD

With all the responsibilities of parenthood—changing dirty diapers, applying bandages to scraped knees, checking homework, driving to games and lessons, taking photos of the prom dress or tuxedo—it's hard to imagine that one day it all will end. You won't stop being a parent and loving your sons and daughters, of course, but you *will* come to a point where you will say, "It's done. I'm finished. I've given my children all the insight and guidance and wisdom I can, and unless they ask for more of my help, it's now up to them."

When that moment arrives, we urge you to cherish it. Celebrate! You've participated in one of the great privileges of life—preparing young souls for a bright future on earth, and an even better one in heaven. If you've given your all and tried to follow the plan laid out by our heavenly Father, you'll have the great satisfaction of hearing those wonderful words: "Well done, good and faithful servant. Come and share your master's happiness!" No reward could be more fulfilling.

To encourage you and help you anticipate that incredible moment, we leave you with this prayer from our hearts:

Heavenly Father, I yearn to be the kind of parent that You desire of me. My highest ideal on this earth is to hear Your approval of the way I lead my children. Yet I feel so inadequate! It's frightening to realize how much my own example will influence my children in what they do, and in what they believe about You. But I take comfort in knowing that You only expect me to do the best I can. Thank You for the positive parenting examples You've given me in my own family and elsewhere, and for the eternal, guiding wisdom of Your Word. Help me to lead and teach to the best of my ability the beloved sons and daughters You've placed in my care. I pray most of all that our family circle will remain unbroken when we gather to celebrate and praise Your name in heaven. Thank You for my kids! Amen.

God bless you and your precious children…and don't forget to turn out the light.

Jim and Shirley Dobson

The publisher and author would love to hear your comments about this book. *Please contact us at:* www.multnomah.net/nightlight

WEEK ONE

Sunday: "Footsteps" by Dennis Rainey. From *Parenting Today's Adolescent* by Dennis and Barbara Rainey with Bruce Nygren. © 1998. Thomas Nelson, Inc. Used by permission. All rights reserved.

Tuesday: Statistics from "Teens and Adults Have Little Chance of Accepting Christ As Their Savior," *Barna Research Online,* 15 November 1999, as quoted in *Bringing Up Boys* copyright © 2001 by James Dobson, Inc. Published by Tyndale House Publishers, Inc. Used with permission. All rights reserved.

Saturday: Prayer from *Bringing Up Boys* copyright © 2001 by James Dobson, Inc. Published by Tyndale House Publishers, Inc. Used with permission. All rights reserved.

WEEK TWO

Sunday: "Living and Learning" by Robin Jones Gunn. © 1998. Robin is the award-winning, bestselling author of over fifty books including the Christy Miller series for teens and the Glenbrooke series. Visit her Web site at www.robingunn.com. Used by permission of the author. Spiritual training checklist from *Emotions: Can You Trust Them?* by Dr. James C. Dobson (Ventura, Calif.: Gospel Light Publications, 1980). Used by permission.

Monday: Danae Dobson quote from *What My Parents Did Right,* compiled and edited by Gloria Gaither (Nashville, Tenn.: Star Song Publishing Group, 1991).

Saturday: McQuilkin family material from *A Promise Kept* by Robertson McQuilkin (Wheaton, Ill.: Tyndale House Publishers, Inc., 1998).

WEEK THREE

Sunday: "Innocent Petitions" by Robin Jones Gunn. From *Mothering by Heart* by Robin Jones Gunn (Sisters, Ore.: Multnomah Publishers, Inc., 1996). Robin is the award-winning, bestselling author of over fifty books including the Christy Miller series for teens and the Glenbrooke series. Visit her Web site at www.robingunn.com. Used by permission of the author.

Thursday: Illustration adapted from *Growing a Spiritually Strong Family* by Dennis and Barbara Rainey with Bruce Nygren (Sisters, Ore.: Multnomah Publishers, Inc., 2002).

Monday: Illustration adapted from *Illustrations Unlimited,* edited by James S. Hewett (Wheaton, Ill.: Tyndale House Publishers, Inc., 1988).

Tuesday: Illustration adapted from *Bringing Up Boys* copyright © 2001 by James Dobson, Inc. Published by Tyndale House Publishers, Inc. Used with permission. All rights reserved.

Friday: Illustration adapted from *Bringing Up Boys* copyright © 2001 by James Dobson, Inc. Published by Tyndale House Publishers, Inc. Used with permission. All rights reserved.

Saturday: Illustration adapted from "Circle of Love" by Jeannie S. Williams. © 1998.

WEEK NINE

Sunday: "Three Days of Joye" by Sandra Byrd. © 2002. Sandra Byrd is the author of numerous books, including the Hidden Diary series, the Secret Sisters series, *Girl Talk,* the *Inside-Out Beauty Book,* and *Heartbeats.* She and her husband, Michael, have two children. Used by permission of the author.

Wednesday: Statistics and illustration from "The Parent Trap," *Newsweek,* 29 January 2001; and the University of Michigan Institute for Social Research and the Surface Transportation Policy Project of Washington, D.C., as reported by Cox News Service, 26 July 2000.

Thursday: Illustration adapted from "A Walk with a Child" by Faith Andrews Bedford, *Country Living,* May 1998.

WEEK TEN

Sunday: "Standing Tall" by Steve Farrar. From *Standing Tall* by Steve Farrar (Sisters, Ore.: Multnomah Publishers, Inc., 1994). Used by permission.

WEEK ELEVEN

Sunday: "Love Wins" by Patsy G. Lovell. From *Focus on the Family.* © 1993. Used by permission of the author.

WEEK TWELVE

Sunday: "Run, Tami, Run" by John William Smith. From *Hugs for Mom* (West Monroe, La.: Howard Publishing Co., Inc., 1997). Used by permission.

Tuesday: Illustration adapted from *What Kids Need Most in a Dad* by Tim Hansel (Old Tappan, N.J.: Fleming H. Revell Company, 1984).

Wednesday: Illustration adapted from *Mothers Have Angel Wings,* compiled and edited by Carol Kent (Colorado Springs, Colo.: NavPress Publishing Group, 1997).

Friday: Illustration adapted from *Leaving the Light On* by Gary Smalley and John Trent (Sisters, Ore.: Multnomah Publishers, Inc., 1994).

WEEK THIRTEEN

Sunday: "Finders, Keepers" by Faith Andrews Bedford. From *Country Living*. © 1996. Faith Andrews Bedford is a freelance writer living in Tampa, Florida. Used by permission of the author.

Wednesday: Illustration adapted from *Living in Light of Eternity* by Stacy and Paula Rinehart (Colorado Springs, Colo.: NavPress, 1986).

Thursday: Study released from *Rich Kids* by John Sedgwick (New York, N.Y.: William Morrow and Company, 1985), as quoted in *Solid Answers* by Dr. James Dobson (Wheaton, Ill.: Tyndale, 1997).

Saturday: Illustration from *The Treasure Principle* by Randy Alcorn (Sisters, Ore.: Multnomah Publishers, Inc., 2001).

WEEK FOURTEEN

Sunday: "A Father's Blessing" by Morgan Cryar. This article was taken from *Decision,* June 1998. © 1998 Billy Graham Evangelistic Association. Used by permission. All rights reserved.

Tuesday: Illustration adapted from *The Prayer of Jabez Devotional* by Bruce Wilkinson with David Kopp (Sisters, Ore.: Multnomah Publishers, Inc., 2001).

Friday: Statistic from "Expenditures on Children by Families: 2000 Annual Report," USDA Center for Nutrition Policy and Promotion. http://www.govspot.com/news/reports/family.htm (accessed 16 July 2002).

Saturday: Illustration adapted from "Special Occasions" by Faith Andrews Bedford, *Country Living,* November 1999.

WEEK FIFTEEN

Sunday: "Holding On to Innocence" by Dale Hanson Bourke. From *Everyday Miracles* by Dale Hanson Bourke (Nashville, Tenn.: Word Publishing, 1989). Used by permission of the author.

Monday: Quotes from Ellen Goodman, "Battling Our Culture Is Parents' Task," *Chicago Tribune,* 18 August 1994, as quoted in *Bringing Up Boys* copyright © 2001 by James Dobson, Inc. Published by Tyndale House Publishers, Inc. Used with permission. All rights reserved.

Tuesday: Illustration adapted from *Bringing Up Boys* copyright © 2001 by James Dobson, Inc. Published by Tyndale House Publishers, Inc. Used with permission. All rights reserved.

Thursday: Nazi methods from "Courageous Choices," *Focus on the Family,* 24 May 2001; quote from "Media Tied to Violence among Kids," *Associated Press,* 26 July 2000, as quoted in *Bringing Up Boys* copyright © 2001 by James Dobson, Inc. Published by Tyndale House Publishers, Inc. Used with permission. All rights reserved.

WEEK SIXTEEN

Sunday: "Double Life" by Michael Fitzpatrick © 2000. Used by permission of the author.

Tuesday: Illustration adapted from *Parables, Etc.* newsletter, April 1989.

Wednesday: Material from Ellen Sorokin, "Conservative Groups Scold Powell," *Washington Times,* 16 February 2002, and "Sexually Transmitted Disease Surveillance, 2000," Centers for Disease Control and Prevention, Atlanta, Georgia, U.S. Department of Health and Human Services, September 2001 (www.cdc.gov/std/stats/TOC2000.htm), as quoted in *Family News from Dr. James Dobson* newsletter, May 2002.

Thursday: MTV material from *Bringing Up Boys* copyright © 2001 by James Dobson, Inc. Published by Tyndale House Publishers, Inc. Used with permission. All rights reserved.

Friday: Quotes from Peter Singer, *Practical Ethics,* 2nd ed. (Cambridge, U.K.: Cambridge University Press, 1993), 191, and Paul Zielbauer, "Princeton Bioethics Professor Debates View on Disabilities and Euthanasia," *New York Times,* 13 October 1999, B8, as quoted in *Family News from Dr. James Dobson* newsletter, May 2002.

WEEK SEVENTEEN

Sunday: "Sweet Dreams" by Jeannette Clift George. From *Mothers Have Angel Wings,* compiled by Carol Kent © 1997. Used by permission of NavPress/Pinon Press. All rights reserved. For copies call 1-800-366-7788.

Monday: Illustration adapted from *Bringing Up Boys* copyright © 2001 by James Dobson, Inc. Published by Tyndale House Publishers, Inc. Used with permission. All rights reserved.

Tuesday: Illustration adapted from "Awards Ceremony" by P. R. from *Sons: A Father's Love* by Bob Carlisle (Nashville, Tenn.: Word Publishing, 1999).

Saturday: Illustration adapted from Martha Sherrill, "Mrs. Clinton's Two Weeks out of Time: The Vigil for Her Father, Taking a Toll Both Public and Private," *Washington Post,* 3 April 1993, C1, as quoted in *Bringing Up Boys* copyright © 2001 by James Dobson, Inc. Published by Tyndale House Publishers, Inc. Used with permission. All rights reserved.

WEEK EIGHTEEN

Sunday: "Chase and the Beanstalk" by Dale Hanson Bourke. From *Everyday Miracles* by Dale Hanson Bourke (Nashville, Tenn.: Word Publishing, 1989). Used by permission of the author.

Monday: Illustration adapted from *Focus on the Family* radio broadcast, 20 January 1986.

Wednesday: Illustration adapted from "Do What?" by Carole Mayhall. © 1997.

Saturday: Illustration adapted from "True Generosity" by Elizabeth Cobb. © 1999.

WEEK NINETEEN

Sunday: "I Wasn't Prepared for a Prodigal" by Gigi Graham Tchividjian. From *Currents of the Heart* by Gigi Graham Tchividjian (Sisters, Ore.: Multnomah Publishers, Inc., 1996). Used by permission.

WEEK TWENTY

Sunday: "Yerr Out!" by Clark Cothern. From *At the Heart of Every Great Father* by Clark Cothern (Sisters, Ore.: Multnomah Publishers, Inc., 1998). Used by permission.

Monday: Illustration adapted from *God's Little Devotional Book for Dads* (Tulsa, Okla.: Honor Books, 1995).

Wednesday: Illustration adapted from "Fare Is Fair" by Lucille Lind Arnell, *Reminisce Extra*, February 1999.

Friday: Statistic from "Census Bureau Says 7 Million Grade-School Children Home Alone," U.S. Census Bureau, 31 October 2000. http://www.census.gov/Press-Release/www/2000/cb00-181.html (accessed 16 July 2002).

WEEK TWENTY-ONE

Sunday: "It Is Well with My Soul" by Jennifer Rothschild. From *Lessons I Learned in the Dark* (Sisters, Ore.: Multnomah Publishers, Inc., 2002). Used by permission.

WEEK TWENTY-TWO

Sunday: "Infamy on Ice" by Phil Callaway. From *Who Put the Skunk in the Trunk?* by Phil Callaway (Sisters, Ore.: Multnomah Publishers, Inc., 1999). Used by permission.

Saturday: Illustration adapted from *Weatherproof Your Heart* by Gigi Graham Tchividjian (Old Tappan, N.J.: Fleming H. Revell Company, 2000).

WEEK TWENTY-THREE

Sunday: "Perceptive" by Gary Smalley and John Trent. From *Leaving the Light On* by Gary Smalley and John Trent (Sisters, Ore.: Multnomah Publishers, Inc., 1994). Used by permission.

Wednesday: Illustration adapted from *Designed for Excellence* by Lori Salierno with Esther Bailey (Anderson, Ind.: Warner Press, 1995).

WEEK TWENTY-FOUR

Sunday: "Neighborhood Secrets" by Sandra Byrd. Reprinted from *Heartbeats,* copyright © 2000 by Sandra Byrd. Used by permission of WaterBrook Press, Colorado Springs, Colorado. All rights reserved.

Tuesday: Illustration adapted from *Standing Tall* by Steve Farrar (Sisters, Ore.: Multnomah Publishers, Inc., 1994).

Saturday: Illustration adapted from *Being a Great Mom, Raising Great Kids* by Sharon Jaynes (Chicago, Ill.: Moody Press, 2000).

WEEK TWENTY-FIVE

Sunday: "Our Girl" by Max Lucado. From *Six Hours One Friday* by Max Lucado (Sisters, Ore.: Multnomah Publishers, Inc., 1989). Used by permission.

Friday: Illustration adapted from Erma Bombeck, "Fragile Strings Join Parents, Child," *Arizona Republic,* 15 May 1977, as quoted in *Bringing Up Boys* copyright © 2001 by James Dobson, Inc. Published by Tyndale House Publishers, Inc. Used with permission. All rights reserved.

WEEK TWENTY-SIX

Sunday: "Season of the Empty Nest" by Joan Mills. Reprinted with permission from the January 1981 *Reader's Digest.* Copyright © 1981 by The Reader's Digest Assn., Inc.

Monday: Illustration adapted from *Weatherproof Your Heart* by Gigi Graham Tchividjian (Old Tappan, N.J.: Fleming H. Revell Company, 2000).

Thursday: Illustration adapted from *Bringing Up Boys* copyright © 2001 by James Dobson, Inc. Published by Tyndale House Publishers, Inc. Used with permission. All rights reserved.

SEARCHING FOR
TIMELESS TRUTH?
FIND IT IN THESE DOBSON CLASSICS

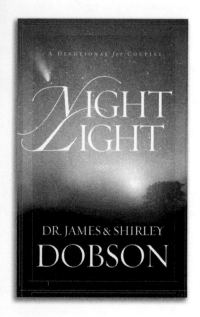

Night Light
Dr. James & Shirley Dobson

Whether you're just married or are celebrating your golden anniversary, you need regular, quiet moments with your mate—times to renew love and intimacy between each other and with the Lord. *Night Light*, by Dr. James Dobson and his wife, Shirley, will help you do just that. This daily devotional offers the personal, practical, and biblical insights that have sustained the Dobsons' marriage for forty years and encouraged couples and families around the world. Let *Night Light* enrich your marriage too—tonight and every night.

ISBN 1-57673-674-1

Love for a Liftime
Dr. James Dobson

The bestselling Gold Medallion winner *Love for a Lifetime* has brought hope, harmony, and healing to millions of homes worldwide, giving men and women powerful and biblical insights for building lasting marital harmony. Encouraging and practical, this proven classic is perfect for every husband and wife who want to strengthen and celebrate their marriage relationship.

ISBN 1-59052-087-4

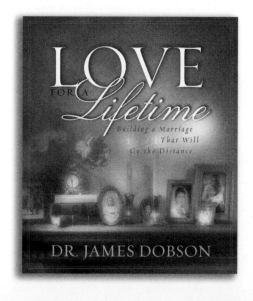